Sam Peckinpah's Feature Films

Bernard F. Dukore

University of Illinois Press
Urbana and Chicago

© 1999 by the Board of Trustees of the University of Illinois
Manufactured in the United States of America

♾ This book is printed on acid-free paper.

Library of Congress Cataloging-in-Publication Data
Dukore, Bernard Frank, 1931–
Sam Peckinpah's feature films / Bernard F. Dukore.
p.   cm.
Filmography: p.
Includes bibliographical references (p.) and index.
ISBN 0-252-02486-9 (cloth : alk. paper)
ISBN 0-252-06802-5 (paper : alk. paper)
1. Peckinpah, Sam, 1925–1984—Criticism and
interpretation. I. Title.
PN1998.3.P43 D85   1999
791.43′0233′092—dc21   99-6064
CIP

1 2 3 4 5 C P 5 4 3 2 1

Contents

Preface

With love, affection, gratitude, and happy memories, I dedicate this book to my late wife, Joyce Dukore (1943–1971), and Frederick P. W. McDowell, who were there at the beginning. I wish both were here at the culmination.

The beginning was July 1969, in Austin, Texas. At what was then the Humanities Research Center of the University of Texas at Austin (now the Harry Ransom Humanities Research Center), I was doing research on what would become *Bernard Shaw, Playwright* (1973). At the HRC, I met Frederick P. W. McDowell, a Shavian whose writings I admired. Eating lunch and dinner together when the HRC was closed, discussing GBS and life in general, Fred and I soon became friends. One night, we decided to see a movie. Neither of us had heard of *The Wild Bunch,* which just opened, or its director, but the cast looked good and the film seemed more promising than the other options available to us.

The promise was more than fulfilled. *The Wild Bunch* overwhelmed us. Although we were not inclined to pronounce a play or film a "classic" on just one viewing, we recognized how extraordinary this movie was and knew we had to see it again. I phoned my wife, Joyce, in New York, told her about it, and asked her not to see it until I returned in a few days so that we could go together. We did. She was as electrified as I had been and was again, and she wanted to see it again. Both of us did. By the time we went again, its producer had made major cuts in it. Joyce was appalled by the mutilation, as I was.

Advertisements of Peckinpah's next movie, *The Ballad of Cable Hogue,* appeared. We saw it in its first week and subsequently. When we were in London in late 1969, we saw *The Wild Bunch* again, realized it had flashback scenes that had been excised from the American print first released, and discussed whether that extra minute made the film better or worse.

Back in New York, we searched out other Peckinpah films. *Major Dundee* appeared on TV, on which we infrequently watched films, since editing for general consumption, arbitrary deletions to make a movie fit into an inflexible time slot, pan-and-scan reformatting for TV screens, and advertising inserts were standard practice. Clearly, *Major Dundee* had been mutilated, and while we had no knowledge of this film's painful history, we longed (in vain) to see the full version. Later, *Ride the High Country* dazzled us. Peckinpah's movies were subjects of much happy and lively discussion.

Joyce, who had cancer, died in October 1971, before *Straw Dogs* opened. I miss her in so many ways that I hope I do not trivialize her memory and my loss when I attest that not seeing and discussing all of Peckinpah's feature films with her or hearing her criticisms of this book as it underwent various revisions (she was my most astute and helpful critic) are among the ways.

I last saw Fred McDowell in November 1992 at an international Bernard Shaw conference ("1992: Shaw and the Last Hundred Years") that I organized in Blacksburg, Virginia. He asked if I remembered, as I was on the verge of asking if he remembered, seeing *The Wild Bunch* in Austin, Texas, in July 1969.

Let me take this opportunity to thank other people and institutions. Foremost is Virginia Polytechnic Institute and State University, where I served as University Distinguished Professor of Theatre Arts and Humanities from 1986 to 1997. Virginia Tech, as this university is usually called, provided me with time and support to compose and complete over 95 percent of this book, and gave me the opportunity to teach cinema as well as dramatic literature. I am especially grateful to Tony Distler, director of Virginia Tech's School of the Arts, and Don Drapeau, head of its theater arts department, for their encouragement. In fall 1997, I was Hoffman Eminent Scholar in Florida State University's School of Theatre. I thank Dean Gil Lazier and Joanna Dolloff, his assistant, for their aid in completing the book.

I am particularly indebted to Richard Leskosky of the film department of the University of Illinois, who was an anonymous reader of my manuscript for the University of Illinois Press. His comments, adverse as well as favorable, were models of criticism—carefully considered, detailed, specific, clear, and reflective of great knowledge of Peckinpah. They helped me enormously. I did not learn his name until this book was accepted, and I look forward to meeting him one day so that I may thank him in person. Thanks, too, to Michael Bliss, a colleague at Virginia Tech, for having read a portion of a very early draft and for his useful criticism. Although I hope they approve of the use I have made of their suggestions, anything blameworthy is my own responsibility.

1

What He Did

"I don't care what you meant to do," the chief clerk berates a young teller when robbers enter the bank during the opening credit sequence of *The Wild Bunch*, "it's what you did I don't like." His speech may summarize the response of some of Sam Peckinpah's early critics to the violence in this film and in *Straw Dogs*, which followed two years after. However, as we recognize today, more than a quarter of a century later, the brutality they depict pales before the savagery in many recent movies. Whatever blemishes or imperfections may attach to *The Wild Bunch*, as Stanley Kauffmann perceived when he reviewed it in 1969 during its initial release, "the faults recede because the violence *is* the film. Those who have complained that there's too much of it might as well complain that there's too much punching in a prizefight: to reduce it would be to make it something else."[1]

The quotation that starts the previous paragraph also summarizes the response of many producers and studio executives, who objected not necessarily to the violence but to other aspects of what Peckinpah did, such as his editing and the length of the director's films. To make his art conform to their standards, they reedited and shortened the running time of several of his movies, among them *Major Dundee*, thereby raising the films to their level, in their view, or lowering it to that level, in the director's estimation. Accounts of the director's cut suggest *Major Dundee* contains little of the violence characteristic of *The Wild Bunch* and *Straw Dogs*, but the film is one of his most seriously mutilated works. Charlton Heston, its star, judges: "There's the smell of a great film in there somewhere, among the ruins."[2] Rightly, I believe, Heston emphasizes both the greatness and the ruins. Of course, one must assess a film on the basis of what is on the screen rather than what a director wanted to be there but, for whatever reasons, was unable to put there. To adapt Sir Walter Scott's well-known phrase, good intentions butter no parsnips. Thus, critics may be justified in stressing the ruins and concluding that this is what Peckinpah did with *Major Dundee*. Yet such an assessment does not end the matter, since elements of greatness or even its whiff are, to those with an acute sense of smell, also part of what he did, perhaps the chief part. With *Pat Garrett and Billy the Kid* recently restored to what is pretty much the director's cut, we are able to see for ourselves that Peckinpah was accurate when he asserted that Metro-Goldwyn-Mayer mutilated this film for its initial release.[3] Apart from such aspects as the strikingly different opening sequence and episodes that were excised in their entirety, there is, to cite another, specific example, the music. In the maimed version that was first released, Bob Dylan simply sings his songs on the sound track; in Peckinpah's version, Dylan's songs are scored—by Dylan, possibly with some input from or supervision by Jerry Fielding, who also collaborated with Peckinpah on *The Wild Bunch, Straw Dogs,* and *Junior Bonner*. Fielding left the project when the studio executives preferred Dylan's singing his songs to Dylan's and/or Fielding's cinematic scoring, and he had his name removed from the credits when the film was released.[4] Because the restored version of *Pat Garrett and Billy the Kid* validates Peckinpah's comparison between it and the MGM version, statements by him and Heston, among others, that studio executives butchered *Major Dundee,* have acquired greater credibility than they had before the former work's distribution in restored form.

In the case of films that emerged close to the way Peckinpah wanted them to, such as *The Wild Bunch* as it was first released (and has since been restored), *Bring Me the Head of Alfredo Garcia,* and *Cross of Iron,* one may admire or detest what he did. Since criticism is not a mathematical science, or indeed any kind of science, one cannot prove conclusively that what Peckinpah did was masterful or abominable. At best, one can make a case—a legal brief, as it were—justifying one's conclusions and hoping that readers and film viewers—a jury, as it were—will find in one's behalf. *The Wild Bunch* has done better than stand the test of time, it has gained more widespread critical recognition of its excellences; and its detractors now seem, like those of Ibsen in the nineteenth century now seem, to have been myopic in their judgment of the work's value and its author's artistry. The chief premise of this book is that Sam Peckinpah's feature films establish him as a major film director, one of the best America has produced, who is worth serious attention. What he achieved, "what he did" (to quote this chapter's title) on the big screen, is what makes him important, and it is the subject of this volume. His earlier work on television, which is treated in other studies, is beyond this book's scope.

His breakthrough film was *The Wild Bunch,* which William Bayer says "may be one of the great films of our time."[5] "More and more, as time goes on," according to Stanley Kauffmann over a decade after *The Wild Bunch* opened, this film "becomes a landmark." Without losing an iota of historical veracity, Peckinpah moved the western from "John Ford's domain of retrospective, myth-exaltation," from "veneration and idealization of the past" into contemporary sensibilities that include a "rowelling of the present." According to Kauffmann, Peckinpah, "who may never have heard of [Antonin] Artaud," seems to have been impelled by Artaud's drives to create thunderous images that would "open the audience to the long-suppressed elemental in itself." Peckinpah "reclaimed violence from the balletics of the gun duel and from anaesthetized, remote, random butchery. He made violence hurt and thrill and he did it through conviction of *fulfillment of being* by bloodshed and by the expression of it—the only word—beautifully." Thus, he struck "the Artaudian blow, past our civilized disdain, to the animal in us that wanted waking—or at least to test our civilizing."[6] This may be true, and it is true that Artaud and his Theater of Cruelty were "in the air" in America in the 1960s, a part of the intellectual and dramatic ambience of which Peckinpah may have partaken. Yet let us be wary of imputing causality where affinity but not causality exists. Peckinpah did not study this theatrical theorist at school. Artaud's *The Theater and Its Double* was not published in the United States until 1958, after Peckinpah had left the University of Southern California.

Perhaps more important, to Kauffmann's suggestion let us add that Peckinpah struck a Brechtian blow. As a graduate student in USC's School of Drama in the late 1940s and early 1950s, he not only could not have avoided exposure to the plays and ideas of Bertolt Brecht (to whom, as will be indicated below, he explicitly refers in *Cross of Iron* and in comments about making films, such as *The Killer Elite*), he also developed "an interest" in this influential German dramatist, whose works were among the "plays or cuttings" he directed at USC.[7] With what might be Brechtian historification, Peckinpah prompts us to criticize the laundered and conventionalized treatment of human beings in the cinematic Old West, to evaluate them in terms of his own more realistically depicted society that was the West, to appraise that society as well, and to apply such judgments to contemporary people and society. For Sam Peckinpah, for the western genre, and for cinema in general, *The Wild Bunch* was unquestionably a breakthrough. After it, his work was not the same and the western was not the same; even non-western films have reflected its impact. *The Wild Bunch* may well be the most important American motion picture since *Citizen Kane*.

The movies that follow Peckinpah's first, *The Deadly Companions,* are unmistakably his works. Whoever produces them, whoever edits them, and whoever receives credit for their screenplays, they bear his imprint. On some occasions, he receives explicit recognition for his textual contributions to them. He has screenplay credit (in collaboration) for *Major Dundee, The Wild Bunch, Straw Dogs,* and *Bring Me the Head of Alfredo Garcia,* as well as story credit (likewise in collaboration) on the last work, for which he wrote one piece of music (also credited). Yet even films that do not cite him as cowriter might well do so. "The one thing I learned [on *The Deadly Companions*]," he maintained, "was never to agree to direct a picture unless you have script control. Since then, I've learned that sometimes even that is not enough."[8] In the words of film editor Lou Lombardo, who worked on many films with him, Peckinpah the director "takes hold like a bulldog and doesn't let go of any aspect of the show." He reviews "every piece of film cut by cut and frame by frame."[9] Confirming Lombardo, Monte Hellman, one of the editors of *The Killer Elite* and before then a well-known director himself, recalls the San Francisco airport fight sequence, which he edited until he considered it good enough to show Peckinpah. The director "looked at it and had the idea to intercut it with a dialogue scene. It was incredible the way it turned out. I wouldn't have thought to do that."[10] Peckinpah's intercutting of the two scenes in the editing room was, in effect, a rewriting of them, for he transformed events in a fight sequence followed by a scene explaining these events into a single, compact, and intense scene that, by dramatizing exposition and cutting some or much of the cackle, gives the fighting episodes enormous impact and makes the dialogue more consequential than it otherwise might be.

As Paul Seydor puts it, Peckinpah is "a genuine auteur who often wrote his own material or so changed the material given him that it became his own."[11] In his own words, Peckinpah the director is also Peckinpah the writer. "No matter how good a script is," he says, "you have to adapt it to the needs of the actors."[12] Every script "changes at least thirty percent" from the time you agree to direct it: "ten percent while you fit your script to what you discover about your locations, ten percent while your ideas are growing as you rehearse your actors," and "ten percent while the film is finally being edited. It may change more than this but rarely less."[13] In brief, as Marshall Fine states, "Peckinpah routinely rewrote" scripts he directed.[14]

Documentation on Peckinpah's uncredited revisions of screenplays is abundant. "The producer, Richard Lyons, and the head of the MGM studio at that time, Sol Siegel, brought me in to rewrite the N. B. Stone script [of *Ride the High Country*] and shoot the picture," says Peckinpah, for example, "and they gave me a free hand."[15] According to Lyons and Joel McCrea, who played Steve Judd, Peckinpah rewrote some 80 percent of the dialogue, reconceived the characters of the two old westerners, and had Judd rather than the other old-timer die at the end; furthermore, Peckinpah's copy of the original shooting script, which he gave to a typist, authenticates how massive his revisions were.[16] Warren Oates, who played Henry Hammond, reports that the scene in which Hammond's brothers give him a bath was Peckinpah's invention, as is the religious hymn the brothers sing, ironic in context, as they ride to the wedding in the mining town's brothel.[17]

According to cinematographer Lucien Ballard, Peckinpah "must have rewritten half of *The Ballad of Cable Hogue* while shooting it," and Stella Stevens, who played Hildy, maintains that once she signed to do the film he reconceived the role for her; Marshall Fine flatly states that Peckinpah and Gordon Dawson "rewrote the script, though they didn't receive credit."[18] Jeb Rosebrook, the screenwriter of credit for *Junior Bonner,* admits the director "helped me a great deal" in revising the script and calls him "a master rewrite man."[19]

The opening sequence of *The Getaway,* filmed at Huntsville Prison, Texas, was Peckinpah's concoction, and he directed actors Al Lettieri and Sally Struthers in improvising dialogue.[20] Take one exchange between Doc McCoy (Steve McQueen) and Rudy (Lettieri) in the second draft of Walter Hill's screenplay of *The Getaway:*

> *Rudy:* Aren't we going a little too hard?
> *Doc:* How's that?
> *Rudy:* It's a walk-in bank. You don't have to be Jesse James for this one.
> *Doc:* I'm not like Jesse James. He got killed.
> *Rudy:* Okay.[21]

Compare it with the corresponding exchange in Peckinpah's film:

> *Rudy:* Aren't we going a little bit hard? (*He throws down the bulletproof vest Doc offered him.*) That's a walk-in bank, man. Piece of cake. You don't

have to be Dillinger for that one. (*He clicks his flashlight on, pointing to Doc's face.*) Bang.
Doc: Dillinger got killed.
Rudy: Not in a bank.
Doc smiles.

In the 1994 remake of *The Getaway,* directed by Roger Donaldson from a screenplay coauthored by Hill and Amy Jones, the exchange, which is different from both passages just quoted, is also less felicitous than in Peckinpah's film:

Rudy: Why do we have to go in so hard? We've all got to be John Dillinger for this one.
Doc: Dillinger got killed.
Rudy: Yeah. Well, Johnny got shot in the back. (*He clicks his flashlight on and off three times.*) Bang, bang, bang.

"Rewriting was imposed" on *Pat Garrett and Billy the Kid,* maintains Rudolph Wurlitzer, the sole writer to receive screen credit for this film, and he confirms that the director actually did some rewriting.[22] In 1989, sixteen years after the film's original release, Metro-Goldwyn-Mayer/United Artists released the director's restored final print in large-screen venues (cinema houses) and for small screens (videocassettes). By comparing the restored film with Wurlitzer's published screenplay, as well as with the first videocassette version, which conforms to the print initially released by MGM, readers are in a position to certify the claim that Peckinpah, more than Wurlitzer, is author of the film itself.[23]

In *The Killer Elite,* the automobile scene between James Caan and Robert Duvall, who played Mike Locken and George Hansen, was mainly improvised by the director and the actors. Asked whether the script underwent any changes since the start of shooting, Caan replied, "I haven't looked at it. Sam hasn't looked at it. Sam will say, 'What do you think?' And I'll say: 'I don't know. What do you think?' . . . Sam will make something out of this." For this film, Peckinpah shot several endings, including one he called "Brechtian."[24] Robert Visciglia declared that Sterling Silliphant, who is officially credited as coauthor, "would write at night and Sam would change it during the day."[25]

According to David Weddle, Peckinpah and Walter Kelley spent four months revising the screenplay of *Cross of Iron,* both writers adding new scenes and Peckinpah then "acting as the final editor, cutting, pasting, and rearranging the scenes again and again." Such finality was only relative, for after Peckinpah completed his editing, says Ron Wright, "The real basis for the final script evolved during that week of rehearsal between Sam and the actors" before shooting began.[26] Where evidence exists, endnotes for chapter 4 will point out important differences among Peckinpah's films, their novelistic sources, and their screenplays.

Ironically, the intervention of studio executives confirms rather than refutes the view that Peckinpah's films are "his." Columbia Pictures removed fifty-five minutes from *Major Dundee* in its first release, more minutes subsequently, and as for what remained, in the director's words, "it's wrongly cut [edited]." The studio took out "all of Dundee's motivation (what it was that made him the man he was)."[27] These missing minutes may not reveal a mutilated masterpiece, as I suspect they do, but what remains discloses dismemberment of a directorial vision. "It didn't work," says Peckinpah of the version of *Pat Garrett and Billy the Kid* first released to the public by "those emotional eunuchs back at MGM," who "cut all of the character and humor and drama out leaving, or at least trying to leave, only the shoot-outs."[28] The results clearly "didn't work." Although, as indicated, "his" film vindicates his statement, one mark of the value of even the mutilated versions of *Pat Garrett and Billy the Kid* and *Major Dundee* is not that they differ so much from Peckinpah's other work, which they do, but that they have so much in common with it. Even the remnants—the "ruins," to use Heston's term—bear Peckinpah's distinctive artistic signature. So does the director's last motion picture, *The Osterman Weekend,* which was released in 1983, the year before he died, and which producers Peter S. Davis and William N. Panzer recut. I was greatly surprised when I learned of the recutting eleven years later.[29] When I saw the film about half a dozen times during its initial release, and more often years later on videocassette, it not only seemed to bear Peckinpah's distinctive stamps, it appeared, and still appears, to be a superb artistic accomplishment. Perhaps what Peckinpah said of producer Phil Feldman's interference with *The Wild Bunch* before it was released—"90 percent of the mutilation helped it"[30]—holds for *The Osterman Weekend* as well. Perhaps, too, his view of *The Osterman Weekend* resembled his view of *Straw Dogs* while he was making it. One of his comments suggests as much. "'It's a piece-of-shit script of some fifth-rate Robert Ludlum novel that I'm just trying to put some life into!'" he told Paul Seydor while he was preparing *The Osterman Weekend.* As Peckinpah knew, says Seydor, "there is little difference between his preview . . . and the version eventually released."[31]

Take, by way of further illustration, another motion picture that we have been able to see in Peckinpah's version and in the producer's butchered version. When *The Wild Bunch* opened in the United States in July 1969, it ran two hours and twenty-three minutes. A few weeks later, the producer (Phil Feldman) cut it to two hours and fourteen or fifteen minutes.[32] Until recently, this version, or versions still shorter by some fourteen minutes, was the one that played in America. In the film's release in Great Britain, it ran one minute and twenty seconds longer than the print first released in America, the additional time occupied by flashbacks showing how Pike Bishop (William Holden) was wounded. Before 1984, the shortest edition was available in movie houses in America; that year, the fullest edition, the British print, was released, and two years later, it was issued in videocassette in the United States. I have seen many of these versions, on both large and small screens. Any of the extremely truncated variations is a good film; each of the others, with and without the eighty seconds of the British print, is a great work of art. More important to our present purpose, each of them is unmistakably "a Peckinpah film," since each contains his unique stylistic artistic signature (chapter 3 focuses on his editing, which one critic rightly calls "much imitated but never equalled")[33] and his distinctive thematic preoccupations (which chapters 2 and 4 analyze).

By attending to every detail of film production, including writing and editing, Peckinpah makes his feature films "his." These works demonstrate "what he did."

Among other things, what Peckinpah did was to create dramatically exciting feature films. *Dramatically* exciting: the chief viewpoint from which this book will examine his artistry is as intensely dramatic cinema. However, I will not arbitrarily divide his films into dramatic acts and scenes, or impose playwriting structural patterns on them—critical methods that are nowadays suspect even for stage plays. Rather, I will examine his movies from viewpoints familiar to dramatic and theatrical criticism, such as thematic sources and patterns, the pacing that is a directorial technique in both media, scenic stratagems, and variants of the play-within-a-play. Chapter 2 explores the thematic underpinnings of his movies, which are existential. The structure of his dramatic depiction of violence, in which his famous editing methods are prominent, is the subject of chapter 3. Chapter 4 returns to a frequent concern of dramatic criticism, the author's consistent thematic preoccupations. This book does not focus on the personal aspect of how Peckinpah managed to do what he did, which has been the subject of a great deal of oral and published reports. Many of these tales—such as those examining the varieties and amounts of booze and pharmaceuticals he ingested, the frequency of his temper tantrums, and the ways he bullied actors and behind-camera personnel—are so fascinating that they have assumed the stuff of popular lore. They surely make absorbing listening and reading. Since several, many, or most of them derive from people who like to spin good yarns or from interested parties, perhaps some with scores to settle, all the stories about Peckinpah are not verifiable, although a number of them, be that number small or large, may be accurate. What is important is that none of them would engage our attention if what Peckinpah did, did not engage our attention. "What He Did" in his dramatic feature films is our concern.

2

Their Own Laws, Their Own Trails, Their Own Ways

As reviewers and critics have frequently remarked, Sam Peckinpah's heroes are flawed. In traditional American serious cinema, heroes display weaknesses, especially toward babies and mothers, but inherent flaws in their character, temperament, or outlook are quite another matter. In this regard, as in others, Peckinpah's films are unusual. The flaws of their chief characters take various shapes. They may be faults or deficiencies, imperfections or shortcomings, mistakes of judgment or errors in basically decent, honest, honorable, or even noble people, however one defines "noble." Conversely, they may be marks of decency, honor, principle, or goodness in vicious, immoral, or bad people, such as outlaws and criminals. As Bernard Shaw insightfully observes, "It is generally admitted that even good men have their weaknesses; what is less recognized is that rascals have their points of honor."[1] Knowing that this is so, Sam Peckinpah understands that just as a flaw in a good person may bring about his defeat, so an ethical action by a bandit or felon may result in his downfall. Such complexities mark characters in Peckinpah's motion pictures, none of whom is a paragon of traditional virtues but many of whom have integrity and stature that are rare in contemporary cinema and stage drama.

"Cliché or not," says Doug McKinney, "Peckinpah subscribes to the ideal of the Boy Scout Law: Steve Judd in *Ride the High Country,* as an ideal character, is trustworthy, loyal, helpful, friendly, courteous, kind, obedient, cheerful, thrifty, brave, clean, and reverent. But," McKinney adds shrewdly, "Peckinpah is even more concerned with what it takes to maintain any of those virtues, drawn more to those who struggle short of ideals, or who strive to maintain them despite the cost." Some of "what it takes" is pride in one's professionalism, which derives from commitment, "and a character can retain that pride even without successful achievement: believing in commitment is half the battle."[2] Acting upon that belief is the other half. Such commitment and the price one pays for it put Peckinpah's figures far beyond the ideal of the Boy Scout Law, regardless of the extent to which this commitment resembles that law.

Take the quotation from which the title of this chapter derives: "I . . . have no other law but mine. . . . I must blaze my trail. . . . [E]very man must find out his own way." This passage might seem to come from an early draft of one of Peckinpah's movies, probably a western, or from one of his unfilmed screenplays. It does not. Rather, it is from Stuart Gilbert's translation of act 3 of Jean-Paul Sartre's *The Flies*. Here is a fuller quotation, in which Orestes tells Zeus about himself: "Outside nature, against nature, without excuse, beyond remedy, except what remedy I find within myself. But I shall not return under your law; I am doomed to have no other law but mine. . . . I must blaze my trail. For I, Zeus, am a man, and every man must find out his own way. . . . I am free."[3] Is this coupling of the Left Bank and the Old West, or of ancient Greece and the New World, farfetched, an ex-post-facto rationalization that employs both ideas and terminology that are remote to a film artist's frames of reference? In Peckinpah's case, no. In the late 1940s, after leaving the United States Marine Corps, he attended Fresno State College and then the University of Southern California. While at both institutions, he read voraciously. Marie Selland, his wife at the time, explicitly identifies a few of his major reading interests: "'Aristotle's *Poetics* was something that seemed to grab him and he was constantly referring to it.'" Camus also interested him, not only *The Stranger* and *The Rebel* but the collection of essays in *The Myth of Sisyphus* as well.[4] Peckinpah "knew Aristotle's *Poetics* cold," says Paul Seydor.[5] It "gave him the foundations for dramatic writing," notes David Weddle, "and he became a strong believer in the philosopher's theory that great drama provides an audience with a catharsis through which they can purge their own pain, rage, and fear." Such contemporary French writings as Sartre's *No Exit* and *The Flies,* adds Weddle, also fascinated him. The writings of Sartre and Camus "articulated feelings that had been evolving within Sam."[6] His "favorite novel" was *The Stranger,* reports Seydor, who cites Katy Haber (dialogue director, production assistant, or assistant director to Peckinpah on five films) as stating that "Peckinpah was greatly pleased when he read of *The Rebel* being used as a way to explicate some of the underlying ideas that are dramatized in *The Wild Bunch.*"[7] The Department of Drama of the University of Southern California reinforced these foundations.[8] There, he read Plato as well as Aristotle, and he began to write a thesis on theories of tragedy from ancient to modern times, getting as far as Ibsen in his notes and drafts.[9]

During the period that Peckinpah attended Fresno State and USC, the plays, novels, essays, and philosophical writings of Jean-Paul Sartre and Albert Camus were largely responsible for the great impact that existentialism had in this country, certainly among young professors and students at our colleges and universities. These French artist-philosophers were exciting, they were "in." Those were heady days, and to be *au courant,* although the younger American professoriat and students did not necessarily think of the subject in terms of voguishness, they devoured the plays, novels, and essays of Sartre and Camus. A number of those who were not philosophers or students of philosophy even went as far as to read these Frenchmen's philosophical writings. In western America, Peckinpah imbibed the existentialist essays and plays associated with Paris's Left Bank. In both Fresno and Los Angeles, he read *The Flies* (in the translation quoted above), *No Exit,* and *The Wall* by Sartre and *The Stranger, The Plague, The Rebel,* and *The Myth of Sisyphus* by Camus.[10] Years later, he described *The Ballad of Cable Hogue* as "a new version of Sartre's *The Flies* with a touch of Keystone Cops."[11] With Peckinpah's films in mind, we find that at least one passage in *The Myth of Sisyphus* fairly leaps from the page, for it links philosopher and bandit: "If one believes Homer, Sisyphus was the wisest and most prudent of mortals. According to another tradition, however, he was disposed to practice the profession of highwayman."[12]

To use the existentialist vocabulary of Sartre and Camus, existence precedes essence, which is to say that what human beings are or should be follows their actuality or appearance on earth. According to the humanistic type of existentialism of these writers—who were philosophers, essayists, novelists, and dramatists—there is no outside force or purpose, deistic or other, to give human beings meaning prior to their existence. Kenneth Burke's distinction between essence and existence cleverly follows the notion of a six-year-old child, who told him, "'There *is* an Easter bunny, but he isn't *real.*'" Says Burke, "I saw the application immediately: the Easter bunny has a *being,* or *essence,* but he does not *exist.*"[13] According to the existentialists, human beings are a higher form of life than Easter bunnies. Since the core or moral foundations of human beings are not predetermined or fixed in advance, people are free to choose and are thus responsible for what they are.

In the words of Sartre, "Freedom is choice."[14] Through will and through action, by which one implements one's will, each human being defines his essence, his being, himself. As Camus says, "There always comes a time when one must choose between contemplation and action. This is called becoming a man."[15] In choosing, and in acting upon that choice, each man—the generic term of course includes woman[16]—assumes responsibility for everyone, since morally speaking he chooses and creates a model. If he rejects an opportunity to kill someone in anger, he establishes this choice as an exemplary moral law for everyone. If he kills people and accepts these murders as justifiable and honorable under certain conditions, which he defines, as Orestes does in *The Flies,* then he establishes his motives for this act as right and honorable for everyone, simultaneously rejecting the morality of those who consider the action in itself to be wrong and dishonorable, whatever the motives. Although morality is subjectively determined, its enactment as a model implicates mankind.

What if one refuses to choose, as each of the three main characters of *No Exit* does? According to Sartre, refusal is itself a choice, since one chooses not to define oneself by action and either to exist without self-definition or to accept the definition of others. Willy-nilly, one defines oneself—either positively by choices and deeds, or negatively by evasions and inaction. Even an apparently external force involves choice. To quote Sartre: "If I am mobilized in a war, this war is *my* war; it is in my image and I deserve it. I deserve it first because I could always get out of it by suicide or by desertion. . . . For lack of getting out of it, I have *chosen* it. This can be due to inertia, to cowardice in the face of public opinion, or because I prefer certain other values to the value of the refusal to join in the war (the good opinion of my relatives, the honor of my family, etc.). Any way you look at it, it is a matter of a choice."[17]

In separate interviews, Peckinpah virtually echoes these views: "In a land for all intents and purposes without the law"—that is, a world in which one's morality is not predetermined—the outlaws of the West "made their own," and "The outcast is the individualist. I see color, conflict, a wish for something better, in the man who strikes out for himself."[18] Peckinpah paraphrases his father: "When the time comes, he used to say, you stand up and you're counted. For the right thing. For something that matters. It's the ultimate test. You either compromise to the point where it destroys you or you stand up and say, 'Fuck off.'" In other words, you choose, and in doing so you make your choice a model for mankind. But one must act upon one's choice, not merely talk about it. "I'm not an anti-intellectual, but I'm against the pseudo-intellectuals who roll like dogs in their own verbal diarrhea and call it purpose and identity," Peckinpah declares. "An intellectual who embodies his intellect in action, that's a complete human being. But sitting back and quarterbacking from the stands is playing with yourself."[19]

Peckinpah's feature films, which are his major works of art, conform to what Camus says of the great novels, that they are works by "philosophical novelists" and thereby "the contrary of [works by] thesis-writers." The preference of the former authors for creating "in images rather than in reasoned arguments" reveals that to them a work of art "is the outcome of an often unexpressed philosophy, its illustration and its consummation. But it is complete only through the implications of that philosophy."[20] Peckinpah's films, which are certainly replete with imagery and which only occasionally contain reasoned arguments or thesis statements (and these arguments and statements are usually deficiencies that one must overlook in view of the overall excellences of the films), are products, illustrations, and consummations of his philosophy, which is existentialist. With this in mind, let us examine some of the implications of his movies.

* * *

Perhaps Peckinpah's unrecognized, therefore unacknowledged, affinities to A. S. Fleischman's screenplay *The Deadly Companions*, to be analyzed in chapter 4, revolve around its existentialist aspects, which are embodied in the conventional trappings of its genre, the western. As authored by Fleischman and as directed by Peckinpah, the defining moments of the protagonist, Yellowleg, are those in which he chooses to admit the truth (although Kit's son accidentally died in the crossfire that resulted from the bank robbery, he confesses to her, it was he who shot the boy); to accompany Kit to Siringo; to return to her to protect her from Apaches rather than continue his pursuit of Turk, who fled the previous night; and to have a life with Kit rather than lose her by killing Turk. What is most significant about Peckinpah's disputes with the film's producer, as chapter 4 will document, is that Charles B. FitzSimons diminished Peckinpah's fidelity to Fleischman's scene of the final altercation between Yellowleg and Billy. At this point in the novel/screenplay/film, Yellowleg swiftly, unhesitatingly shoots Billy, who stands in the way of his revenge upon Turk, as he would dispatch a barking dog who got in his path. Until the protagonist redefines, thereby recreates himself when Kit forces him to choose between abjuring vengeance and forsaking her, he is his revenge, marking his being by a dedication to this purpose, which includes eliminating whoever stands in the way of fulfilling it. To FitzSimons, Yellowleg's concentration on his vendetta means ignoring, not ruthlessly stamping out, any impediment to it. Far from exemplifying existentialist choice, although neither Fleischman nor Peckinpah would probably put it in these terms, such intense focus would remove it from the reality created by the characters who demand that on each occasion a conscious choice be made.

* * *

Complexities mark characters in *Ride the High Country*. Joshua Knudsen's language and rules of conduct cue audiences to consider him not only a harsh and inflexible religious fanatic, an unyielding, moralistic despot who may have driven his wife, Hester (probably named after the heroine of *The Scarlet Letter*), to seek affection elsewhere—that is, to commit adultery—but also a tyrannical father. Despite his protestations that he wants his daughter Elsa to marry, she believes that he considers no man good enough for her. He calls the mining town, Coarse Gold,[21] "a sinkhole of depravity, a place of shame and sin," and he asserts that Billy Hammond, who wanted to marry her and whom she wants to marry, is "evil" and "sinful." One of the film's first shocks occurs when viewers, having sided with Elsa against her father, see Billy in Coarse Gold, because they quickly recognize the irony that the assessment of the rigid Knudsen was entirely accurate. In refusing to permit her to go there and marry him, the flawed father acted in his daughter's best interest. She learns this, although she does not explicitly say so, after the wedding ceremony and she begins to suspect it only a short time before, when she reunites with Billy. Although spectators have regarded Heck Longtree as a callous, love-her-and-leave-her ne'er-do-well, they recognize, also ironically, that despite the flaws revealed by his early actions, he is, unlike the man she initially wants to marry, decent.

There is additional irony in that the unblemished and sympathetic Steve Judd, the "reliable" and "honest" man the bankers want, whom the critic quoted earlier compares to a Boy Scout, has what Gil Westrum accurately calls an "ironbound code of ethics." Partly because his reliability, honesty, and ethics are valued by most audiences, partly because he has the saving grace of a sense of humor (the hole in his boot, he quips, was made to his specifications according to "the principle of ventilation"), partly because his coeval, Westrum, plans and commits a felony, partly because he is protective of young Elsa and forgiving of young Heck, but mainly, I believe, because the ethics of the more apparently rigid Knudsen seem more severe than Judd's, one tends not to think of Judd in these terms. Yet his values are every bit as inflexible and harsh as those of Knudsen. Unlike Elsa and Heck, this legalistic man agrees to abide by the decision of the Miners Court on whether Elsa must stay with Billy Hammond, whom she married the night before, or leave with Judd. To Judd, the law is the law; but to the criminally intentioned Westrum, it is manipulable, and he unhesitatingly thwarts the law (though not justice) by taking, at gunpoint, Judge Tolliver's license to perform marriage ceremonies so that, at the Miners Court, when Westrum asks the judge whether he possesses that license, the judge can truthfully reply in the negative (it is in Westrum's physical possession). Whereas Knudsen expresses his values in off-putting terms and seems to embody the father figure as a relentless moral taskmaster, all three words descriptive of malevolent figures in westerns, Judd expresses his own ethics endearingly. He has learned "the value of self-respect," which, while worth little in the open market, has a great value to him. In perhaps the film's most quoted line, derived from Peckinpah's father, Judd says, "All I want is to enter my house justified." In short, Judd seems to embody the best qualities of the traditional western hero. There is a further irony: despite the different ways each manifests them, the essential values of both Knudsen and Judd are good.

This is not to say that their values are identical. Near the end of the film, Peckinpah makes it clear that they are not. "My father says there's only right and wrong, good and evil, nothing between," says Elsa. "It isn't that simple, is it?" "No, it isn't," replies Judd. "It should be, but it isn't." Yet while he will testify in court for Heck, so that Heck's punishment will not be too harsh, he will not testify for Westrum. His reason: "Because he was my friend." Judd's ability to forgive goes only so far; to put the matter another way, he is flawed. Yet—another complexity—this flaw is part of a virtue, his persistent refusal to believe that his friend is dishonest, despite so many of Westrum's suggestions that point to this conclusion, until he catches Westrum in a dishonest action (attempted theft).

Unlike these characters, who are flawed decent people, the Hammond brothers are flawed indecent people. The flaw that undoes them is their sense of what Billy calls their "family honor." During the shootout in the mountains, after two brothers are killed, Billy and Henry urge Elder Hammond to leave with them. "You're getting out?" Elder asks incredulously. "You got two brothers dead and you talk about running!" This sequence prepares viewers for the final shootout, wherein the three surviving Hammonds, for the sake of family honor, accept Judd's and Westrum's challenge to a straight-up, in-the-open gun battle. In this battle, the older, more experienced gunfighters defeat them.

Although Peckinpah rewrote a great deal of Richard E. Lyons's screen-play, as Weddle points out, he "made only one structural change." Yet this change "was crucial." Weddle says, "Instead of Westrum getting killed in the final gun battle, he switched things around; Judd would die and Wes-trum would survive. It was an inspired move, not only because it flew in the face of the genre's conventions (the villain must always die for his sins), but because it threw the story's theme into sharp focus. With a few quick strokes of the pen, Peckinpah had made Westrum the protagonist and the upstanding Judd the antagonist."[22] Since both characters seem to be prom-inent, the conception of a single protagonist is problematic in *Ride the High Country*. Nevertheless, Weddle has hit upon a salient point.

Despite Westrum's efforts to persuade Judd to steal the gold, which apparently present Judd with a series of ethical choices, they are not real tests, for Judd has clearly made his moral choices before the film begins. So apparently, but only apparently, has Westrum, whose first appearance has him fleecing a hick in a rigged carnival shooting booth and who joins Judd for the express purpose of stealing the gold on the way back from the mining camp. When Judd makes Westrum his prisoner, Westrum determines to escape—believing that his poverty, after many years of law enforcement, justifies his attempted crime and rejecting Judd's view that neither of them has a right to claim he is owed anything for those years. Only after he returns from the high country, where one might say, truly though perhaps tritely, that he has acquired higher values, and sees his old friend, young friend, and the girl they befriended trapped by the Hammonds, who are about to kill them, does he make an existential choice to join the force of good against that of evil, despite the possible cost to himself. When he and Judd are victorious, even though Judd is fatally wounded, he chooses morality. "Don't worry about anything," he tells his dying friend of the gold. "I'll take care of it. Just like you would've." "Hell, I know that," says Judd. "I always did. You just forgot it for a while, that's all. So long, partner." Neither Westrum's change of mind nor change of heart is corny, partly because his status as Judd's friend suggests that his criminal actions are aberrations and partly because his existential choice is earned, coming as it does from the core of his being. "A few years ago," says Sartre, "someone pointed out to me that the characters in my plays and novels make their decisions abruptly and in a state of crisis, that, for example, in *The Flies,* a moment is enough for Orestes to effect his conversion. Of course!"[23] It takes a crisis to force a choice. Experiencing a crisis, Westrum makes an existential choice.

* * *

With *Major Dundee,* whose two chief characters are more pointedly antagonists, we come to an aspect of existentialism known as "bad faith." As Sartre says, bad faith is essentially self-deception, "a lie to oneself." Since one cannot lie about something one is ignorant of, the essence of bad faith is that "the liar actually is in complete possession of the truth which he is hiding." He may be hiding an unpleasant truth or he may be presenting a pleasing untruth as true, but the deceiver and the deceived are the same person, "which means that I must know in my capacity as deceiver the truth which is hidden from me in my capacity as deceived." The person who acts in bad faith may view evidence, but he does not fully consider it, since bad faith "is resigned in advance to not being fulfilled by this evidence, to not being persuaded and transformed into good faith." Rather, it is resolved "to adhere to uncertain truths." Bad faith forms "contradictory concepts which unite in themselves both an idea and the negation of that idea." Instead of coordinating or synthesizing them, the person acting in bad faith simultaneously "seeks to affirm their identity while preserving their differences."[24] Bad faith is more complex than this paragraph's summary may suggest. To deceive oneself, the lie must to some extent, however superficially, be plausible. Part of what makes it plausible is that it contains one or more elements that are true.

Of the complex, flawed, forceful, principal personages of *Major Dundee,* let us begin not with the title character but with his rival, the initially imprisoned Confederate Lieutenant Ben Tyreen, who virtually paraphrases a statement by Orestes to Zeus in act 3 of *The Flies:* "I am no criminal, and you have no power to make me atone for an act I don't regard as a crime." Tyreen has been indicted and convicted of three crimes. The one crime of which there appears to be no doubt is the murder of a prison guard. In attempting to escape from the Union prison, Tyreen and four enlisted men clubbed a Union soldier, who died. In command of the prison, Major Dundee, acting as judge and jury, finds him guilty.

Some time earlier, Dundee was one member of a five-officer military court whose four other members were equally divided on whether to find Tyreen guilty of killing a fellow officer. Dundee cast the deciding vote: guilty. In the dramatic present, Tyreen protests that he killed his opponent in a duel, which he claims the southern-born Dundee should recognize to be an honorable form of combat that exempts the victor from the charge of murder. With our twentieth-century view of this form of nineteenth-century honor, which, to be sure, not everyone in that century thought honorable, we may simultaneously accept Tyreen's subjective view as valid for him and also remain skeptical of its validity. "Still blaming me instead of yourself?" Dundee asks him and, intimating that Tyreen is acting in bad faith, "When are you going to learn you've made all your own troubles?" Suggesting Tyreen's bad faith later in the film, Dundee calls him "a would-be cavalier, an Irish potato farmer with a plumed hat," which he does not deny, for he is an Irish immigrant who sports a plumed hat.

The third crime is treason, a charge Tyreen denies when Dundee tries to recruit him to fight the Apache. "Captain Tyreen, does the prospect of serving under your country's flag once again seem more attractive than dragging its chains in this prison?" "It is not my country, Major Dundee. I damn its flag and I damn you." Tyreen does not need to respond to Dundee's later accusation—"You're a traitor to your country, Ben. Are you going to blame me for that, too?"—since he wears the uniform of what he considers another country, the Confederate States of America, and he has already denied that the United States is his country. However, the issue is not that simple, for he joined the Confederate army after the Union army expelled him. Complicating the point further, he admits that he has "killed men in a hopeless war" for the Confederacy, does not deny that he was, in Dundee's phrase, "fighting for a white-columned plantation house you never had and never will," and despite his having called the Civil War "hopeless" for his side, declares, "After the war, Amos, the Tyreens of County Clare will become the landed gentry of Virginia." The extent to which Tyreen has lied and still lies to himself is a source of the character's complexity. Has he defined his essence, or has he let others define it, using bad faith to justify his deeds? "Don't you ever have any doubts about who you are?" asks Dundee at a time when he himself has doubts about who he is. "I've been three men already, Amos," Tyreen replies. "That's enough for one lifetime." Between them, Dundee and he name the three men: "Irish immigrant." "Cashiered American officer." "Confederate renegade."

During the film, Dundee defines Tyreen's essence, of which Tyreen admits only what suits him. Before crossing into Mexico, when a troop of Confederate cavalry appears on the horizon, Tyreen has an opportunity to lead his prisoners-turned-Union-soldiers to join them.

Major Dundee: We don't have much time. Your word is worth about as
    much as your cause.
O. W. Hadley: Then why don't you release him from it?
Major Dundee: Ben, you gave it; you break it, and be damned to you.

Sergeant Chillum: What do you want from us, anyway?
Major Dundee: I've got what I want, Sergeant. I've got his word.

Tyreen keeps his word, which suits his view of himself as a southern gentleman. Otherwise, he becomes Dundee's, and the Union's, man. In Mexico, he defuses a potential race riot that Jimmy Lee Benteen creates by
belittling Aesop, when he steps in to compliment Aesop on the professionalism with which Aesop and the other "coloreds" in the Union army
had crossed the Rio Grande. Although he executes O. W. Hadley rather
than permits Dundee to kill him, he does so after he unsuccessfully pleads
with Dundee to let him deal with the issue of O.W.'s desertion on the
ground that the Confederate members of the expedition should take care
of their own, a caretaking that would obviously not culminate in O.W.'s
death. Here, more clearly than in the earlier episodes, Tyreen becomes that
which he claims not essentially to be, the Union's or Dundee's officer.[25]
Tyreen's costume reveals his change. As Jim Silke says, his and Peckinpah's
aim was to have the costumes "reflect certain changes" in the characters.
"I did one—the Richard Harris character, Tyreen—showed him as a prisoner; then as he puts together a uniform, half Union, half Confederate;
then as he deteriorates into an animal."[26] Acting in bad faith, Tyreen is
defined by Dundee. At the end, Tyreen symbolically saves the Union,
which he had earlier denied, when he rescues its flag from the French
commander who seizes it, and hands it to Dundee, following which the
French officer shoots him in the back; he then kills the Frenchman and,
with his own death imminent, dives headlong into the midst of the enemies of what has become his country. Revealing this engagement to be
national rather than personal, Dundee pointedly displays his country's
flag, which he did not do in his previous combat with the French.

Whereas some of the enigmatic, puzzling, or unclear characteristics of
the title character may be deliberate ambiguity on the part of Peckinpah,
others may derive from the studio's cuts. While recognizing that what has
been deleted might unexpectedly come to light and change this interpretation of what presently exists, one is bound to analyze the film on the
basis of what remains of it. Let us recognize what we do not know.

When Dundee voted Tyreen guilty, did he cast his vote, as Tyreen
charges, to please the generals and thereby receive a promotion, or did
he do so, as he says, because Tyreen killed a fellow officer? Dundee does
not respond to Tyreen's accusation. The structure of the film that survives
suggests that Peckinpah may have kept the answer ambiguous or that
Dundee himself does not know, for perhaps his motives were mixed.

"Have you ever stopped to think why they made you a jailer instead of a soldier?" Tyreen taunts him. Dundee is forced to do so earlier, when his second-in-command, Captain Frank Waller, tells him, "You should recognize that your transfer to this post was a disciplinary action, pure and simple. And if you try to fight your own war again, as you did at Gettysburg, they'll break you." What did he do at Gettysburg to warrant disciplinary action? Of what did "[his] own war" consist? We do not know, and partly because the Durango sequence—which dramatizes his personal obsessions, the war within him—appears to be one of the most, if not the most, extensively butchered in the film, one may legitimately infer that while his actions at Gettysburg may or may not have been clarified in Peckinpah's print, the nature of his personal war and his own obsessive demons probably were. Very likely, Richard Slotkin is accurate when he maintains, "Dundee regards the actual politics of the Mexican revolution/civil war as irrelevant to his mission and tries to limit his engagement with the French and the Mexicans to tactical exercises. He seeks to follow his own script"—or as I would say, congruent with the title of this chapter, his own laws, trails, and ways—"of rescue, revenge, and personal redemption."[27] However, parallels between the Mexican and the American Civil War may be clearer in Peckinpah's version than in the film now available.

Despite what we do not know about Dundee and his motives, the fact that he is driven by mixed or ambiguous forces, and the actions that we see him commit and fail to commit, make him a rich, powerful character. "They won't break me," he tells Captain Waller, "not if I get Charriba and those kids. . . . I am a professional soldier, I'm not a prison keeper. Now, this is something that's got to be done and I'm going to do it—now." "Are you pursuing the Apache, Major, or a promotion?" asks Waller. "Whatever my reasons are, Frank, you'd better get down on your knees and pray to God I don't take you with me." In referring to what motivates him, Dundee uses the plural. In dramatizing his errors of judgment and his successes, the film demonstrates that Dundee is what he calls himself, a professional soldier. What he aims to do, despite daunting odds, is, as he says, something that needs to be done. He may be pursuing a promotion (or a transfer) as well as the Apache, but whatever personal triumph he may acquire, his pursuit of the Apache is justified.

What gives Dundee his stature is that, in Peckinpah's words, "through all the shit, through all the lies, through all the drunkenness and the bullshit that Major Dundee goes through, he survives and continues!"[28] However flawed he is, however mistaken some of his judgments are, he perseveres. Soon after the beginning of the film, when Sierra Charriba has destroyed the Rostes ranch, tortured and murdered soldiers and civilians, and abducted the three Rostes boys, Dundee swears to Potts, "I'll get the children and I'll get him." From the outset of his venture, his self-imposed mission is twofold, retrieving the kidnapped boys and bringing the murderer-abductors to justice. "Until the Apache is taken or destroyed"—the phrase becomes a mantra, repeated although not chanted by Dundee, Tyreen, and even Sergeant Gomez at various moments of the film.

When the old Apache returns the Rostes boys, some of Dundee's skepticism vanishes. Tyreen's statement of purpose is somewhat misleading:[29]

> *Lieutenant Tyreen:* Are you going back now that you've got what you came for, Major?
> *Major Dundee:* Everything points to that old man talking straight. Potts is half convinced. I'm more 'n half.
> *Lieutenant Tyreen:* Did it ever occur to you that Charriba gave us what we wanted because he intends to take it back again?
> *Major Dundee:* It's occurred to me.

What Dundee does is partly sagacious and partly unwise. The shrewd aspect is ensuring that he will keep what Sierra Charriba has given him: he has three soldiers take the three Rostes boys back to the fort. Thus, whatever the outcome of his decision to attack Charriba, he accomplishes one of the two parts of his mission, rescue. His faulty judgment lies in obeying the more than half of his mind that is convinced, and he leads his troops into Charriba's ambush. If Peckinpah had made Dundee try to attack Charriba before sending the children safely home, the major would be a fool. If he had made both of Dundee's decisions successful, the major would resemble a traditional western hero. One result of the different outcomes of his decisions is a rich ambiguity. Another is reinforcement of Dundee's determination. "Major, we can't follow the Apache," urges Tyreen. "I'm not letting go of that Injun," insists Dundee.

The film seems strongly to stress Dundee's inabilities and insecurities: his need of Tyreen's assistance in order to accomplish his self-imposed mission, his helplessness when Tyreen might break his word and join his fellow Confederate soldiers, and his noninterference in the apparently imminent race riot, leaving Tyreen to handle the problem, all of which may suggest greater stature for Tyreen; his apparent self-doubts, which we sense by the nagging questions of his reasons for being where he is and for pursuing the mission; his splitting the command by his insistence that O. W. Hadley be executed; his real self-doubts after his blunder in going to an unsafe area results in his being wounded; his deterioration in Durango. These weaknesses, compounded by Charriba's triumphs, including the ambush and the wounding of Dundee, which results from a slip-up in fundamental security when Dundee dallies with Teresa, may tend to overshadow his successes. What is important is that we recognize both. After liberating the village, Dundee orders his men to get drunk so that the captured French troops can escape and his men will not have to tend them, which prompts Tyreen to declare, "You are either a seventy-dollar, red-wool, pure-quill military genius or the biggest damn fool in northern Mexico." Dundee's response emphasizes ambiguity: "No question of it." Following this exchange, his guerrilla strategy with the French army is successful. Then, when he is wounded while in Teresa's company beside a river that is beyond his security zone, Tyreen insists that he give up command so that he can go to a doctor in Durango. However, Tyreen's outburst at Dundee is so splenetic, one should be wary of accepting what he says at face value, which most viewers and writers, following Dundee's lead, do: "You ought to give up soldiering altogether. You were trapped at the river. Ambushed like a shavetail. You caused a boy's death and you split your own command. And now, just straying outside your own picket line. What are you doing, Major? Easing your own conscience in the arms of a woman—a woman, if I might say so, of rather doubtful virtue? Just what the bloody hell are you doing here in the first place, Amos?" Remember Tyreen's motives in humiliating Dundee. Although the major split his command, Tyreen himself was the man who elected to shoot the "boy" (O. W. Hadley, hardly a boy), who was a fellow Confederate soldier. Perhaps more important, the woman whose virtue Tyreen calls dubious rejected him in favor of Dundee. Whatever legitimate self-doubts Dundee may have, the behavior of Tyreen, who acts in existentialist bad faith, is shabby at best, monstrous at worst.

Since Columbia Pictures cut most of the motivation for Dundee's degradation and self-humiliation in Durango, all we know is that he progresses through a series of degradations and humiliations. What one writer on existentialist philosophy says of bad faith seems, and I emphasize this verb, to characterize Dundee at Durango: "Acknowledgment of guilt for all things becomes a device in bad faith by which one may avoid being held guilty for any one thing."[30] What I want to stress is that Dundee overcomes degradation and self-humiliation, and realizes himself as a soldier, that is, he establishes his *bona fides,* his military expertise. First, he defeats the Apache by the same means the Apache defeated him, disguise and ambush, thereby achieving the second of his two objectives. Acknowledging that Dundee "destroyed" the Apache, Tyreen proposes to fight him.

Dundee agrees, but the arrival of the French army forces them to postpone their battle, which would be the usual climax of a conventional western: two antagonists delay fighting to the death until the end of the film. In *Major Dundee,* a shoot-out, knife-fight, or fistfight does not occur. What happens instead is Dundee's second demonstration of expertise in military strategy. He forces the French, who hold a superior position, to attack on conditions favorable to him, rather than to hold their position and fight on their own terms. Thus, he enters what Tyreen sarcastically calls "a real war," with what Lieutenant Graham, who frequently quotes Napoleon, pointedly dubs "the pride of Europe." Not only is Dundee victorious, but the dynamics of battle create such momentum that, as indicated earlier, Tyreen himself hoists the Union flag that he earlier said was not his flag.

In summation, the sometimes self-doubting Dundee achieves both of his objectives, thereby vindicating himself, and he defeats an army that is larger than his own, thereby outdoing himself. By contrast, Tyreen achieves none of his objectives: he does not survive to lead his Confederate veterans home, which upon the capture or defeat of the Apache Dundee agreed to, and he does not kill Dundee. Is Dundee's victory tainted? Insofar as he has decimated his troops in order to accomplish his goals and insofar as Tyreen is so forceful a character that his death clouds Dundee's victory, yes. Given the terms of the film, however, Dundee vindicates himself. Perhaps Peckinpah's version of the movie would cast doubt on this conclusion. If so, its restoration will prompt a reassessment of this summation.

* * *

As David Ansen wrote in his reappraisal of *The Wild Bunch* upon its re-release, fully restored, more than a quarter of a century after it first opened, this film "threw out the moral compass points we expected from a Western."[31] The film does so almost from the outset. Rugged-looking men in army uniforms observe children whose innocent-looking countenances, we discover as one of the moral compass points collapses, flow from their delight at watching a scorpion and a cluster of ants fight each other to the death. After the soldiers arrive in the center of town, they dismount and, led by Pike Bishop, march down the main street. When he and a woman accidentally bump into each other, she drops her packages. "I beg your pardon, ma'am," he apologizes courteously as he smiles and picks them up. "Allow me," says Dutch, taking them and carrying them, while Bishop offers her his arm, escorting her. Like the cherubic youngsters, the soldiers are not what they seem but, we soon learn, are bank robbers in disguise. Before they enter the town bank, we see, on a rooftop, men waiting in ambush, led by Harrigan, who represents the railroad and the law.

Where are our sympathies? With the good guys, of course. But who are the good guys? Are there, in fact, good guys? "If they move, kill 'em!" exclaims Bishop after the soldier-uniformed robbers enter the bank. Since it is a truism that one would not associate this statement with a so-called good guy, exit another moral compass point. When Deke Thornton notices members of the South Texas Temperance Union marching down the main street, he foresees that they will be caught in the crossfire. "They should have been told," he reproves Harrigan, a railroad official who represents the law and who has laid a trap for the bank robbers. "Told what?" Harrigan asks scornfully and uncaringly. "How long do you think anybody in this manure pile could keep his mouth shut?" Out goes another moral compass point. Like Bishop's order, Harrigan's question is not a phrase one would associate with a nominal good guy. Bishop's regret, when he learns of the ambush, is only that executing the robbery will be more difficult than he had planned. He orders the chief teller to be shoved out the door to draw the first gunfire so that the gang might get away safely. As Ansen notes, the violent slaughter that ensues, in which blameless townspeople as well as predators and prey are killed or wounded, "is played off the reactions of terrified but awestruck children including terrified but fascinated children" and is "doubly disorienting because the audience can't tell the good guys from the bad."[32] In Weddle's words, "The bounty hunters are every bit as sleazy and ruthless as the outlaws, neither group displaying a glimmer of guilt as they blow away innocent bystanders caught in the crossfire."[33] Peckinpah even shows Harrigan shooting an innocent bystander. The only feeling anyone shows that is akin to remorse is momentary regret, when Thornton hesitates to kill his former comrade, Bishop—a pause that, however fleeting, is long enough for a tuba player to get in the way and take the bullet when Thornton, despite his passing contrition, fires his pistol—and Harrigan duly reprimands him for the missed opportunity. Harrigan more fully reveals his indifference to the massacre when prominent townspeople condemn him: "We're holding you and your whole damned railroad responsible for this carnage" and "Innocent people are dead—women dying, men—because you used our town as a battlefield." "I'm trying to catch a band of outlaws," he justifies himself. "We represent the law."

By default, our sympathies go to Harrigan's antagonists and to Thornton, who leads the bounty hunters for Harrigan but whose sympathies are with those he pursues. "We're after men," he later tells the other railroad deputies, whom he denigrates as "gutter trash," "and I wish to God I was with them." When Harrigan taunts him with wanting to join the title characters, he explains, "What I like and what I need are two different things. Listen, Mr. Harrigan, I don't want to go back to prison"—where, a few moments later, a quick flashback shows he was whipped. "I gave you my word," he insists, and then bitterly asks Harrigan, "How does it feel? Getting paid for it? Getting paid to sit back and hire your killings, with the law's arms around you? How does it feel to be so goddamn right?" "Good," is Harrigan's succinct answer, in which he effectively condemns himself and justifies those he is intent on killing.

Thornton does not act in bad faith, for he does not deceive himself as to why he behaves as he does. Although he disapproves of his actions, he accepts them as necessary and desirable conditions for being released from prison, on which he places a higher priority than tracking down his former comrade. Nevertheless, he recognizes that he has become what Beatrice-Joanna calls herself in Middleton and Rowley's play *The Changeling*, "the deed's creature."

In *The Wild Bunch,* the character who acts in bad faith is Angel. Furious and frustrated because Mapache, who killed his father, is the man with whom his fiancée ran off, he demands that a village elder tell him this man's whereabouts. "Why do you wish to know? For your father or for the whore?" asks the old man. Bishop gives Angel an ultimatum: "Either you learn to live with it or we leave you here." Angel subsides: "I go with you, Jefe." In Agua Verde, when the apparently noble Angel sees Teresa caressing Mapache, he kills her, not Mapache, whom he has as good an opportunity to shoot. In the village elder's terms, he murders the whore, not his father's killer. None of the characters who populate *The Wild Bunch* is unambiguously noble or ignoble. Harrigan has good reasons to kill or apprehend the Bunch, and even Mapache rises to the occasion when, later, in the midst of defeat by Pancho Villa's forces, a boy in uniform looks at him admiringly, reminding him of his obligation to his disciples.

Ironically, Thornton's mission makes his actions absurd. During the train robbery, while he and the bounty hunters chase the Bunch, Sergeant McHale wakes up, notices that the railroad deputies have gone, concludes that they have robbed the train, and orders a soldier to telegraph this news to headquarters. When the cavalry he dispatches to find the deputies catches up with them, one of the deputies shoots a soldier. When the other troops report this incident upon their return, it will confirm the sergeant's telegram. For this reason, if Thornton were to return to the United States after accomplishing his mission, he might still be sent back to jail.

In any case, Harrigan's monosyllabic rejoinder to Thornton after the Bunch escapes from the border town links Harrigan with Mapache, who like him symbolizes the law's authority. Later, Dutch contemptuously refers to the Mexican, "Generalissimo, hell! He's just another bandit grabbing all he can for himself." "Like some others I can mention?" quips Bishop, to the laughter of the other members of the Bunch. "Not so's you'd know it, Mr. Bishop," retorts Dutch. "We ain't nothing like him. We don't hang nobody." Despite the irony that they themselves kill people, Dutch is essentially right. As the film's title tells us, the Bunch is wild—untamed, unrestrained, free; but they are not corrupt. They take pride in professionally executing their jobs, not in murdering people in the name of abstract justice or authority.

They are also distinguished in that they are bonded together voluntarily and stand by each other. "When you side with a man you stay with him," Bishop admonishes one of the Bunch when a problem threatens to create a falling-out, "and if you can't do that you're like some animal." This code of loyalty and honor precipitates the final catastrophe. Bishop may be "the best," as Thornton calls him, but he is the best only because "he never got caught." "Being sure is my business," says the man who is "the best," and the words echo in the sound track; but this does not make him an exemplar of greatness or even of wisdom. He is flawed. He was sure that the knock on the hotel or brothel door to the suite in which he and Thornton were enjoying themselves with a group of prostitutes was room service, not the law; and as a result of his being wrong, Thornton was caught. If Bishop had had any sense, he admits, he would have killed the husband of the woman he loved, but he did not, and the man returned to kill her and wound him (as Dundee was wounded, in his thigh). "I was careless," admits the man who says his business was being sure, and he was also careless, during the rapidly moving events of the getaway from the bank, in forgetting to order Crazy Lee, who held the hostages at bay ("Till hell freezes over or you say different"), to leave with the other members of the Bunch. As Weddle points out, Bishop is not "a macho stick figure" but "a tragic character of great complexity: a man haunted by his failures in both the distant and recent past, who fails time and again to live up to the ideals and ethics he has set for himself,"[34] although, I maintain, his failure ends at the movie's finale, when he does live up to them.

A tragic character: as Camus says, if the myth of Sisyphus is tragic, "that is because its hero is conscious." Sisyphus, "powerless and rebellious, knows the whole extent of his wretched condition" and says yes. Thus, ironically, "One must imagine Sisyphus happy." "If death is not the free determination of our being," notes Sartre, "it can not complete our life." Meaning does not come from outside oneself; it "can only come from subjectivity."[35] In *The Wild Bunch*, death is the free determination of the outlaws, who give it their subjective meaning. In the words of Camus, people are "killed for the ideas or illusions that give them a reason for living," since "what is called a reason for living is also an excellent reason for dying."[36]

When a real man sides with another, as I have quoted Bishop saying, he does not abandon him.[37] The Bunch's decision to affirm their bond with Angel, one of their own, knowing that their free election to do so will probably mean their death, raises them above animals. Despite all other considerations, it gives them integrity and elevates their stature to that of tragedy. "Well, he had guts," says Lyle, who with his brother Tector had an almost fatal altercation with Angel. "He played his string out to the end," affirms Dutch, whose life Angel saved during the train robbery. Thornton too gave his word, Bishop reminds the Bunch. "Gave his word to a railroad!" exclaims Dutch, contemptuously. "It's his word!" insists Bishop. "That ain't what counts!" counters Dutch. "It's who you give it to!" Is this what distinguishes Thornton's pledge to the railroad official from Tyreen's promise to Dundee? Since no rejoinder comes from Bishop, one may take Dutch's last two exclamations as either conclusive or ironic. Either way, Thornton like Angel plays his string out to the end, which unlike Angel's is not death. Thornton does what he promised to do, but he will do no more. After the battle between the scorpion-gringos and Mapache's ant-army, which is the film's finale, Thornton picks up the gun of his fallen former comrade (personal memento and symbol of the extent to which each goes to demonstrate his integrity), sends the other bounty hunters back, probably (and actually, he soon learns) to their death, and joins Sykes and the revolutionists.

Is this code of honor that revolves around loyalty merely commonplace, sentimental machismo? Although one can, and some have, dismissed it as such, it is these belittling terms that are trite, not the actions of the quartet who, standing and walking as proud, purposeful, and free men, assert their values by putting their lives on the line. They choose to do so because of who they are, which quality informs how they act. After the failed bank robbery, Bishop says, "I'd like to make one good score and back off." After the successful train robbery, he and the other members of the Bunch have made a good score and can back off, but as Paul Seydor keenly observes, "if he were to leave now, he would only add another increment of shame to a load of guilt which has already become nearly intolerable"; and his and their "'no' contains an implicit 'yes,' like the 'no' of Camus's rebel," whose "no" means that a point has been reached, beyond which the rebel insists that one not go. "In other words, his no affirms the existence of a borderline."[38] According to Simmons, "That they die the way they lived *of their own choice* . . . is essential, for it gives them the personal integrity that is denied to the hundreds they kill as well as to the bounty hunters who grotesquely parody them in the battle's aftermath." Seydor perceives that the irony which permeates the film "turns in upon itself and becomes its opposite. When the Bunch attacks a whole army on behalf of their fallen comrade, theirs is a sacrificial gesture of human solidarity not so very different in principle from the values for which the revolutionaries are fighting."[39]

* * *

As quoted earlier, Peckinpah called *The Ballad of Cable Hogue* "a new version of Sartre's *The Flies* with a touch of Keystone Cops." I take Peckinpah's statement at face value, for I see no reason why he would deliberately try to mislead or trifle with readers, but I suspect that his remark is applicable chiefly in general and thematic terms. Although *The Ballad of Cable Hogue* has no visual passages parallel to Mack Sennett's Keystone Kops (as the word is usually spelled), it has affinities to them in some of the farcical action. Hildy throws a bottle at Hogue, which misses and breaks a window; when she kicks a door to open it, her foot breaks the wood; she throws a chamber pot at him, which misses him, but in trying to avoid it he trips on a rope, thereby untying it and bringing down a preacher's tent; and as he tries to mount his horse to ride away, he falls off and then chases the horse. There are also likenesses to Sennett's Kops in Peckinpah's speeded-up camera shots and in fast movement by actors: Sloane runs away from snakes; Hogue tidies up his home for Hildy; and Hildy, surprised by a stagecoach while she bathes in an outdoor tub, wraps a skimpy towel around herself and races into the house as the coach driver, his shotgun rider, and the passengers gape.

Similarly, *The Ballad of Cable Hogue* has affinities to *The Flies*. As Alan Casty states, "*Cable Hogue* pictures an absurdly comic world in which a god, when importuned, may bring you water, wealth, and the possibilities of love, but ends up getting you run over by a newfangled car when you are impulsively trying to save a man you had vowed to revenge yourself on."[40] Like the world of *The Flies*, that of *Cable Hogue* is absurdist.

"What emptiness! What endless emptiness, as far as the eye can reach!" exclaims Orestes in act 2, scene 1, of Sartre's play, using words that are applicable to the desert that is Hogue's universe. "Cable Hogue was born into this world, nobody knows when or where," says Joshua Sloane in his funeral sermon, and he adds, "Lord, he was a man." In Sartre's view, man appears, turns up on the scene, for no discernible reason. He might just as well not be as be, and he might just as well be somewhere else as where he is. In this sense, his existence is absurd—as absurd as the appearance of strangers in a desert in an automobile, Hildy's arrival in another automobile, and Sloane's entry on a motorcycle. God, whether Zeus or Jehovah, is capricious, and he is irrelevant to human beings, who define themselves by determining their own purposes and acting upon them. Seemingly by accident, Hogue finds water where, the film reiterates, there was none; and not only has no one else found any before, no one else can find any nearby after Hogue locates the one water hole in miles. He might just as easily have not discovered it. Is the water a gift from God, a reward for his humility before God after his arrogance toward God, as Seydor proposes?[41] If so, does God also give Hogue clothing and furniture when luggage and goods, apparently absurdly and fortuitously, fall from a stagecoach as it hurries away from him? If so, does God also make Taggart and Bowen arrive, as they apparently do by chance, at Hogue's water hole, which has become a coach stop? If so, what of Hogue's death, which seems as absurd and as fortuitous as his finding water, which is the basis of his prosperity? If God causes him to find water and to obtain clothing and furniture, and if God is responsible for Taggart's and Bowen's arrival, why does God cause Hogue to die after Hogue renounces vengeance and prepares to leave and live for love? "I'll live to spit on your graves!" he cries to Taggart and Bowen when they abandon him to death by thirst in the desert. Perhaps his vow and his later revenge on Taggart please the God of Vengeance. If they do, or even if they do not, Hogue's abjuration of revenge may displease such a god, who by causing his death casts him out of the water hole that Sloane calls "this cactus Eden." If these are so, the film might suggest that in embracing the Gods of Mercy and Love, Hogue has transcended the God of Wrath.

One may recall the admonitions of the preacher in the tent, while Hogue prepares to make love to Hildy in her room above the saloon: "The devil seeks to destroy you [he pauses for emphasis] with [he pauses longer for greater emphasis] machines" and "In vengeance are the words of Satan." Upon hearing him, Hogue stops. Does the preacher serve as God's surrogate or do his references to the devil remind Hogue of property rights?

The film does not say, but the preacher's sentences, one of which anticipates the film's conclusion while the other ironically reproves one of Hogue's intentions, may simply remind Hogue that he left another preacher to guard the water hole. When Hogue returns to resume lovemaking that night, he does so after he has staked his claim.

In act 2, scene 1, of *The Flies*, Zeus admits that he has the "bitterness of knowing men are free," and in the same scene Orestes recognizes, "I am free, Electra. Freedom has crashed down on me like a thunderbolt." Freely, in defiance of the God of Vengeance, Hogue defines himself anew or perhaps he redefines himself to conform to what he was before betrayal by his erstwhile comrades caused him to recreate himself in terms of vendetta. Essentially a humane man, Hogue's first words in the film, as he observes a gila monster, are, "Sorry, old timer, but you're only part poison and I'm hungry for meat." When he takes out his knife to kill it, Taggart or Bowen blow it to bits with a rifle shot, thereby depriving all three of food and demonstrating a different, unjustifiable slaying of animals. "You peckerwoods just raised hell with our supper," says Hogue, reprimanding them and holding up a leftover, meatless strand of the gila monster's skin. As the sobriquet suggests, Taggart and Bowen are kin to the similarly dubbed Hammond brothers who pan for gold in the high country and the "gutter trash" employed by Harrigan to catch the Bunch. Before killing Taggart, Hogue kills one other person, his first customer, who refuses to pay him to drink the water he found. However, Hogue does not shoot him for nonpayment of ten cents; he does so because of self-defense: the man has pulled a gun on him.

"The wrath of God cometh on the children of disobedience," declares a passenger on a stagecoach, demanding that the driver stop talking idly and vainly to Hogue, who indicated he would not accept the offer to ride to town on the coach, and get on with the journey; and the passenger cites his source, "Ephesians, chapter 5, verse 6." His words are a faithful paraphrase of Scripture: "Let no man deceive you with vain words: for because of these things cometh the wrath of God upon the children of disobedience." If this is the case, God is selective as to which admonitions man should obey, for the verses prior to this urge against fornication, uncleanliness, covetousness, and jesting—sins of which covetousness is the only one Hogue is not guilty.

Another biblical reference, which is uttered twice by different characters, may be more apt. After the paraphrase just quoted, the stagecoach driver, as directed by the passenger, whips the horses to top speed as the passenger's goods fall off, and he yells, "'The Lord giveth and the Lord taketh away.' Matthew, chapter 1, verse—" but the verse number is drowned out by the sound of horses. Later, Reverend Sloane utters the same statement without citing its source. Actually, the quotation is not in any verse of chapter 1 in the book of Matthew, although a similar one, with the same meaning, lies elsewhere in the Bible, in the Old not the New Testament: "The Lord gave, and the Lord hath taken away." Its source is the book of Job (1:21), where a capricious God, like the gods of *The Flies* and *The Ballad of Cable Hogue,* gives and takes away, humbling Job as he humbles (if it is he who humbles) Cable Hogue in the wilderness. *The Ballad of Cable Hogue* seems to emphasize the arbitrariness of God, a dramatization that is consistent with the god of *The Flies.*

* * *

When an author—Bernard Shaw, for instance—writes a preface to a play, the preface often does not reveal insights only into the play it introduces. Since he composes it after he has completed the play, it also, perhaps more so, illuminates his next play, which he may have begun to consider or have started to write. Mutatis mutandis, the same holds true for Peckinpah's statement on *The Flies* and *The Ballad of Cable Hogue.* While he was editing *Cable Hogue* in late 1969, producer Daniel Melnick approached him to direct a movie version of *The Siege of Trencher's Farm,* which became *Straw Dogs.* He was working on David Zelag Goodman's first draft of the screenplay in March 1970, when *Cable Hogue* opened. Shooting of *Straw Dogs* began in January 1971 and the film was released at Christmastime the same year. It is fair to say that when Peckinpah gave the interview, the latter film was at least as much on his mind as the former. Terence Butler may have been the first critic to spot the influence of Sartre's play on *Straw Dogs,* which Butler considers Peckinpah's "most self-consciously Sartrian movie" and whose protagonist, David Sumner, is "a kindred spirit to Sartre's Orestes."[42]

Straw Dogs revolves around themes of commitment and responsibility. Its hero, who in a scene with the local minister appears to reject the view that religion gives life meaning or purpose, finds his own way, blazes his own trail, commits himself, chooses to act, and becomes responsible for his actions. I have quoted Camus as saying, "This is called becoming a man." Becoming a man is what the exemplary hero of *Straw Dogs* does. He achieves this status by defending a man who is incapable of defending himself, by killing people who would kill both of them as well as his wife, and by assessing his conduct as justifiable and honorable in these circumstances, as Orestes assesses his deeds in *The Flies*. By acting upon his commitment, the protagonist of *Straw Dogs* defines himself.

The long avoidance of responsibility and the climactic assumption of it are also true of David Sumner's English wife, Amy. We first see her walking down a village street, wearing a light-weight white sweater that highlights the nipples of her unbrassiered breasts. Walking behind her is Janice Hedden, a teenager who wears a very short miniskirt. Although both flaunt their sexuality, it is Amy's sexual actions and emotions, not Janice's, that are the focus of some of the movie's hostile critics, who attack Peckinpah for them. Molly Haskell gratuitously calls him "an old geezer" (he was in his mid-forties when he made *Straw Dogs*) and stridently asserts, not analyzes: Amy "struts around like Daisy Mae before the brier-patch yokels, and then gets it once, twice, and again for the little tease she is. The provocative, sex-obsessed bitch is one of the great male-chauvinist (and apparently, territorialist) fantasies, along with the fantasy that she is constantly fantasizing rape."[43] If anything in the film suggests that Amy fantasizes rape, Haskell does not cite it and I have not seen it. Moments before the rape, in fact, Amy tells Charlie Venner, her former lover, to leave once he has finished his drink, and although, after he begins to rape her she stops fighting and submits to him, her response is far from enjoyment when Norman Scutt sodomizes her.[44] Later, her memories of both assaults unnerve her. Apart from a tendency to infer from the film more than it contains, including a deduction of what the director's ideas may be from the actual or presumed views of one or more characters, which is unsound criticism, these and similar revelations of Peckinpah's view of women are highly selective in the evidence they present, when they present any, and they ignore women in other films by Peckinpah, notably Hildy in *The Ballad of Cable Hogue* and Carol McCoy in *The Getaway*. (To them, we may add Ali in *The Osterman Weekend,* which Peckinpah made after Haskell wrote her book.)

In a similar vein, Pauline Kael labels *Straw Dogs* "a fascist work of art," "a fascist classic," and a "movie [that] taps sexual fascism," which seems to mean little more than that she interprets Peckinpah's theme and viewpoint as "machismo." She claims that Amy "wants to be raped" and that "we [the plural is a rhetorical ploy aimed at inducing agreement] can see that she's asking for it, she's begging for it, that her every no means yes."[45] Ironically, the view that Haskell and Kael attribute to Amy and Peckinpah is that of the lecherous local louts, not of Amy or Peckinpah. Amy is neither "asking for it" nor "begging for it" but is simply displaying pride in her sexuality. In terms of the former phrase, both she and Janice get "it," although "it" differs for each (rape in one case, murder in the other). Not only do their punishments not fit the crimes, but neither provocative attire nor an attitude that another person might interpret as provocative is a crime in civilized society. As subsequent events demonstrate, civilization in the town near Trencher's Farm has a thinner veneer than Amy realizes, and the veneer cracks.

Because she becomes upset over a minor spat with David about an electric heater, she goes outside and laughingly flirts with Cawsey and Scutt. Later, when she gets out of her automobile, she notices and examines a run in her stocking, exposing her legs as she does so. Cawsey and Scutt, as well as Riddaway and Venner, her former boyfriend, who are fixing the garage at Trencher's Farm, stop their work to gape at her. "They were practically licking my body," she complains to David. Not knowing it was her legs that drew their leers, not her breasts, to which his attention, like ours, is drawn in the first scene, he asks, "Why don't you wear a bra?" "Why should I?" retorts Amy, who unlike him knows what provoked their gazes. She may therefore be irked by what she thinks is a non sequitur and considers it her right to dress as she alone sees fit. "You shouldn't go around without one and not expect that type to stare," David explains. Although she takes out her anger on him, taunting him for cowardice, her temper is short-lived, for she apologizes and they make up. She goes upstairs to take a bath and, once above, removes her sweater. "Don't forget to draw the curtain," he reminds her when she is about to pass an open window, on the other side of which the local men, of whom she just complained, are working on the garage roof. Her resentment at her husband for suggesting that she was in some way responsible for the men's ogling makes her defiant. Instead of drawing the curtain, she stands by the window for a moment as the men stop work and stare at her, and then leaves for the bathroom. In having her act as she does, Peckinpah pointedly dramatizes her rejection of responsibility.

In the film's climactic siege, she refuses to accept responsibility for Henry Niles and demands that David surrender him to the village bully-boys. Even after David forcibly stops her from leaving him to join those men and reminds her that by killing the magistrate they have gone too far to do anything but kill them too, since he and she know what the men did, she resists commitment. Only when Riddaway, the sole surviving intruder, is about to kill her husband, who pleads with her to shoot Riddaway, does she commit herself by action: she fires the shotgun, killing the intruder. She has waited longer than he has to engage herself, take sides, and define herself and her values by action.

Far from portraying David Sumner as an innocent victim, Peckinpah dramatizes him as being partly responsible for the long battle that concludes the film, since at various stages "he could have stopped the whole thing. He didn't. He let it go on."[46] Until the local ruffians invade his home to drag out Henry Niles, he refuses to take a firm stand, to commit himself. Soon after the movie starts, David observes, through a window in the pub, Charlie Venner putting his arm around Amy's neck. Since David cannot hear what they are saying, he does not know that she tells him to remove it, but while the sight disturbs him, he neither tells her what he saw nor orders Venner not to work on his garage, which he just hired him to do. By refusing to make an issue of the incident, he takes no stand. After he observes Amy laughing with Cawsey and Scutt in the short scene mentioned above, he says nothing about what looks like flirtation; but by choosing to make no comment on her assertion that she sometimes thinks him strange, as they do, he downplays or avoids acknowledging her tacit alliance with them in this matter. Neither does he take a stand after he discovers that Amy has altered his complex mathematical equation on the blackboard by changing a plus sign to a minus sign. "What does she think I'm doing here? Playing games? That this is a grammar school?" he mutters—to himself, not to her. By not making an issue of her action, he diminishes himself in her eyes, since he does not accept the challenge implicit in her action. Thus, she becomes still more upset with him, and when she is provoked she raises the ante.

His refusal to take a stand links to earlier refusals to commit himself. In the context of 1970–71—Weddle observes that on 18 May 1970, when Peckinpah was working on the script of *Straw Dogs,* Ohio National Guardsmen killed four and wounded eight students at Kent State University[47]—there is political resonance in Amy's charge, "You left [America] because you didn't want to take a stand, commit." In rejecting her charge and refusing to recognize his avoidance of committing himself, David reveals his bad faith: "Commit to what? I was involved in my work. You want something out of me that is not mine to deliver. That [work] is what I was there for." His argument has enough truth to persuade himself, but it is insufficient to invalidate her accusation. When she alleges that he left America for England "because there's no place else to hide," he denies the allegation: "I'm here because you once said you thought we could be happy here. Remember?" "I'm sorry," she concedes. Although he seems to win the debate, he undercuts himself by calling after her, as she goes upstairs, "By the way, I never claimed to be one of the involved," which is an admission of his refusal to make a commitment and a revelation that he has acted in bad faith.

His avoidance of taking a stand makes him more vulnerable to the villagers who work for him than he otherwise might be. When he starts to drive into town, they laugh at his difficulty in starting his car. Cawsey, the rat catcher, giggles when he inadvertently turns on his windshield wipers; and they all guffaw when he accidentally shifts the manual gear into reverse. On the narrow road from the farm to town, he follows their slow truck. The driver, Riddaway, motions him to pass, which he does, and thus almost collides with a tractor that Riddaway and the others know is moving toward him—a very near miss. In town, he sits in his car, waiting for the men to arrive, and watches them go into the pub, which he then enters. Instead of sacking them for deliberately causing him almost to crash his car and perhaps injure or kill himself and the tractor driver, he raises his glass and says, "Cheers." Because they are unchallenged, they are dominant and do not repeat the one-word toast. When the magistrate enters, telling him, "I was about to call up to your farm to welcome you into our little community," David says, for the benefit of the men, "I've just been welcomed." His irony is insufficient to give him command of the situation over the toughs who nearly killed him: it displays weakness, whereas firmness is required. Before leaving with the magistrate, he gives the bartender money to buy drinks for the house. His workers, to use the British phrase, "take the piss" on him: they taunt him mockingly while being outwardly polite and they deferentially say goodbye to the magistrate but not to him, which confirms their dominant position and their contempt toward him. By not responding, David concedes his powerlessness. His bad faith makes the locals regard him as vulnerable.

Ultimately, as is always the case, he is aware that he has acted in bad faith, and he tries to compensate for it. At home he expends his aggressive feelings on the minister, a battle he wins through intellect and irony, tactics congenial to him. Although neither his stratagems nor his victory raise him in Amy's esteem, the former suggests that his intellect is a weapon and it foreshadows his triumph over the village hooligans when, abjuring bad faith and acting upon his inner convictions, he uses his mind to defeat them, a victory against immense odds.

Had David confronted them in the pub, either sacking them or threatening to do so if they continued to mock him or to play another dangerous trick on him, they might not become emboldened to enter his house bullyingly and menacingly later, to demand the surrender of Henry Niles. Nor might they do so if he were to confront them, as Amy urges him to do, about the cat he finds strangled in his bedroom closet. Instead, he evades the issue and tries to deflect his noncommitment by blaming his avoidance on her: "Why didn't you ask them, instead of making me look like an idiot with that bowl of milk?" After he returns from the "hunt," where the ruffians mocked him, and determines to take a stand by firing them, he displays his avoidance of responsibility by not opening the closet door to hang his coat but putting it on a bedpost instead. Amy's indictment is accurate: "If you'd have said something to them ages ago"—which means the day before, and her phrase indicts herself as well as him— "about the cat, this would never have happened, none of it," the last phrase referring to her rape, about which he knows nothing. Although he seems to suspect that something has happened during his absence, he does not inquire, for he is unprepared to commit himself fully.

When he sacks the villagers the next day, it is too late to regain esteem in their eyes, his wife's eyes, or his own eyes. It is too late to prevent them from treating him as if he were irrelevant, which they do when they demand that he surrender Henry Niles to them. Had David committed himself earlier, this situation might not become the crisis or test of his manhood that it turns out to be. By the time he does, his entire being is at stake. Forced to choose between commitment and capitulation, he selects the former: "He's staying here with me until the doctor and the police arrive. He's my responsibility." When the ruffians incredulously ask him why, the only answer he can think of is, "This is my house." In his house— for the house, which throughout the ages has symbolized the person who inhabits it, has become his self—he takes his stand. It is Amy who seeks to avoid doing so when she adamantly demands that he surrender Niles despite David's reminder that the men will beat him to death. To David's surprise, she truly does not care. On this issue he defies her and finally takes a stand, for he cares, and he perceives that violence against Niles or against the house is a violation of himself. After the accidental shooting of the magistrate, Amy, who is Electra to his Orestes, still urges appeasement, but like Orestes he assumes the burden of responsibility: "This is my affair." The result is an epic battle in which the aptly named David defeats all but one of the village Goliaths and, unlike Orestes, prompts his female partner to take responsibility in defeating the aggressors and killing the last of them.

Pauline Kael's description is accurate: "Not surprisingly, the audience cheers David's kills; it is, after all, a classic example of the worm turning.

It's mild-mannered Destry putting on his guns. It's the triumph of a superior man who is fighting for basic civilized principles over men who are presented as mindless human garbage." Yet she intends these terms to be put-downs, for she sees the director setting up the "primitive moviegoer's soul" to cheer David on rather than, as I do, creating a resonant myth. As we have seen, her accusation, "As the situation has been set up, every possibility for nonviolent behavior has been eliminated," is inaccurate.[48] In my judgment, her colleague John Simon is closer to the mark: "The slow stages by which David, despite his reasonableness, cleverness, and mild charm, lost the audience's sympathy, are matched by his regaining (in the midst of utter mayhem) first our admiration, then that of his recalcitrant wife, and finally her and our love. . . . [S]ince it is his scientific and logical resourcefulness that enables David to prevail over such great odds, a highly rational expertise is clearly seen as a prime factor in victorious commitment."[49] At the end of the film, by his commitment in words and deeds, which give him integrity, the formerly irresolute David becomes an existentially heroic figure. Furthermore, as Alan Casty observes, the conclusion of *Straw Dogs* "has none of the romantic dignity or glory given to it in the traditional Western's structure of feeling."[50] It and its hero achieve dignity and glory on their own terms, not by generic association, although it is partly through such association that *Straw Dogs* achieves mythic resonance.

* * *

"To them as has their roads ahead," toasts Ace Bonner, standing beside his family, which includes two grandsons. On another occasion his older son, J.R., nicknamed Junior, affirms, "I gotta go down my own road," a common western locution that also paraphrases Orestes and reveals J.R.'s kinship to his father, who continues to go down his own road even if that road takes him as far as Australia. In *Junior Bonner,* both father and son, despite their ages, insist on following their individual paths. Junior's first words in the movie, after he has been thrown from a bull in a rodeo, are, "Maybe I ought to take up another line of work." As Steve McQueen's delivery of the speech indicates, Junior's suggestion is facetious, an effort to lighten his mood. When his mother asks when he will stop being a rodeo contestant, he changes the subject. Buck Roan, a contractor who provides rodeos with livestock and who is considering expanding his business to include more rodeos, offers J.R. a job as his assistant. J.R.'s response is friendly but conclusive: "Don't think so, Buck." And that is that. When his brother Curly offers him "another line of work," he does not bother to reply; but when Curly, linking the advantages of real estate development with a slur on their father, "I don't want you to turn out like the old man, that's all," he reacts by punching Curly so that Curly falls through their mother's porch window. If J.R. considers going down a trail other than the one his life and actions have made his own, this motion picture makes clear, he does not do so more than momentarily, after which he promptly rejects the notion.

The nickname "Junior" probably derives from the initials of his given names. Characters who deal with him formally call him "J.R.," initials that are prominently displayed on his horse trailer. "Junior" suggests not only a youngster but also a person in a lower or lesser position in a hierarchy. The character Junior Bonner is no longer young, and several personages consider him to be over the hill. Sympathetically, Buck urges him, "You might as well face it: you're just not the rider you was a few years back," and he calls J.R. "a champion in his day." Junior's old car is dented, as he himself is. During the opening credit sequence, he painfully wraps a large bandage around his midriff after having been thrown by the bull Sunshine, and the bandage remains in place overnight. Both automobile and driver need oil to keep functioning: literally forty-weight motor oil for the car and the symbolic oil of victory for Junior. Although he claims that he needs the victory in the bull-riding contest because the rodeo is being held in his home town, he also needs it for self-validation.

Camus observes that

> during every day of an unillustrious life, time carries us. But a moment always comes when we have to carry it. We live on the future: "tomorrow," "later on," "when you have made your way," "you will understand when you are old enough." Such irrelevancies are wonderful, for, after all, it's a matter of dying. Yet a day comes when a man notices or says that he is thirty. Thus he asserts his youth. But simultaneously he situates himself in relation to time. He takes his place in it. He admits that he stands at a certain point on a curve that he acknowledges having to travel to its end. He belongs to time, and by the horror that seizes him, he recognizes his worst enemy. Tomorrow, he was longing for tomorrow, whereas everything in him ought to reject it. That revolt of the flesh is the absurd.[51]

Although J.R.'s life has not been entirely unillustrious, since people recognize him as a former champion, that time is long, or long enough, past. Not at age thirty but past forty (Steve McQueen was forty-two when he played the role), he recognizes age to be what Camus calls one's "worst enemy." Absurdly, and recognizing the absurdity, he revolts against the flesh, determined to persevere despite his age, rejecting tomorrow, and concentrating on today.

"Hey, how's the bull rider?" asks the more successful rodeo contestant Red Terwilliger, as their cars move on the highway parallel to each other. The occupants of Red's car, which is newer, or younger, than J.R.'s, include two pretty young women. "Lonesome," says Junior. "Not for long," answers one of the women, who tosses a beer can to him before Red's car passes Junior's old heap, just as Red surpassed J.R. in the last rodeo. While the woman in Red's car considers Junior attractive, she is in Red's car, not in Junior's. J.R. is as lonely in his world as Orestes is in the universe. Like Orestes, he is, as quoted above, "without excuse, beyond remedy, except what remedy I find within myself." His commitment is total. He does not place a time limit on himself, saying that he will quit after he wins a particular rodeo, after he competes in a specified number of rodeos, or after a fixed number of years from today. The totality of his commitment constitutes its pureness and integrity. J.R. might die in an automobile accident on his way to the next rodeo. If so, or if not, the value and meaning of his life are determined by his present actions. On the day that is the concern of the film, he rejects alternatives, pursues his own road or trail, and wins, thereby validating his way of life, his values, and his existence.

The question of values is central to *Junior Bonner*. "Money?" Buck tactfully asks J.R., meaning, "Do you need any?" Self-reliant, Junior answers with similar tact, "Well, money's nobody's favorite, Buck." Actually, it is the favorite of a number of people, notably Curly, who boasts, "Hey, boy"—a subtle effort to place J.R. in a "junior" status and himself in a senior position—"I'm just making money hand over fist." Curly's financial success conspicuously contrasts with Junior's lack of it, which J.R. summarizes to his father: "I'm busted. . . . Flatter'n a tire." As Curly disparagingly phrases their dissimilarity, "I'm working on my first million and you're still working on eight seconds"—the time required to stay on a bull to qualify for a rodeo prize.

Each brother exemplifies one trait of their father, Ace Bonner, who was a rodeo star and remains a gold and silver prospector. Junior follows their father's cowboy tradition, Curly his entrepreneurial tradition. Whereas Junior has not repeated Ace's success in winning, or even performing, at Madison Square Garden in New York City, Curly has been, unlike Ace, enormously successful in business. By further contrast, whereas Ace was a loner, an individualist who prospected for precious metals, Curly's business involves others and is on a larger scale: real estate acquisition, land and property development, and sales. Unlike Ace's business practices,

Curly's are exploitative. He buys his father's land for less than its fair market value, with the self-serving justification that no matter how much money he might give his father, Ace would squander it on drink, gambling, and women. Instead of staking his father's gold-mining venture in Australia, where Ace would also raise sheep, Curly proposes to put the old man on a weekly allowance if he remains in the area. Although Curly supports his mother, he stints, so that she must supplement his stipend by taking in boarders, and he plans to sell her home, moving her into one of his model trailer houses, where she would demonstrate its virtues and at the same time run a curio shop.

Furthermore, Curly's actions suggest that he would replace his father as patriarch, for he tries to assign roles to the other members of his family. In addition to employing his mother, he hopes to hire his brother to sell his real estate. Curly's sales pitch to Junior proposes opportunity ("You may not know it, but you are in the right place at the right time. That's here. There's a regular land boom, Junior") and employs family ties ("We're family. I don't care what you do. You can sell a lot or a hundred lots. I'm just trying to keep us together"). Rejecting his brother's reasons, Junior makes the statement, quoted above, that links him with his father and Orestes, "I gotta go down my own road."

Both Ace and Junior are fiercely independent. "Not penny one will I take from him!" Ace exclaims, referring to Curly's proposal to give him a weekly allowance if he remains in Prescott, Arizona, and does not emigrate to Australia. Nor will Junior become a salesman for Curly in the Prescott area. Like his father, Junior is an individualist as well as a rodeo champion. Individualism, and putting oneself and one's skills on the line in competition with the best, demonstrates integrity, which despite their weaknesses both Ace and Junior have. When J.R. tells Buck that he and his father will work together in the cow-milking contest, Buck remarks admiringly, in terms of poker, "That's a pair to draw to." Peckinpah couples father and older son dramatically not only by showing the contest—from which, in terms of their relationship, they emerge as winners, as Junior points out— but also by picturing them together atop Junior's horse in the Frontier Days parade. After J.R. wins the major rodeo contest by successfully riding the bull Sunshine, he demonstrates how unlike his brother he is and how unlike his brother's values his are: he buys his father a first-class plane ticket to Sydney, Australia. Like father, like this son. Alone and in disregard of his years, in a profession that tests his individual skill each time he practices it, Junior goes beyond junior to senior status, making his own way and validating his ethos with the utmost integrity.

* * *

We first see Doc McCoy, the protagonist of *The Getaway,* in prison, where he has completed four years of a ten-year term for armed robbery. Like Junior Bonner, McCoy might ask, "Maybe I ought to take up another line of work." Unlike J.R., Doc—who is played by the same actor, Steve Mc-Queen—appears to have asked himself that question seriously. His answer is a decision to retire from his profession the way Bishop of *The Wild Bunch* hopes to, after making one big score. In Doc's case the robbery is more necessary than in Bishop's, since in addition to giving him the wherewith-al to leave his life of crime, it is payback to the man responsible for get-ting him out of jail. Doc also resembles Bishop in his devotion to one woman, in Doc's case his own, not another's wife. Like the wife of the principal character in *Straw Dogs,* Doc's wife is sexually unfaithful to him, although unlike Amy, who is raped, Carol McCoy's action is voluntary. In Carol's case, sexual infidelity is a price—unlike her husband, she gives the fee in advance—which she pays to gain his parole. Like Bishop, and Amos Dundee as well, Doc is a flawed hero, and like Dundee especially, his errors create grave difficulties for him.

True to its title, *The Getaway* is about a getaway, or series of getaways: from prison, from the area of the bank Doc robs (so that he and Carol will not be injured by diversionary explosions they have timed), from those who would take the money he stole, and from America into Mexico. In all these efforts, Doc and Carol are successful. As the film dramatizes, he is a professional thief with considerable skills. As it suggests, his expertise has limitations—or else he would not be in jail in the first place—and Peckinpah hints at Doc's deficiencies when he shows Doc losing at a chess game in the opening credit sequence.

The limitations that Peckinpah dramatizes revolve not around theft, at which Doc demonstrates aptitude, but around killing. He murders not because he enjoys doing so, but because he must, and he is insufficiently brutal to blast people away in order to ensure that the job has been done properly. When he recognizes that Rudy, having killed Jackson, wants to shoot him for the loot, Doc fires first, hitting him. From a distance, Doc fires two more bullets, the first missing him, the second not. Assuming that Rudy, who had scorned the bulletproof vest Doc proposed he wear, is dead, Doc does not go closer to ensure Rudy's decease by firing point-blank into his head, as the chief of a military firing squad would do. Iron-ically, Rudy had donned the bulletproof vest, which saves his life. When policemen locate Doc near a radio and television store, he demolishes their car with a twenty-gauge shotgun, but he does not shoot them. His goal is to stop their pursuit, and he can accomplish that goal without killing or wounding them. Later, he again outwits Rudy, who has found him, and knocks Rudy unconscious with his pistol. He is about to finish the job by shooting Rudy at point-blank range, but he hesitates and decides instead to take Rudy's gun—his only gun, Doc incorrectly assumes—and leave him unconscious, an action that soon requires Doc to kill a revived Rudy in self-defense, when Rudy tries to kill Doc and Carol. Underscoring Doc's decency is his surprise encounter, after killing Rudy, with one of Beynon's men who has just tried to kill him. Doc points his gun at the man's head before the man can raise his own gun and commands, "Don't do it. Don't. Just run away. Now. Run away." The man puts away his gun and flees. Doc would kill that man only if it were necessary, which it is not.

Despite his quick-thinking inventiveness when he is cornered, Doc has limited skills. Failing to remember or to anticipate possibilities, he betrays major errors in judgment. Although Doc is perceptive enough to notice the scratch marks on the lock on the lavatory door of the train in which the luggage thief tries to escape, and thereby to catch the man, Doc fails to search the thief's pockets for bank money he may have put there, which he did and which enables the police to connect the man who beat him with the bank robber. Carol's purchase of a car with a poorly functioning radio does not indict Doc's or even her wit, for the radio seems like a writer's device to put them in a threatening situation and demonstrate Doc's resourcefulness in getting them out of it, which he does: he buys a shotgun, destroys a police car, drives away, and takes a bus back through the locale where he shot the police vehicle.

Nevertheless, he is skillful. His masterful planning of the robbery involves surveillance of bank employee entry and position patterns, blueprints of electrical circuits, split-second timing, and diversionary explosives. Despite Jackson's panic, which results in his shooting a bank guard, everything functions according to plan. Alert, Doc notices that a car-hop at the fast-food drive-in has recognized him. Resourcefully, he jumps into a dumpster with Carol to escape the police. Yet his skill is not boundless. A major mistake is his decision to go to Laughlin's El Paso hotel, the planned rendezvous point in case something went wrong, in order to get identification documents to escape into Mexico. After retrieving the suitcase, he considers, "If Rudy was by himself we're okay. If he worked for Beynon, Beynon's people'll be waiting for us at Laughlin's in El Paso." A shrewder man would not take the chance and would go elsewhere. In fact, a shrewder man would have remembered that Beynon's brother was present when Carol told the robbery team about Laughlin's hotel.

Doc has integrity. Unlike Rudy, who seeks to double-cross him, and unlike Beynon, who uses the robbery partly as a cover-up for previous embezzlement and who would double-cross Doc by taking his wife, he is trustworthy—unless and until he is betrayed. Carol tries to dissuade him from going to Beynon's house to split the money.

> *Carol:* Do you trust him?
> *Doc:* I don't figure he's gonna try to cross us. At least not until he gets his money.
> *Carol:* Well, let's just send his cut and get going.
> *Doc:* If we make a mistake, he's gonna burn us. If you make a deal you're better off keeping up your end.

A prominent aspect of *The Getaway,* which elevates it above the status of a superior potboiler (a high status, at which I do not scoff), is the relationship between Doc and Carol, a subject I will consider further in chapter 4. Among the actions that demonstrate their love are their cavorting, fully clad, in a lake, which symbolizes (as it partly does in *Major Dundee*) both love and freedom, and his cooking breakfast for her the morning after his release from prison (which is something that a more cinematically conventional criminal would not do). Carol is obviously not a mere gun moll. In contrast to the marriage of Harold and Fran, who willingly indulges in sex with Rudy, even to the point of openly mocking her husband, the marriage of the McCoys is solid. However, their alliance is tested by a deed that is distasteful but necessary, with which each, existentially, must come to terms. In *The Getaway,* Doc's first words, to Carol, are telegraphic: "Get to Beynon. Tell him I'm for sale. His price. Do it now." Each believes the price to be a robbery; neither considers that it will be sexual. It is both. To get a reprieve for her husband, Carol humiliates herself by committing adultery with Beynon. "Thank you," says Doc the morning after his release. "For what?" she asks. "For getting me out." "It was a pleasure," she says ironically. When Doc delivers the money to Beynon, Beynon taunts Doc with his sexual and political prowess, implying that he won Carol from Doc. She underscores her choice of her husband over Beynon, whom she apparently conned about his prowess, in what would seem to be the clearest possible way: she shoots Beynon. To Doc, whom Beynon's words have "got to," her deed is insufficient, and he angrily asserts that Beynon "got to" her. Only after severe tribulations, when each, in turn, proposes splitting the money and leaving the other, does Doc come to terms with the deed that he initiated; he gives it his (and her), not society's, valuation: a painful necessity that does not affect their love and that he must forget. At the end of the film, the truck driver who takes them across the Mexican border virtually validates their union. "Hey, I'm glad!" he exclaims when they confirm that they are married, because "That's the trouble with this goldanged world: there ain't no morals." Never mind the robbery and the killings: Doc and Carol are truly married, which casts them, albeit against type, as "the good guys."

* * *

Probably the most felicitous and suggestive description of *Pat Garrett and Billy the Kid* was made by its producer, Gordon Carroll: "a man who doesn't want to run is being pursued by a man who doesn't want to chase him."[52] Intentionally or not, Carroll suggests that the title characters live in bad faith. Whereas *The Ballad of Cable Hogue* and *Straw Dogs* may be, as Peckinpah says the former is, variants of Sartre's *The Flies, Pat Garrett and Billy the Kid* may be a variant of Sartre's *No Exit*. Like the three principal characters of *No Exit*, the titular characters of Peckinaph's film, as William Barrett says of Sartre's play, practice bad faith, "the surrendering of one's human liberty in order to possess, or try to possess, one's being as a *thing*." They "have no being other than what each has in the eyes of the others," who in determining their essence, deprive them of "their own subjective being" and make them exist "not as free beings for themselves but as beings in the eyes of others."[53]

Emblematic of their bad faith, and of the absurdity of their situation, are the sequences involving Alamosa Bill (that he is a namesake of Billy the Kid is surely not accidental). It is absurd that Alamosa Bill is Pat Garrett's deputy: the job results from their chance encounter in a barbershop-saloon, where Garrett, to Bill's visible surprise, states that he is making Bill his deputy, an assigned role to which Bill offers no resistance. Passively, he accepts Garrett's definition of his being as if he were not a free man capable of determining his own essence subjectively, but a man who has no choice other than to accept another person's valuation and treatment of him as a thing. It is absurd that Bill meets the second title character at a trading post, which they visit at the same time, another chance encounter. It is absurd as well that Bill and Billy duel: they fight not because they want to, but because they cannot figure out how to avoid dueling, which means that each abnegates his free will, accepting the roles their meeting has given them. Furthermore, in killing Alamosa Bill, Billy is killing Pat

Garrett's deputy, or surrogate, who since Garrett is Billy's alter ego, is also himself. The scene also foreshadows Garrett's killing Billy near the end of the film, because in doing so, Garrett kills a part of himself.

"A man who doesn't want to run is being pursued by a man who doesn't want to chase him." On at least two occasions, screenwriter Rudy, or Rudolph, Wurlitzer emphasizes in explicitly existential terms Billy's disinclination to run: "Billy at some point made a fascinating existential choice." He "chose to be Billy the Kid." Elsewhere, says Wurlitzer, Billy decided "not to flee, to accept the consequences of his own myth, no matter how unreal, even though it meant his death."[54]

In a single, thematically clear-cut scene between Billy and Maria, whose relationship with each other and whose thematically explicit dialogue Peckinpah wisely alters in the film, Wurlitzer's screenplay spells out Billy's bad faith. "You have to go now," she tells him. "*Pronto—esta noche.* You've been here six weeks. People know you are here. Garrett, he knows you are here." Denying his knowledge, which he reveals later, that Garrett is purposely giving him time to get away, Billy responds, "Pat don't know how to look no more. He's lost that." Then, he adds, accurately, "He's tied to a game he ain't dealin'." Billy also evades acknowledging the result of his staying: "I would have figured you'd want me here." "I want you to stay," she replies, "but I want you alive more." "I'm known here. I ain't never goin' to be forgot here," insists Billy, alluding to his mythic status. "In Mexico I'd be another drunken gringo whorin' and shittin' out hot chili peppers and gettin' old."[55] In the film, Peckinpah eliminates the statements that resonate the myth of Billy the Kid, and he renders the remainder implicit by making Billy wrong in some instances, right in others, and by using only some of the dialogue and dispersing it between two different characters, neither of whom is Maria. "Come to Mexico, Billy," says Billy's Mexican friend Paco in the film, as Paco prepares to leave for Mexico. "People know you are here." Not Billy but Luke, one of Billy's gang, raises the objection that Wurlitzer has Billy make in the screenplay: "Hell, in old Mex he ain't going to be nothing but another drunken gringo shittin' out chili peppers and waitin' for—nothin'." By making Paco urge Billy to leave, Peckinpah connects the admonition with Billy's decision to return after having made up his mind to depart. When Billy finds Chisum's men torturing Paco and raping Paco's daughter, Billy kills them. "Well, that tied it," he says when Paco dies. "I'm going back."

What Billy makes himself believe is that there is no exit for him, no way to evade his fate, and that he may as well stay put. This belief is as much an evasion as the belief of the damned in Sartre's play that they have no exit. They do have an exit: the door that inexplicably or absurdly opens gives them an opportunity to define themselves by action, by leaving, which is an opportunity they refuse to take. Billy too has an exit, southward to Mexico or westward to California, which he too refuses to take. There is no evidence that the brutality of Chisum's men toward Paco and Paco's daughter would be similarly inflicted on Billy, for he could, if he wanted to, leave their jurisdiction and—unlike Paco, who believed that since he had no quarrel with Chisum, Chisum would not harm him—simply keep out of their way. "That" has tied nothing but Billy's resolution to define his essence by action. Rather, he accepts being defined by others and, in doing so, he creates the conditions for Garrett to kill him.

Wurlitzer is correct that Billy chooses to enact a role assigned by others, to live up to his reputation as an outlaw, to be hunted and shot in a certain locale instead of to flee and recreate himself elsewhere. Billy chooses the role, not death itself. As Sartre says, "If death is not the free determination of our being, it can not *complete* our life." Death does not confer "a meaning on life from the outside; a meaning can come only from subjectivity. Since death does not appear on the foundation of our freedom, it can only *remove all meaning from life*."[56]

"A man is what he wills himself to be," says Garcin in *No Exit,* triggering Inez's challenge: "Prove it. . . . It's what one does, and nothing else, that shows the stuff one's made of." "I never figured to hear you brag on bein' a workin' man. Ain't figured you for the law either," Billy tells Garrett in the Lincoln County jail. It is a statement that is more diplomatic to his old friend than those he later makes to Bell, one of Garrett's deputies, that Garrett "signed himself over to Chisum and every other damned landowner" and "I ain't sold my side like you and the rest of the town boys, Bell." "It's just a way of stayin' alive," Garrett responds to what Billy tells him, adding, "I aim to be rich, old, 'n' grey." He does not achieve the first objective, and he knows, although he does not admit it, that he "sold [his] side." "I understand you been ridin' for Chisum," Sheriff Baker tells Garrett in a subsequent scene. "I'd rather be on the outside of the law than packin' a badge fer that town of Lincoln and them that's a-runnin' it." "It's a job," says Garrett, defensively; "there's an age in a man's life when he don't want to spend time figurin' what comes next." Shortly before this exchange, however, he expresses as much contempt to the rich landowners who run the territory as they do to him. One of them calls him "a man who's half outlaw himself" and warns him that "in this particular game there are only a few plays left. I'd advise you to grab onto a winning hand while you have a chance." In retort, Garrett tells them to shove the down payment of reward money up their asses and set it afire. This landowner's unveiled assertion of his power differs only in style from the more urbane Governor Lew Wallace (author of *Ben Hur,* published in 1880, the year before the early scenes of this film take place), who on the same occasion tells Garrett, "This territory is vast and primitive. There is money here, growing investments, and political interests. We must protect these investments so that the area can continue to prosper and grow."

"This country's getting old, and I aim to get old with it," says Garrett to Poe, whom Governor Wallace deputized to keep an eye on him. "Now, the Kid don't want it that way. He might be a better man for it, I ain't judgin'." Garrett's statement is untrue, for he is judging, and his verdict, which he refuses to admit to himself, is that Billy is right. Garrett knows that in contrast to Billy, he has allied himself with, indeed has made himself the lackey of, men and forces he despises. What he has done constitutes bad faith, a life composed of a lie, which ultimately fails to deceive Garrett himself. Although Garrett is a flawed but not a tragic figure, he is an alienated personage. Ultimately, his actions alienate him from himself. "When are you going to learn you can't trust anybody, not even yourself, Garrett?" asks the coffinmaker before he curses Garrett. The role is played by Peckinpah, and since the line is not in Wurlitzer's published text, one may assume that Peckinpah composed it and that it is significant. What it signifies is Garrett's bad faith and metaphysical alienation.

Because of Garrett's bad faith, his pursuit of Billy, which he does not acknowledge to Poe, consists of deferral and procrastination. This is why Billy decides, albeit temporarily, to go to Mexico for a few months. "I reckon he's given me 'bout all the time he can," he tells Eno, one of his gang, acknowledging, as Wurlitzer's Billy does not acknowledge to Maria, that he knows Garrett is allowing him an opportunity to leave the territory. After Garrett shoots Billy, whom, the film suggests, Garrett considers the better part of himself, Garrett sees his own reflection in a mirror. He shoots it, then stares at himself in the shattered glass, as if looking at a stranger. One recalls a statement by Camus: "A man is talking on the telephone behind a glass partition; you cannot hear him, but you see his incomprehensible dumb show: you wonder why he is alive. . . . Likewise the stranger who at certain seconds comes to meet us in a mirror . . . is also the absurd."[57] As James Coburn, who plays Garrett, speaks the words, "I shot him. I killed the Kid," Garrett seems surprised that he has killed his friend. When Poe, who was too frightened to kill Billy when he had a chance to do so (chapter 3 explores this scene in greater detail), brutally cries out, "I want his trigger finger. I want it cut off. I want him nailed to a post, and then I want him taken back to Lincoln," and leans down, picking up Billy's right hand as if to sever the finger, Garrett yells, "No!" He hits Poe with his pistol, kicks him away from Billy's body, and speaks slowly and deliberately, as if to, or about, himself as well as to Poe: "What you want and what you get are two different things"—an echo of Thornton's assessment of his situation in *The Wild Bunch* ("What I like and what I need," Thornton tells Harrigan), which is equally bitter, for both involve the requirement to kill a former comrade. As Garrett rides out of town alone, a boy throws stones at him. Garrett seems fully alienated. Reinforcing the view that in killing Billy, Garrett has killed part of himself, the movie slowly dissolves to 1909, the time of the opening credit sequence (to be analyzed in the next chapter), in which Garrett is shot by agents of the same people who had hired him to kill Billy. With each enacting a role defined by others, the deaths of the two men merge.

* * *

In *Bring Me the Head of Alfredo Garcia* as well, the doom of one man, Bennie, merges with that of another, Alfredo Garcia, whose decapitated head Bennie carries. Both have been lovers of Elita, which in the terminology of a macho world, including the United States military, in which Peckinpah served as a marine, makes them "blood brothers." At the end of the film Bennie, while transporting the head, is shot to death by the underlings of El Jefe, who commanded the head to be brought to him.

When we first encounter Bennie in Mexico City, he is singing and playing a piano for tourists at a sleazy bar, adorned by bar girl–prostitutes. Bennie's dark sunglasses, which he wears inside the poorly lighted saloon, seem designed to hide the view of a "loser" that his naked eyes might reveal. A subordinate of Max, one of El Jefe's henchmen, sees him without the dark glasses and instantly sizes him up in precisely that word, and the man considers Bennie to be so insignificant, he is unconcerned that Bennie hears his snide evaluation. "Nobody loses all the time!" Bennie snaps back.

This episode encapsulates much of the film. By deeds, not words, Bennie tries to break his pattern as a loser and remake himself into a winner. "I go all the way or I pass," he proposes, persuading Max to offer him ten thousand dollars for Garcia's head instead of the thousand proffered by Quill and Sappensly.[58] Bennie's need and commitment are so total that he does not argue when these gangsters refuse to give him more than two hundred dollars for expenses—which establishes that they are in control, not he—and he fails to consider how ambiguous Max's agreement to pay him ten thousand dollars is: "Well, my friend, one must do what one must do." As he learns later, these men would sooner kill him than pay him.

To Bennie, the money means more than dollars. It is, as he maintains, "a way out." "I could have died in Mexico City or T.J. [Tijuana] and never known what the hell it was all about," he tells Elita at one point. "Now I've got a chance. A ticket. And we're not going to miss it." Whereas Pat Garrett and Billy the Kid see no exit from their dilemma, Bennie seizes the possibility of an exit, no matter how dangerous, the moment he glimpses it. Because he makes an existential choice, he gives his own valuation to the social and religious strictures against chopping off a corpse's head with a machete. "You want to desecrate the grave," Elita charges, initially refusing to join him in his mission. "Don't give me that crap," he counters. "There's nothing sacred about a hole in the ground. Or a man that's in it."

As he commits himself to the deed "all the way," so he commits himself to Elita, whom he agrees to marry in a church. "Bullshit, Bennie," she says in disbelief." "No, I mean it this time." When, at her request, he formally asks, "Will you marry me?" she cries with happiness. She stops Bennie from interfering with a motorcyclist who prepares to rape her at gunpoint while another motorcyclist holds a pistol to Bennie. She asserts her dignity, derived partly from Bennie's commitment to her, by slapping the man twice, although she knows he will slap her in return and rape her anyway, and by calmly requesting, "Please don't. Please," which she knows may be equally futile. Although the rapist makes her give herself to him in a way that appears voluntary, she does so in order to spare herself more physical abuse by surrendering what he would otherwise take by force. Bennie defines the totality of his commitment to Elita by knocking his captor senseless with a frying pan when the man is momentarily off guard—again affirming his willingness to take an exit, despite its danger, when he glimpses one. He seizes the man's gun, kills the would-be rapist in time to prevent the rape, then shoots the revived cyclist who held him captive. Defining himself and his relationship to Elita, Bennie proves his essence by his action, then does so again when he forces a hotel clerk to acknowledge Elita and him as a married couple, not as a man with a whore. Defining her commitment to Bennie, she politely but firmly demands, "The best room in the house, please." In their hotel room, he repeats his love for her, which she accepts.

Because Bennie does not exist in a social vacuum, he must redefine himself when circumstances change. Literally, he rises from the grave, symbolically reborn, after having been knocked unconscious and buried alive by the thugs sent by Sappensly and Quill to oversee his actions and, by killing him, avoid paying him ten thousand dollars. Elita, whom they have also buried, is less fortunate. Born anew, Bennie has a mission, to avenge his betrothed, but he goes further. He becomes his mission, defining himself by acting on his self-imposed goal. No longer does he want money as a way out: he determines to learn who ordered Max to get Alfredo Garcia's head, since this person is ultimately responsible for Elita's death. Linking himself with the dead man, he tells the head, "We're going to find out, you and me."

Bennie expresses his new status by killing every level of the hierarchy that led to Elita's murder. He slays the two men immediately responsible. He dispatches Sappensly (one of Garcia's relatives kills Quill), but he does not execute the old man who is the sole survivor among Garcia's relatives, whom Sappensly and Quill exterminated, for he has no quarrel with this man and his revenge does not involve him. Bennie liquidates Max and his minions, but not before he gets the business card that has El Jefe's name and address.

He then travels to El Jefe's well-guarded mansion, where he uses the card to gain entry. When El Jefe's daughter realizes what Bennie is carrying, sees her father give him an attaché case containing a million dollars, and hears Bennie tell El Jefe that the first time he saw Garcia, Garcia was dead, she allies herself with Bennie, ordering him to kill her father, which he does. Like Bennie, she seizes an exit, in her case from domination, and with that exit, revenge on the man who ordered the death of her child's father. She urges Bennie to leave as quickly as he can. "Come on, Al, we're going home," he tells the decapitated head as he takes it and the money. He is indeed going home, but the home to which he leaves has a location he does not fully comprehend. It is to Garcia's home, death, for El Jefe's guards kill him after he smashes his car through the gate of El Jefe's compound. Having become his deed, having fully accomplished his self-imposed mission, Bennie moves to the next stage, oblivion.

* * *

As professional killers, Mike Locken and George Hansen, the chief mercenaries of *The Killer Elite,* resemble Pike Bishop and Deke Thornton of *The Wild Bunch.* Their services are for hire—by political organizations in the later film, by Mapache and the railroad owners in the earlier—although the contemporary aristocrats of death-dealing have at their disposal a greater variety of weaponry than the outlaws of the old west and are habitually contract workers who kill or protect, whereas the gunslingers are usually independent operatives. Both types take pride in their skill, and the older group might agree with "a credo of the company" (ComTeg) that Hansen cites with approval, "Always operate on the six-P principle: Proper Planning Prevents Piss-Poor Performance." The alliterative tenet is a mark of the professional. Like Bennie in *Bring Me the Head of Alfredo Garcia*, Locken becomes vengeance.

Foreshadowing Locken's actual betrayal by Hansen is an apparent betrayal. Hansen reads a letter, supposedly from a doctor to the woman with whom Locken had sexual intercourse the previous night, informing her that she has a vaginal infection. Before Hansen confesses that the letter is a fake, one of a batch he had printed, Locken, who is annoyed that Hansen did not prevent him from infecting himself, promises, "I'll get even." "You'll have no chance," says Hansen, who has planned to kill the Eastern European defector that the CIA hired ComTeg to protect and to shoot Locken's left elbow and knee, thereby incapacitating but not killing him.

With a pitilessly demeaning prediction—"That leg of yours will never be anything but a wet noodle"—Weyburn assigns Locken the role of invalid and retiree. Cap Collis proposes to give Locken the role of office worker, "a decent, dignified job," using a term whose sly cruelty is not lost on him. But Locken refuses to be, as his name might suggest, locked into their definitions of his essence. Instead, by traditional therapy, untraditional therapy (Chinese martial arts), and, transcending both, sheer will and dogged action, he unlocks what constrains him, creating a different, ironic meaning of his name, forging his own trail, and defining his essence: vengeance against Hansen, whose name, associated with leprosy ("Hansen's disease," after the Norwegian physicist who discovered the bacillus that causes it), carries among its secondary, symbolic meanings a deterioration of moral values.[59]

Weyburn gives Locken the chance to kill Hansen, who has accepted a job to assassinate Chung, by accepting Locken back into the company and assigning him the task of protecting Chung and, while he is about it, of murdering Hansen. Locken seizes the opportunity. For him, the secondary mission becomes primary. "Too many windows," observes Miller, one of his three-man team, when he sees the hide-out Locken selected for Chung. Mac, the third team member, concurs, calling it "a mouse trap." When, inside the house, Locken predicts, "They'll be here. I know him. I can just feel it," Mac recognizes that this is the real reason Locken chose the site as supposed refuge. Unlike Bennie, Locken is prevented from completing his mission. When Miller kills Hansen, saving Locken's life by doing so, Locken is so angered that he punches Miller.

Whereas Bennie locks himself into the role he chooses, Mike Locken does not. The reason is largely his mentor, Mac, who was so disillusioned by those who employed him that he retired, but who returned out of friendship for Locken. He presses Locken to join him in withdrawal: "I know the rationale. Self-defense. God and country. Another assignment in national interests. . . . You're so busy doing their dirty work, you can't tell who the bad guys are." Since all of the sides are in one way or another trying to hurt him, he concludes, all of them are the bad guys, "all full of bullshit." Ironically, it is Collis who confirms him. When Locken accuses Collis of being paid by everyone—"our side, their side"—Collis answers, "Side, side: all full of shit. They all want the same thing: to be in charge." According to Collis, "they" include his Asian protégé. "Do you think your Oriental friend is any different? Just another ambitious politician." But why should Locken, or we, accept the word of Collis, whom the film discredits? Why, for that matter, should he or we accept the word of Mac, who admits that his knowledge is limited and whose self-deprecation might be more accurate than his conclusion: "What the hell do I know?"

Weyburn promises Collis's job to Locken at a large increase in salary. Chung offers Locken the opportunity to fight for democracy in Asia. When Chung tells Locken that he cannot pay him, the professional killer instantly refuses. "Walk away," Mac proposes. "Come with me, be a civilian. You're not going to stay with this son-of-a-bitch Weyburn, after he set you up too." Mac's statement echoes that of the Tutor in act 1 of *The Flies:* "your mind is free from prejudice and superstition; you have no family ties, no religion, and no calling; you are free to turn your hand to anything. But you know better than to commit yourself—and there lies your strength." Whereas Locken's freedom recalls that of Orestes, his dilemma is reminiscent of the dispute between Sartre and Camus on political action. According to Sartre, one must engage oneself, dirty one's hands, in order to change the world, since avoidance is evasion and refusal to act is to cede change to others, who would alter the world according to their will, not yours. By the reckoning of Camus, however, to choose between immoral alternatives is an immoral act, because one chooses from odious terms set by others, whereas refusal to choose is a demand that the terms be changed, and with different terms come different alternatives. At the end of *The Killer Elite,* Locken seems to side with Camus. As he and Mac leave, walking away from both Weyburn and Chung, Mac asks where they are going. "Don't know where we're going," Locken admits. "Don't know where we been. But I know where we was wasn't it." The two men sail away.

The conclusion is open. Two statements by Chung resonate: "It's in the manner of living and dying one finds relevance" and "Many times, men's decision betrays their confusion. One must develop clear roads to follow." Although both Locken and Mac recognize the speciousness of Chung's decision to engage his political enemy in combat by sword in order to prove himself capable of leading his country (after all, the two skills are independent of each other), neither contests the statements just quoted. Locken suspends judgment. Like Orestes in the first act of *The Flies*, Locken is "free as air," and like Orestes he might say, "My mind's my own, gloriously aloof." Unfettered by revenge, ComTeg, or Chung, he is free to redefine himself.

* * *

Cross of Iron is more complex than *The Killer Elite* and its protagonist, Corporal (soon Sergeant) Rolf Steiner, is more complex than Locken. Like Locken, however, he is a professional killer who takes pride in his skill and who has become disillusioned with the organization he serves. More so than Locken, Steiner's disillusionment extends beyond the organization to the ideals of his country and its government. Steiner's disenchantment has soured into contempt and hatred. Unlike Locken's, his feelings began long before the slice of action depicted in the movie. What Dutch, Bishop, and Angel feel about Mapache and his cause, Steiner feels about the officers of the German army, Germany's aristocratic class, Hitler, the Nazis, and the war itself. Bishop assures Mapache's German military expert that the Bunch has little in common with its government; Steiner has nothing in common with his.

"I hope you've memorized our serial numbers, our mothers' maiden names correctly," Steiner tells Zoll, a Nazi Party man and member of the special action squad, whom Stransky transferred to Steiner's platoon to keep tabs on the soldiers in it. "I wouldn't want the Gestapo to come and arrest the wrong man, woman, or child." To Steiner, the Iron Cross is "just a piece of worthless metal." "You think that just because you and Colonel Brandt are more enlightened than most officers that I hate you any less?" he asks Captain Kiesel in Brandt's presence. "I hate all officers—all the Stransky's, all the Triebigs, all the Iron Cross scavengers, and the whole German army. . . . Do you know how much I hate this uniform and everything it stands for? God!"

Steiner is alienated existential man, a flawed hero, a professional whose exceptional skill virtually everyone acknowledges. "He's a first-rate soldier, and so we look the other way" admits Brandt. "Steiner is a myth," adds Kiesel. "But men like him are our last hope, and in that sense he is truly a very dangerous man." "A myth": Kiesel does not use the term in the sense that Steiner exists only in the imagination or that his deeds are not verifiable, but in the sense that because only superior phenomena like him can save them and that because such men are so awesome as to become the stuff of legend, lesser beings are beholden to them and are for this reason in their power. Peckinpah does not ask us to take their word for Steiner's abilities. Instead, he shows Steiner in action, defeating or escaping from various enemies: individuals, notably, his principal antagonist, Captain Stransky; a machine gun emplacement; and tanks. Peckinpah also shows Steiner tempering killing with mercy and justice. Steiner spares a captured Russian soldier, not more than a boy, whom Stransky wants killed. He does not kill the captured female Russian troops, does nothing to them when they kill one of his own soldiers, a naive youth, and virtually castrate Zoll, a bullying brute. He leaves Zoll with them for their revenge when he departs with the rest of his men.

This alienated man lives in an absurd world. His meeting the Russian lad, who the film suggests reminds him of his own children, is, he tells the boy, "an accident, an accident of hands—mine, others', all without mind." It is, in short, absurd. In the middle of no-man's-land, he makes an equally absurd gesture: he tells the youth to go home to his own people. Absurdly, these people think him an enemy and shoot him, which pains Steiner so much that he screams in agony.

To be alienated is to be free. "I am free," says Orestes in act 2, scene 2, of *The Flies,* and the heavier his deed is for him to bear, "the better pleased I shall be; for that burden is my freedom." Wherever his path may lead, "it is my path." The sentiments are Steiner's, too. When he is trapped behind enemy lines, his whereabouts and very existence unknown to his battalion and his foes alike, he admits, "I'm beginning to enjoy it. What do you want—sitting in some mud hole someplace, waiting for the top of your head to be blown off? At least here we're free." This situation, brief as it is, exemplifies his alienation and freedom. "I have no home," he tells the nurse earlier. When she proposes to share her home with him, he does not accept her offer. Nor can he accept commitment to this woman, who does not understand that her final words to him, "Long live Germany!" are anathema to this man, who told his military superior that he hates everything his uniform represents. Yet this free man willingly accepts a burden, the safety of the men in his company, whose lives are entrusted to him. He has committed himself to the soldiers he leads in combat. Near the conclusion of the film Schnurrbart acknowledges Steiner's burden: "You've been responsible for all of us."

Like Steiner, Schnurrbart is a professional. Although he has less stature than Steiner does, he is skillful enough to save Steiner and the Russian youth who is their prisoner from a dangerous situation. When Steiner refuses to obey Stransky's command to shoot the boy—"You shoot him, sir"—Stransky is about to do so when Schnurrbart stops him, indicating that there is no need, since he will undertake the task. He then leads the boy to safety in the bunker, not death.

Steiner's hostility toward war, despite his professionalism, is not a knee-jerk action but comes from first-hand acquaintance with war. He is also familiar with the writings of war's proponents, as he demonstrates in an exchange with Schnurrbart while they wait for the Russian attack:

Schnurrbart: Rolf, what are we doing here?
Steiner (ironically): We are spreading the German culture throughout a
    desperate world.
Schnurrbart: Didn't someone say that war is the highest expression in life
    for the truly cultured people?
Steiner: Yes. A foolish wise man named Frederick von Bernhardi.
Schnurrbart: Right. And von Clausewitz said—?
Steiner: Von Clausewitz? Ah. Von Clausewitz said, "War is a continuation
    of state policy—"
Schnurrbart (interrupting): "—by other means."
Steiner: Yes. "By other means."[60]

Schnurrbart, whose presence is functional in terms of plot (saving the Russian boy and motivating Steiner to leave the hospital), is also themat-ically integral. He has professional abilities similar to those of Steiner, as do the other members of Steiner's platoon, which increases Steiner's cred-ibility and stature. In addition, Schnurrbart shares and permits the reve-lation of Steiner's grasp of the wider aspects of war.

Some critics consider Kiesel to be one of the "good" characters because Brandt certifies him as a braver man than he thinks he is; orders him to search out, after the war, the "better people" with whom to rebuild Ger-many; and arranges his early evacuation from the front.[61] These analysts might ponder an earlier exchange between Brandt and Kiesel. "What will we do when we lose the war?" asks the colonel. "Prepare for the next one," the captain replies. Is this what Kiesel and the other "better people" will do? Critics who admire Kiesel might also recall his description of Steiner, quoted above, as a dangerous person. In addition to the meanings men-tioned above, Steiner is dangerous because of his independence. After Stransky leaves, Kiesel tells Brandt that with the Wehrmacht going down in defeat, "if they're the last of us, Stransky and Steiner, then God help us." He and Brandt are not sympathetic to what Steiner stands for: they tolerate him—look the other way, as Brandt puts it—because Steiner is a good soldier. Nor are they sympathetic to Stransky and what he stands for, the aristocracy. They are professional officers, members of the military class, and Brandt explicitly calls upon God to bless the German soldier.

Although *Cross of Iron* embraces and insists on the wider social ramifications of its subject, its plot focuses on the conflict between a protagonist, the uncommon commoner Steiner, who believes that "a man is generally what he feels himself to be" and that "talent, sensitivity, and character are no longer privileges of the so-called upper class," and an antagonist, Stransky, who accurately classifies himself as "an officer of the Wehrmacht. I have never been a [Nazi] Party member. I am a Prussian aristocrat," and who demands recognition of the "ethical and intellectual superiority" conferred on him "by blood and by class." Shortly after Stransky leaves battalion headquarters, Steiner returns to the camp. During their first encounter with each other, Steiner is brazenly insubordinate when Stransky orders him to shoot the Russian boy. In their second meeting, when Corporal Steiner does not react to Stransky's information that he has been promoted to senior sergeant, effective immediately, he is more politely insubordinate. "Your promotion doesn't seem to have made much of an impression," says Stransky. "No, it doesn't," admits Steiner. Stransky admonishes him not to overestimate his importance. Lieutenant Meyer warns Steiner that Stransky has "taken a strong dislike" to him.

> *Meyer:* You're not dealing with just another Nazi Party type. This one is pure Prussian military aristocracy. And rich. You know the ruling classes.
> *Steiner:* Now, Lieutenant, what's left for them to rule?
> *Meyer:* Don't be naive. Stransky will survive this war one way or another, and he'll still have his land, his wealth, and his status, but can be very dangerous in defeat. Be careful of him. He doesn't live in the same world we live in.
> *Steiner:* I know. He's living in my world now.

As much as Stransky tries to make Steiner's world into an image of the world with which he is familiar and which he dominates, he cannot do so. Whereas Stransky dominates by exercising his rank and status, Steiner dominates by exercising his personal qualities and abilities. Whereas Steiner defines himself, Stransky is defined by others. Although the Iron Cross is to Steiner a piece of tin without value, Stransky declares, "It's not worthless to me." "Tell me, Captain, why?" asks Steiner. "Sergeant," he confesses, "if I go back without the Iron Cross, I couldn't face my family." Its value, in other words, is determined by others in his social class, not by Stransky himself, and like the heroic military values attached to the titular cross, Stransky's ethical and moral values are defined by these others. Like the medal, Stransky is a thing, whose meaning exists in the perception of others, not himself.

To get the medal, Stransky tries but fails to have Steiner killed. Steiner, who survives by means of his professional skills, augmented by those of his platoon, seeks out Stransky in order "to pay my debts." Although Stransky tries to use his aristocratic bearing to intimidate Steiner into submission, he fails, since what previously propped his authority, the support of the structures created by others, is gone in the rout of the German army. He is alone with Steiner, who needs no one else to authenticate himself. Steiner, the social commoner who is the film's existential hero, dominates the aristocrat. "Where is the rest of your platoon?" demands Stransky in a last-ditch effort to assert his authority. Although Stransky carries a rifle, Steiner has sufficient self-confidence to turn his back on Stransky as he asserts his authority over the Prussian officer who, Steiner knows, ordered Triebig to murder him: "You are, Captain Stransky. You are the rest of my platoon." Stransky may transcend his limitations by accepting the challenge, but he nevertheless places himself under Steiner's command. He now truly lives in Steiner's world. Steiner gives the orders, and he laughs at Stransky's ineptitude when the captain falls in the dirt, dropping his rifle. "My differences with Captain Stransky are personal," Steiner told Colonel Brandt earlier. Despite the defeat of the army that Steiner both serves and detests, he triumphs in personal, subjective terms, which in the social context at the end of the film mark the only terms in which success is possible.

A powerful and complex figure, a man who recognizes the failings of the cause he serves but strives to transcend them, Steiner has stature and integrity. To the extent that he can do so, which given the circumstances is astonishing, he chooses his actions, defines himself, and determines his fate. What he does and what he is display decency, honor, principle, indeed grandeur and nobility. Alienated, he is free, and he makes his own laws. He is sufficiently intelligent to be familiar with von Bernhardi and von Clausewitz, but in Peckinpah's words, as quoted earlier in this chapter, he "embodies his intellect in action," which makes him "a complete human being."

* * *

Despite its visual flair and virtuosity, which are such familiar aspects of Peckinpah's feature films that one almost takes them for granted, and which may entice spectators of *Convoy,* as they often disarm this spectator, *Convoy* is existentialism manqué, which would not matter if it successfully dramatized something else. It does not. Its redolence of existentialism and of Peckinpah's familiar themes reveals *Convoy* to be an empty shell. Its depiction of the individualist in defiance of authority recalls an exchange in act 2, scene 2, of *The Flies.* "You and I harbor the same dark secret in our hearts," Zeus tells Aegisthus: "The bane of gods and kings. The bitterness of knowing men are free. . . . Orestes knows that he is free." Aegisthus recognizes, "A free man in a city acts like a plague-spot. He will infect my kingdom and bring my work to nothing." Rubber Duck, an Orestes-like trucker, seems intended by the director to represent a free man whose actions threaten, to use the term of Sartre's Aegisthus, to "infect" America.

Shortly after the beginning of *Convoy* comes an exchange between the Duck and his principal antagonist, Sheriff Wallace, also called "Dirty Lyle," which contrasts independence and membership in a herd:

> *Rubber Duck:* Hey, Lyle, you're gonna be one of us pretty soon, you know.
> *Wallace:* How's that?
> *Rubber Duck:* Ain't you heard? The Teamsters are going to be organizing the cops.
> *Wallace:* Not this one. I don't want any part of your damned union.
> *Rubber Duck:* It ain't my damned union, Lyle. I'm independent, remember?
> *Wallace:* At least we got one thing in common.
> *Rubber Duck:* . . . There ain't many of us left.

Peckinpah does not pursue the implications of this dialogue. Although Rubber Duck displays his independence, Wallace does not. Dirty Lyle acts in bad faith. After Rubber Duck and his comrades rescue Spider Mike from the Alvarez, Texas, jail, which their trucks demolish, the sheriff emerges from the rubble to rebuke the Duck: "I knew you'd come, but I never figured you'd need help, too." "I didn't bring nobody. They came on their own," says the Duck, truthfully. "This was between you and me. You knew it," persists Lyle, despite the fact that he himself had brought dozens of law-enforcement personnel to help him capture the Duck. Having raised the issue of bad faith, Peckinpah drops it. Because the subject is undramatized, it amounts to putting on airs.

Rubber Duck is an unfeigned, unpretentious individualist who existentially demonstrates his freedom by acting. When Lyle, in a helicopter, tells him to stop driving because of a road block ahead, the Duck points out that his truck is carrying volatile chemicals that might explode, but he does not slow down. Although the law enforcers in the air think he is bluffing, he is not. He proves his mettle in action, willing to take the consequences. He chooses not to die but to test his courage, even if his action results in death, so that if he lives, which he does, it will be on his terms, not in moral or penal servitude but in freedom. The police "blink," as it were, and remove the road block.

Similarly, near the end of the film, he drives his truck at top speed across a bridge that would take him to freedom in Mexico, an action recalling that of Doc and Carol McCoy in *The Getaway,* in defiance of a tank and troops who, far from "blinking," fire a variety of weapons at him and blow up his truck. Rubber Duck's act, freely chosen, may result in death, but death is not its object: freedom is. Although the authorities think he dies in the crash, he does not, which is a happy if arbitrary ending on the part of Peckinpah. The director demonstrates, intentionally or not, that the Duck and the defiant individualism he represents may live, but only in disguise and in hiding, a conclusion that blunts the impact of existential choice, individualism, and defiance.

The Duck proceeds along his own path. Regardless of who may follow him, and regardless of what may result from negotiations with the governor of New Mexico in behalf of the convoy, whose demands—except to permit the Duck, Spider Mike, and Love Machine to evade punishment in Arizona—are unclear, he elects to go to Texas to free Spider Mike, who is in jail and whose need is clear. When Governor Haskins, urging the Duck to stay, insists, "Sometimes you have to sacrifice the individual," the truckers respond with cries of "Bullshit!" The governor promises to help the truckers but insists that they must leave Spider Mike—who, after all, is in another state, outside his jurisdiction—to fend for himself. Knowing that in Mike's situation he cannot fend for himself, knowing too that Lyle and other police authorities are using Mike as bait to trap him, the Duck takes responsibility for his colleague and chooses to engage in action. Working with truckers who, accepting their own responsibility, act by following him to help, the Duck releases Mike. His commitment is fulfilled and he prepares to walk, or drive, away.

What does the titular convoy exemplify? The film's initial release followed the widespread popularity of the song that inspired it and that runs through the sound track. To us, two decades later, the thematic interest of the motion picture lies in its anticipation of the usually vague antigovernmental stance of a number of Americans in the 1990s. The film shows this incipient attitude as imprecise, if not incoherent. "That's incredible," says Melissa of the hundreds of trucks in the convoy. "Where are they all coming from?" "Everywhere," answers Rubber Duck. She wonders why they have joined the convoy. "Don't ask me, ask them," he says, "I'm running for my life myself," which is true. Their next exchange reveals Peckinpah's inability to deal with the issue. "Yeah, but they're all following you," she says. "No they ain't," says the Duck. "I'm just in front." Although Peckinpah does not dramatize this to be the case, Rubber Duck is wrong: they *are* following him. "Is this convoy some sort of protest demonstration, and if it is, what is its purpose?" asks Chuck Arnoldi, special assistant and press representative to Governor Haskins. "The purpose of the convoy is to keep moving," says the Duck. While it is his purpose, since he is trying to escape from the law, others in the convoy give different reasons, among them protests against racism, against higher taxes, against the recently imposed fifty-five-mile-per-hour speed limit (repealed years after this film), and simply "to kick ass."

The last motive, which may seem frivolous, suggests what the film shows to be the two real reasons for the convoy: its members follow a newly revealed leader in a world devoid of leaders whom the people genuinely respect, and they register a complaint, however inarticulate it may be. Rubber Duck seems to understand the first motive: "I don't know what to do about it. I been thinking about all those towns we're going through and all those people who's cheering us, man, people falling in behind us, and I think I figured it out. The only reason they're coming in behind us is who the hell else they got? Nobody, that's who." Like him, Peckinpah seems not to know what to do about it, but while Peckinpah is not obliged to answer this question, he is required to dramatize the dilemma the protagonist states, which he fails to do.

Governor Haskins, whom the people of New Mexico elected, has no understanding. He thinks that the convoy is about "more than the banning of the fifty-five-mile speed limit," but Rubber Duck disabuses him of the notion that it has anything to do with the speed limit. At least, the Duck recognizes the inexactness, therefore the incoherence, of the protest. All that Haskins recognizes is that the Duck has become "the people's leader," which makes the Duck politically useful to him. Since Haskins, like Sheriff Wallace, embodies the government and the laws that frustrate those who are in or who cheer the convoy, he is someone against whom to protest, not with whom to negotiate. Paradoxically, however, as Melissa and even the Duck recognize, they have no choice other than to negotiate—which is another issue that Peckinpah raises and then drops. Ultimately, this problem too is reduced to a posture, as in the exchange between Wallace and the Duck, a feeble echo of one quoted earlier, between Harrigan and Thornton in *The Wild Bunch*. "I am the law. Don't you understand? I represent the law," emphasizes Wallace. "Well, piss on you, and piss on your law," is the Duck's rejoinder. Does *Convoy* aim to dramatize protest reduced to posture? If so, it does not do so adequately and thereby diminishes challenge to attitude.

Convoy dramatizes people who try but fail to control their lives and whose victories are momentary, made meaningless because, except for the rescue of Spider Mike, they are inarticulate demonstrations instead of responsible actions. In the film's conclusion, the truckers leave the governor, who plans to run for the United States Senate, to make speeches without their presence, which would have demonstrated that he had the people's backing. Dirty Lyle, who personifies the villain, expresses solidarity with the truckers when he sees that Rubber Duck is not dead. This finale is a dramatized theatrical gesture that is divorced from the social context to which it purportedly addresses itself. As an existentialist drama to which it seems to aspire, the film has only the outlines and is unfulfilled.

* * *

Despite the presence of a protagonist who is another Orestes figure, John Tanner, *The Osterman Weekend* focuses not on the existential choice of the Orestes character but, to use the perspective of *The Flies,* on life in America under Zeus, who is personified by Maxwell Danforth. Danforth's hired myrmidons, as well as other, unsalaried subjects, consent to exist within the parameters he sets and to live not by their individual, subjective values but by the values he establishes for them. Despite the illusion that they are free, they lack liberty. Peckinpah shows Danforth's control of human lives at the start of the film, which reveals that he made a deal with the Soviets, the details of which he has long since forgotten, sanctioning the KGB's killing an innocent person, the wife of one of his underlings, Lawrence Fassett. When Danforth phones Tanner from his office, Peckinpah visualizes Danforth's deadliness by placing him before a picture window, on the other side of which are rows of tombstones, presumably in Arlington National Cemetery. Tanner's epithet for this man, whose presidential ambitions Danforth first denies, then inadvertently confirms, is apt: "Big Brother Max."

Ironically, it is one of Danforth's agents, Fassett, who before the film begins has made an existential choice that defines himself, to expose this Zeus figure's guilt. Fassett's activities, involving further ironies and complexities, fulfill his goal. Prominent among these ironies is the fact that by his actions he becomes no different from Danforth, whom he manipulates into conducting a covert operation in the way he wants it handled. Fassett becomes a tyrant to whom people's lives are worthless except insofar as they advance his goal. Near the end of the movie, he admits that in causing the death of four innocent people, he resembles Danforth. "My guilt is not in question," he concedes, "but the guilt of this man is." Fassett's existential choice denies choice to others, to whom he, like Danforth, gives the appearance but not the actuality of freedom.

The principal means by which Fassett accomplishes his goal is Tanner, a television muckraker whom he calls "a bigot about truth, democracy, and justice" and whom one of Tanner's friends labels "king of the exposés." Tanner is an independent man, a free agent, whose vocation consists of exposing authorities and questioning their actions, aims, and justifications, which most people ordinarily accept. Our first view of him is his TV interview with an American army general whose prepared statements he demolishes.

At the start of *The Osterman Weekend*, Tanner is controlled by neither Danforth nor Fassett. After he enters the building where he is to meet Danforth, and where he meets Fassett, he rides up a freight elevator, whose door is not solid but has vertical wooden slats suggestive of prison bars; as the elevator passes each floor on its way up, Tanner sees, through the slats, men who resemble guards. Fassett gives him a copy of the Official Secrets Act: "If you want to go for the jackpot, then you must sign it. But I warn you that after the signature, then there is no walking away. You sign it, and your life isn't going to be the same." "I'm not your man," is the initial response of Tanner, who walks away. As he is about to enter the elevator, out steps Danforth, with whom Tanner makes a deal: in return for signing the document and agreeing to do what Fassett and Danforth want, Danforth consents to appear on Tanner's television program and be questioned. "So who's your next victim in the show?" Bernie Osterman later asks Tanner. "Maxwell Danforth." "Oh, yeah, the big one. What did you have to give up to get him?" Tanner does not reply, but the question remains in his and our minds. Although Tanner fathoms that he has surrendered some control over his home and is nervous that he must keep the truth about his mission and about Fassett from his wife, he has ceded more than he realizes. Although his existential choice has made him Fassett's man, he is not completely in thrall to Fassett but remains free to reevaluate his initial choice and to make another choice when new circumstances warrant his doing so.

Fassett manipulates him, and through him others. To manipulate is to deprive people of their free will, of their liberty to choose, and to make them puppets. "No need to worry, John," he soothingly tells Tanner. "Everything is under control." Four of Tanner's house guests are "just on a very long leash." "Who's pulling your strings?" asks Tanner. Fassett smiles, laughs, and mimics a puppet whose strings are being pulled or manipulated; but it is he who controls the strings of the others, whose lives mean nothing to him except insofar as they help him to achieve his objective. "Try to think of them," he tells Tanner after blowing up a camper that contains these four guests, "as fleas on a dog that gets hit by a stolen car, driven by a drunk teenager, whose girl friend's just given him the clap. It will help your perspective."

Visualizing Fassett's, Danforth's, and the Establishment's control over our lives is television, which pervades the movie. Danforth watches a video replay of the execution of Fassett's wife, filmed by a hidden camera. So does Fassett, who uncovered the film, which he shows to Tanner. In *The Osterman Weekend,* television is both a surveillance instrument and a medium that creates docility and compliance. Fassett wires Tanner's home with an elaborate TV system—"state of the art stuff," as Tanner calls it. "Where are you putting all these cameras?" asks Tanner. "Everywhere. The whole house is going to be covered." So, it turns out, are the grounds and the inside of a camper. Fassett shows Tanner videos of Tanner's friends alone, with a financial agent, and together. On a TV monitor in the building Tanner visits to meet Danforth, Fassett observes them concluding their deal. He witnesses Tanner and his wife making love. He inspects Tanner's house guests in their bedrooms, as does Tanner. Television is addictive. "Switch it off, John," Bernie Osterman, a TV writer, tells Tanner when a TV screen near them suddenly goes on, by remote control, showing Fassett. "You know better than that, Bernie," responds Fassett. "It's your business, both of you, addicting people so that they can't switch off"—in other words, cannot exercise free, existential choice. Even Fassett is addicted to TV, mesmerized by the serpent's eye of the camera. During the battle in Tanner's pool, just after the second of his agents is killed, his attention is caught by one of the TV screens that shows a baseball game and, distracted from the life-and-death situation at hand, he watches the game for a few moments.

"In this world you have entered," he states after Tanner signs the Official Secrets Act, "things are rarely as they seem." His saving Tanner's wife and son after their apparent kidnapping is a complex, elaborate hoax that he arranges to ensure Tanner's future compliance. On cue, Tanner tells him, gratefully, "I should have listened to you." Even Fassett's self-introduction to Ali Tanner as an FBI man is not what it seems: this identifica-

tion covers his real identity as a CIA man. A quick cut from the weekend-
ers at a table to a view of them frolicking in a pool is not a jump cut forward in time to the poolside, which it seems to be, but a chronologically
reverse movement, for the pool gambols, which took place during a previous weekend, are in a home movie, transferred to videotape, seen in a
different setting, in time present. The severed head of Tanner's dog, in the
refrigerator, is not real, which it seems to be, but is "a fake," as Osterman
notices when he examines it closely. Fassett persuades his superiors at the
CIA that Mikhailovich is "our old friend, Mr. KGB himself," in Stennings's
description to Danforth, and is the "bag man" of Tanner's friends, known
to them as Petrov, in their income-tax evasion scheme. During the battle
in and around the pool, he is revealed to be in the employ of Fassett, who
according to Stennings, later, "fabricated a KGB dossier on him," and this
dossier is part of what Fassett shows Tanner on a TV screen. Whether
Mikhailovich was really a money launderer before Fassett engaged him
or whether he acted in that capacity under Fassett's instructions, we do
not know. Nor do we know whether he was formerly a Soviet agent whom
Fassett recruited, as he may have been, since as Fassett tells Tanner, "To
us, an enemy agent is potentially our agent."

Even outside the world Tanner has entered, things are not always what
they seem. Before Fassett enters their lives, the Tanner marriage is fray-
ing, despite the good face each tries to put on it. Wearing a white robe
with a white slip beneath it, Virginia Tremayne tells her husband, on the
telephone, that she wears a black gown with nothing underneath. Betty
Cardone makes her husband, Joe, think she had an orgasm when they
made love, but as her retrieval of her chewing gum from the bedpost after coitus makes clear, her enjoyment was not what it seemed to be. "Virginia, don't you ever get tired of playing the bitch in heat?" asks Ali, who
sees through Virginia's act. Later, when Virginia sees her strange, perhaps
stranger-like, cocaine-smeared face in a mirror, she reacts with revulsion
to her self-recognition, "Cocaine bitch!" As Osterman remarks to Tanner,
"The truth is a lie that hasn't been found out," an aphorism appreciated
by Fassett, who overhears it.

When Tanner and Osterman learn the truth about each other, they join
to defeat Fassett and Danforth. Since television is their profession, they
do so through this medium, thereby manipulating their manipulator. "I'm
just wondering how we got into this mess," says Osterman as they prerecord TV clips to set up their antagonists, which recalls Fassett's videotape
of Osterman proposing that he and Tanner's friends set up Tanner during their weekend. "It's called being programmed," quips Tanner, who saw

the videotape. With Osterman in the booth at the video controls and Tanner on camera, Tanner exposes Danforth. As Fassett watches Tanner, who seems to appear live on television, Tanner shows up in person at Fassett's hideout, shoots him, and rescues his family, whom Fassett kidnapped—a real deliverance in contrast to Fassett's earlier apparent rescue of them after a fake kidnapping.

The exposure of Danforth as the man responsible for having Fassett's wife murdered, and as an aspiring president with right-wing rhetoric and a police-state view of order, is truly live on TV, as is the exposure and killing of Fassett, whose manipulations and murders the film dramatizes. Furthermore, the spectators themselves are also exposed, or rather are challenged to prove that they are free, not manipulated. After they see the actual nature of Danforth and Fassett, Tanner's prerecorded voice tells them, and us, "What you just saw, in a way, was a life-size video game. You saw a liar talk to a killer and you couldn't tell them apart. Who cares? It's only television. As you all know, television programs are just the fillers between attempts to steal your money. So if you want to save some, switch off. It's simple. It's done with the hand and what is left of your free will. This is the moment. My bet is you can't do it. Go ahead and try." After a pause, Tanner asks, "Am I still on?" Ironically, the conclusion of this feature film that was made for theatrical release is more effective on television, where viewers have precisely the choice that is offered them. What is left of their, or our, free will? Like David Sumner in *Straw Dogs,* Tanner, an intellectual, proves himself in action and becomes an existentialist hero. Yet *The Osterman Weekend* does not really focus on an exemplary existentialist hero as such. Rather, its crux is ways of being manipulated and of surrendering one's free will. As such, it is a challenge. In terms of *The Flies,* the last of Sam Peckinpah's feature films dramatizes Argos before Orestes arrives.

* * *

This director's feature films exemplify various aspects of the existentialist philosophy of Sartre and Camus. Peckinpah's heroic protagonists—notably Pike Bishop, David Sumner, and Sergeant Steiner—define their essence by their will and by acting upon that will, even if their actions might cost them their lives. In choosing and in acting as they do, they assume responsibility for society, since the enactment of their free choices, albeit subjective, creates models for mankind. When characters of Peckinpah—particularly Ben Tyreen, Pat Garrett, and Billy the Kid—act in bad faith and refuse to choose, whether by self-deception, evasion, or inaction, their refusals are themselves choices, since they elect not to define themselves but, by default, to be defined by others. As quoted above, Peckinpah's paraphrase of his father, a man of the American West, conforms to the philosophy espoused by these French philosophers associated with Paris's Left Bank, that either one stands up for what is important and what is right, or else one compromises to the point of self-destruction.

Let us not fall into the trap of what might be called the thematic fallacy, that a work of art is valuable insofar as it contains important themes. What a character in Steve Martin's play *Picasso at the Lapin Agile* says of a painting applies to all the arts: "if you judge it only by its meaning, then any bad painting is just as good as any good painting if they have the same meaning." Although Peckinpah's films exemplify the existentialist ethic, as this chapter has demonstrated, their embodiment of existentialism is not in itself a badge of merit. If it were, then to use Martin's terms, *Convoy* would be just as good a movie as *The Wild Bunch*. Nevertheless, the dramatically cinematic coherence of existentialism, and its employment or execution as a unifying concept, when it is coherent and is thus employed, help to account for the excellence of Peckinpah's better films and the relative weaknesses of others.

These qualities concern not only plot, but also and perhaps primarily characterization. Despite the stature and integrity of numerous figures in Peckinpah's films, they are flawed, imperfect, or weak, which is to say realistic human beings. Furthermore, their flaws or deficiencies, not their stature, honor, or nobility, may be their dominant characteristics. None of them is a paragon of virtue, traditional or otherwise, and many of them are criminals. When Gil Westrum, Pike Bishop, and David Sumner, for example, realize who they are and what their situation is, when they recognize that they must take a stand, must rise and be counted, or else drift and evade, their realization and recognition, as well as the stand they take, derive from the complex core of their beings and from the fabric of the films that dramatize them and their complexity. In dramatic terms, what precedes these defining moments enables these figures to earn their status and their stature. Junior Bonner's refusal of the inducements of his brother and of Buck bolsters his existential determination to test his mettle against the very best opponent, making his victory, when he gets to act upon his decision, a magnificent achievement. By contrast, Mike Locken's decision to walk away from Weyburn's offer is a considerably lesser accomplishment. This is partly because Locken's characterization is less complex than that of the rodeo rider; partly because the dramatic thrust of the film—his existential determination to overcome, and actions that overcome, his physical deficiencies, which enable him to destroy the man who inflicted them—is dramatically more momentous than his decision concerning Weyburn; and partly because Peckinpah inadequately dramatizes Weyburn's "office politics" as a core dramatic action of the film or as a serious existential choice for Locken, but treats it chiefly in terms of phrasemaking by Mac. In terms of quality, *The Killer Elite* also contrasts with *Pat Garrett and Billy the Kid,* both of which portray alienated killers. However, the bad faith that permeates the titular characters of the latter film, in which it is an organic principle, has no counterpart in the former film, whose characters merely deceive for profit. The coherent social and psychological complexity of *Cross of Iron* that underpins its protagonist's existential actions, every bit as much as the superbly rendered battle scenes, helps to make this motion picture a monumental achievement. Just as psychology and existentialist coherence helps to elevate *Bring Me the Head of Alfredo Garcia,* the absence of psychological and existentialist coherence, plus the mere graftings-on of occasional social and existentialist thematic passages, help to reveal, despite its visual delights, the hollowness of *Convoy.* The dramatization of what I have called life under Zeus in *The Osterman Weekend,* together with the acutely rendered psychological realism of the three marriages, the bewilderment of the two surviving male victims when they recognize the true nature of what has happened, and their actions based upon that understanding elevate this film far above the status of spy story or revenge yarn. When existentialism is wedded to psychological and socially defined characterization, and to dramatic structure, it functions as an informing principle of Peckinpah's movies and in large measure accounts for their artistic success.

Ride the High Country. The race between a camel and a horse. Heck Longtree (Ron Starr) is on the camel.

Ride the High Country. The two old-timers, Gil Westrum (Randolph Scott) and Steve Judd (Joel McCrea), prepare to ride to the high country.

Ride the High Country. The travelers arrive at Coarse Gold, the mining town in the high country. On horseback, from left: Elsa Knudsen (Mariette Hartley), Heck Longtree (Ron Starr), Steve Judd (Joel McCrea), and Gil Westrum (Randolph Scott).

Major Dundee. Major Amos Dundee (Charlton Heston) at Fort Benlin.

Major Dundee. Confederate Captain Tyreen (Richard Harris) gives the American flag, which he retrieved from a French soldier in battle, to Major Dundee (Charlton Heston).

The Wild Bunch. Mapache (Emilio Fernandez), in back seat of car, has his men torture Angel (Jaime Sanchez).

The Wild Bunch. The Wild Bunch march to Mapache's headquarters to get Angel back: Tector Gorch (Ben Johnson), Lyle Gorch (Warren Oates), Pike Bishop (William Holden), Dutch Engstrom (Ernest Borgnine).

The Wild Bunch. Pike Bishop (William Holden) is shot in the back by a prostitute.

The Wild Bunch. The bounty hunters observe the Bunch's battle with Mapache's forces. Coffer (Strother Martin), standing with rifle; Deke Thornton (Robert Ryan), at right, holding binoculars; behind him, T.C. (L. Q. Jones).

The Ballad of Cable Hogue. Bowen (Strother Martin) and Taggart (L. Q. Jones) rob Cable Hogue (Jason Robards), leaving him to perish in the desert.

The Ballad of Cable Hogue. Hogue lobs snakes into a hole that Taggart (L. Q. Jones) and Bowen (Strother Martin) have dug, thinking Hogue hid his money there.

The Ballad of Cable Hogue. Hildy (Stella Stevens) goes to Hogue (Jason Robards) after her car has accidentally run over him.

3

I Would Give You Some Violence

"All right, let's get it on. I promise to do my little number," Sam Peckinpah told William Murray, who interviewed him for *Playboy*. "But I'm not going to talk about violence." "Then we might as well not begin," said Murray. "That's fine with me," the director shot back. The reason he claimed he did not want to discuss violence was that "that's what everybody is trying to nail me on. They think I invented it. They think that's what I'm all about."[1] He then proceeded to discourse on violence.

The year in which this interview appeared, 1972, saw the publication of *Lear,* by Edward Bond, an English dramatist whose plays, like Peckinpah's films, are associated with violence. "I write about violence as naturally as Jane Austen wrote about manners," says Bond at the start of his preface to the play. "People who do not want writers to write about violence want to stop them from writing about us and our time. It would be immoral not to write about violence."[2] Like Bond, Peckinpah invokes the familiar yet valid point that the violence in his work reflects the violence in society. In 1967, two years before the release of *The Wild Bunch,* in a reference to riots in black ghettos in American cities, H. Rap Brown, a spokesman for many black Americans, said that violence "is as American as cherry pie." True, but as Bond's statement indicates, it is equally as English as roast beef and Yorkshire pudding. Furthermore, it is as German as sauerkraut, as Russian as borscht, as Japanese as sushi, and as Italian (or Chinese) as spaghetti. In short, it is worldwide. Nor is it exclusively characteristic of our times. *King Lear,* on which Bond based *Lear,* is rife with such onstage violence as eye-gouging. The title of this chapter misquotes *Hamlet,* in which Ophelia, driven insane by her father's murder by the man she loves, proposes to Hamlet's mother, Queen Gertrude, "I would give you some violets," which are a symbol of faithfulness (act 4, scene 5). She does not do so—perhaps because Gertrude was unfaithful to her husband (although it is unclear how Ophelia would know this), perhaps because in killing Ophelia's father Hamlet was unfaithful to her. In either case, this play too contains violence. Despite Prince Hamlet's initial delay in slaying his stepfather, who murdered Hamlet's father, he executes Ophelia's father as a reflex action, without displaying an iota of remorse afterward, when he discovers whom he killed; he cold-bloodedly causes the deaths of Rosencrantz and Guildenstern; and he unhesitatingly stabs his stepfather upon discovering that the man just poisoned him and his mother.

As Bond says, Jane Austen wrote of manners; but violence was as endemic in her time as in previous ages—as witness, for example, the careers of Attila the Hun, Genghis Khan, and Vlad the Impaler—and in subsequent eras. In 1775, the year of Austen's birth, Bohemian peasants staged bloody revolts and the British crown hired twenty-nine thousand German mercenaries for war in North America. In 1811, the year she published *Sense and Sensibility,* the Marmelukes were massacred in Cairo. Two years later, when *Pride and Prejudice* appeared, war raged throughout Europe. Austen wrote about manners because she was attuned to this motif. Bond writes about and Peckinpah films violence because they are in tune to that theme. All three are adept at their subjects.

In the *Playboy* interview, Peckinpah documents instances of violence in contemporary popular entertainment and classical works:

> Do you think people watch the Super Bowl because they think football is a beautiful sport? Bullshit! They're committing violence vicariously. Look, the old basis of catharsis was a purging of the emotions through pity and fear. People used to go and see the plays of Euripides and Sophocles and those other Greek cats. The players acted it out and the audience got in there and kind of lived it with them. What's more violent than the plays of William Shakespeare? And how about grand opera? What's bloodier than a romantic grand opera? . . . Want to have some fun? Read *Grimm's Fairy Tales.*[3]

The statement is accurate: violence abounds in these adult and children's classics. I have already cited the eye-gouging scene in *King Lear.* The exclamation "kill, kill, kill, kill, kill, kill!" is spoken not by one of Peckinpah's characters about to indulge in an orgy of blood-lust, but by Lear, who fantasizes a mad wish-list for his sons-in-law (act 4, scene 6). To Walt Whitman, "nothing can happen more beautiful than death" (*Starting from Paumonock*, Section 13); to Sylvia Plath, "Dying / Is an art, like everything else" ("Lady Lazarus"). Both quotations are as apposite to Peckinpah's movies as the quotation from *King Lear*. For a germane epigraph to a book on Peckinpah, one of his critics took a 1908 statement by Tolstoy: "I am seriously thinking of writing a play for the screen. I have a subject for it. It is a terrible and bloody theme. I am not afraid of bloody themes. Take Homer or the Bible, for instance. How many bloodthirsty passages there are in them—murders, wars. And yet these are the sacred books, and they ennoble and uplift the people. It is not the subject itself that is so terrible. It is the propagation of bloodshed, and the justification for it, that is terrible."[4] While I am not going to claim that the bloodthirsty portions of Peckinpah's films ennoble and uplift human beings, neither will I avow that Homeric or biblical passages of carnage do so. To be candid, "ennoblement" and "uplift" are not critical terms with which I am comfortable. I would have difficulty justifying *King Lear* or *Hamlet* in these terms, and I find no uplift in *Othello*.

It is equally accurate, as Peckinpah indicates in the first quotation, that his feature films are about and consist of more than violence. Nevertheless, whether he liked it or not—more likely, he liked it and not—he has become as associated with violence as Guildenstern has with Rosencrantz. Whereas Ophelia only offers to give violets, Peckinpah does give violence, a theme to which he is faithful and which he depicts with a mastery that has been imitated but not equalled, and which he dramatizes with a personal, idiosyncratic style that makes his portrayals of the subject recognizably his, and those of directors who are influenced by him or who imitate him, unmistakably not his. Moreover, to call Peckinpah's depiction of brutality "machismo" is true only insofar as his principal characters happen to be men. When it comes to violence, he is an Equal Opportunity Employer. One of the most graphic images in *The Wild Bunch* is a woman, with bandoliers around her breasts, suckling a baby. Those bullet-filled bandoliers are not merely decorative. In realistic terms, she is a killer. In symbolic terms, she nurses murder as well as a child. In this film's final gunfight, a woman shoots Bishop in the back. In *Straw Dogs*, Amy uses a shotgun to kill the last of the village louts who are trying to murder her husband. In *The Getaway*, Carol McCoy employs a pistol to dispatch Beynon. In *Bring Me the Head of Alfredo Garcia*, El Jefe's daughter urges Bennie to kill her father. In *The Killer Elite*, the Asian politician's daughter prepares to exercise martial arts to kill. In *The Osterman Weekend*, Ali

Tanner uses a bow and arrows to terminate two men. As Peckinpah says, "There is a great streak of violence in every human being."[5]

See, as partial evidence of the common association of Peckinpah with violence, the titles of some books about him: *Peckinpah: Master of Violence; Bloody Sam* (a common sobriquet); and *"If They Move . . . Kill 'Em!"*[6] The last title, the most frequently quoted line of any of his films, is spoken by William Holden in *The Wild Bunch,* heralding the directorial credit. It is so well known that the chief villain in *GoldenEye,* a James Bond movie, utters it, although he changes it from plural to singular. On the approximately silver anniversary rerelease of a restored, 70-millimeter print of *The Wild Bunch,* a national magazine reviewed it under the title "The Return of a Bloody Great Classic."[7] Let us unapologetically acknowledge this association. Stanley Kauffmann hits the target, so to speak, when he observes, in a review of *Pat Garrett and Billy the Kid,* that Peckinpah's "violence is still the most shaking on the screen (not the most gory)."[8] "One recalls *sequences* of violence from Peckinpah's work as opposed to single violent shots," notes another critic. "For Peckinpah's violent action is decidedly a matter of action rather than gore," and "there is no lingering over a corpse for sensationalism, only to demonstrate the physical effect of violence." In *The Wild Bunch,* the effect is "the scope of the destruction" rather than "individual gore for shock value."[9]

Apropos cinematic violence, two personal recollections are relevant. In 1985, I asked a friend whether I should see William Friedkin's *To Live and Die in L.A.* "Well, if you like watching people's faces get shot," my friend began with humorous sarcasm, and concluded that I probably should see it, which I did. While watching several skillfully made sequences of faces blasted by shotguns in *To Live and Die in L.A.,* I recalled *The Wild Bunch,* in which Buck, the member of the Bunch who has been shot in the face, asks Bishop to put him out of his misery. Among the striking aspects of Peckinpah's treatment is that while the director does not show Buck's face being shot, the face after it has been shot—the wounded man's hands cover it—or the head into which Bishop puts a bullet, the effect in *The Wild Bunch* is of savage brutality. In *To Live and Die in L.A.,* blood and gore are the focus of the sequences just mentioned, which have great shock value; in *The Wild Bunch,* the focus is chiefly the emotionally and morally painful aftermath of violence, including its effects on the men who perpetrate it. I am not disingenuous enough to claim that Peckinpah refrains from depicting explicit violence. In one of the same film's most horrendous moments, Mapache slits Angel's throat as the camera moves closer to record the moment. Here too, however, Peckinpah uses the moment mainly to spotlight the effect of Mapache's action.

The second example, which occurred in 1990, concerns a woman who admires only two of Peckinpah's movies, *Ride the High Country* and *The Ballad of Cable Hogue*. She has either walked out on his other films or has refused to watch them. She would concur with Judith Crist's disarming admission, "*The Wild Bunch* is simply not my cup of gore."[10] When this woman and I saw Paul Verhoeven's *Total Recall,* I was initially surprised not that she admired it, which I also did, but that she particularly enjoyed the climactic fight between the hero (played by Arnold Schwarzenegger) and the second chief villain (performed by Michael Ironside). Their battle takes them into an open freight elevator as it ascends to the roof. The hero tries to knock his antagonist off the elevator to his death, but Villain 2 grabs the hero's forearms, threatening to pull the hero with him if he falls. As the elevator rises, each of them looks up, sees the concrete roof, and recognizes that when Villain 2's arms make contact with it, he will be dismembered. Verhoeven's editing shows the hero glance upward, cuts to the underside of the roof, then to Villain 2 looking up, next to the roof again, then to both men, and next, from inside the elevator, to the hero and Villain 2 holding each other's forearms as the villain's are severed. The hero holds the dissected arms for a moment before tossing them down, with a quip that he hopes to see the man later at a party he plans to attend. During the dismemberment, the woman clutched my arm with one hand and covered her eyes with the other. Upon reflection, it became clear why she enjoyed this sequence. It foreshadowed what would happen, showed it happening, and filmed the result, which permitted her to enjoy a simple but effective means of formal artistic pleasure and at the same time gave advance warning to avert her eyes at what might become displeasure.[11]

Peckinpah's dramatization of violence is unlike this. He takes one by surprise, as violence in real life often does; he neither tops blood and maiming with a joke nor has anyone toy with prop arms; instead, he maintains simulated reality, wherein such matters are not funny. In his dramatization of the real, as this woman agrees, one finds it difficult to avert one's face from the horrors on screen. This is one quality that draws me to his films as major artistic triumphs and that draws her from them as experiences she prefers to do without. In Peckinpah's words, "You can't make violence real to audiences today without rubbing their noses in it. We watch our wars and see men die, really die, every day on television, but it doesn't seem real. . . . I want them to see what it looks like." One irony of the war in Vietnam was its resemblance to a long-run television series, in which death was often unreal. "When people complain about the way I handle violence," says Peckinpah, "what they're really saying is, 'Please don't show me: I don't want to know; and get me another beer out of the icebox.'"[12] Peckinpah does not glorify violence. Rather, as one of his most astute critics states, "He is instead telling a story about men who occasionally find themselves glorified in violence. To this end he makes the filmmaking style embody from time to time a sensibility that experiences great fulfillment in violence."[13]

Paradoxically, however—and one recollects Bernard Shaw's perception, "Paradoxes are the only truths"[14]—the resources of cinema as deployed by Peckinpah are in many ways more surrealistic or fantasy-like than they are realistic. He is aware of this paradox: "What I do is show people what it's really like—not by showing it as it is so much as by heightening it, stylizing it."[15] Generally, he films scenes of battle or violence with several cameras, one operating at normal speed and others at different fast speeds that, when projected on a screen, are slow-motion, slower-motion, and still-slower-motion; he intercuts them, usually using the slow-motion shots as brief insertions. In editing them this way, he maintains narrative lines: for instance, a body begins to fall from a roof in slow motion, another part of the battle continues at normal speed, the body continues to fall in slow motion, one or more parts of the battle are shown at different speeds, and the body hits the ground in slow motion or at normal speed, which therefore seems faster and more brutal. Except occasionally, to create a special effect—the Bunch blows up a bridge, plunging Thornton and the bounty hunters into the Rio Grande in slow motion, chiefly but not exclusively from one camera viewpoint—Peckinpah, unlike some of his imitators, does not linger on one or two slow-motion shots; he does not overindulge slow-motion violence and he infrequently dwells on slow-motion death. Each type of speed harmonizes with the moment it depicts. As anyone who has experienced pain can verify, the time that elapses seems longer than it actually is. As anyone who has watched a rodeo can testify, and I anticipate *Junior Bonner* here as I anticipated *The Wild Bunch* a moment ago, the eight seconds that the rider tries to stay on the animal seem, and in the movie are, longer.

The various slow-motion speeds represent different viewpoints, as does normal speed, and their juxtaposition creates yet another viewpoint. Through these contiguities, Peckinpah creates distinctive aesthetic experiences. The shocking and beautiful contrast of realism and aesthetic stylization jolt each other, the one preventing empty artiness, the other sup-pressing exploitative violence, and both averting easy empathy with the victim and sympathy for the victimizer. "Balletic," a term often used to describe Peckinpah's cinematic violence, is one of his means; "bloody" is another. What is especially noteworthy is that in his montages of violent action, the manner harmonizes with the matter. Stanley Kauffmann points out another way Peckinpah uses the camera to create violence: "My fa-vorite moment in *Straw Dogs* was just after Dustin Hoffman discovered the hanged cat in his bedroom closet; immediately there was a jump cut to a long shot of the lonely house with only the bedroom window light-ed, then a cut back to the room. In *The Getaway* McQueen and MacGraw are quarreling by their parked car when we suddenly cut to a long shot of them, then suddenly back again. The effect in both cases is to *hit* the scene, to keep it moving, like a boy hitting a hoop."[16]

Professional moralists, state and national legislators, and presidential candidates have written and spoken a great deal of nonsense about vio-lence in the cinema. On this subject, movie critics have long since weighed in. To David Denby, "even excessive violence is often an essential element in great movie art," yet Denby does not explain why or how something that is intemperate can be essential, for if it is organic then it is not ex-cessive. "Violence can be valuable in a movie if it teaches something new about ourselves or other people," he continues; "or if it serves to express emotions that cannot come out in any other way; or if it satisfies our basic desire for action, movement, power, release; or if it is very beautiful or shockingly ugly." Peckinpah, he admits, "accomplishes all of this in his movies," and yet, he adds in another self-contradiction, "we cannot ad-mire him completely without losing some element of sanity and self-re-spect. Despite all his efforts, our sense of the tragedy of violence still out-weighs his certainty of its glory."[17] I confess that I do not understand what the last sentence means, and if Peckinpah attains what Denby says he achieves, I fail to comprehend why admiration entails loss of sanity or self-respect. Pauline Kael too finds Peckinpah's violence disturbing, but she cannot deny his artistry. "The violence in *The Wild Bunch* was out of con-trol," she says—surprisingly, since this movie displays astonishing artis-tic control throughout—and then qualifies her statement, explaining it by reading the director's mind: "but for honest reasons: Peckinpah got caught in the trap of discovering that he was no longer sure what he was trying to do." Her admission, "One no longer knew how to react," reveals that the director prevented her from reacting in her customary ways to cinematic violence, which was one result of his artistic control.[18] More accurate is Stanley Kauffmann, who forthrightly admits, "Fictional killings are fun—when well done." He continues, ironically, since he recognizes the difficulty, "All you need to do is to integrate the violence into suspense and drama." As he sensibly maintains, "If the film isn't intrinsically engaging, the violence seems egregious, possibly offensive. If the film engages, the violence is exciting. Most of the critics who bellyached about *Straw Dogs* were ecstatic about *The Godfather*." More modestly than I, and without naming his colleagues, he proposes elsewhere that "we all lie about this subject as much as about pornography. If a violent picture is entertaining (or better), we may tsk-tsk later but we enjoy it while it's on. If it's not well done, we deplore it because we don't enjoy it." To "the Violence Problem in films," he proposes a solution: "make violent films well." Often, his reaction to Peckinpah's movies fits the formula I mentioned earlier, like it and not. As he says of *The Getaway,* "the picture is smashing. Sam Peckinpah directed, damn him. He is quite clearly a madman with, among other gifts, an extraordinary talent for murder, so powerful that he makes us enjoy blood. 'Down, Peckinpah!' cries civilization. 'Oh, yeah?' grins Sam, knowing the truth about us. Part of that truth is, if you have enough ability and enough conviction, you can make almost anything work in art."[19] My thesis is that Peckinpah has such ability and conviction.

In this chapter I examine the nature of Peckinpah's delineation of violence, which is not always a matter of killing, and try to illuminate ways he and his films are about more than violence. Because he does not photograph or edit every violent scene in the same manner, I also aim to show how his treatment of violence varies, and how its dramatic function differs both in several films and in the same film. In this chapter I do not consider either *The Deadly Companions* or *Major Dundee,* over whose editing he had no control. Nor do I consider the romp, *The Ballad of Cable Hogue,* or the superb *Ride the High Country.* The camera work and editing of the final shoot-out in the latter film foreshadow his later, almost trademarked work in that, under the tutelage of editor Frank Santillo, he uses some flash cuts only two frames long (six frames last a quarter of a second),[20] but despite the excellences of this movie, including the shoot-out, he does not achieve his distinctive style until his breakthrough film, *The Wild Bunch,* whose two most prominent and different scenes of violence I examine in detail first. I then study the violent scenes, lethal and nonlethal, in his major films after *The Wild Bunch: Straw Dogs, Junior Bonner, Pat Garrett and Billy the Kid,* and *Cross of Iron.* In *Junior Bonner,* the destruction of Ace Bonner's house and the climactic scene in which the title

character rides the bucking bull Sunshine are examples of nonlethal violence. I do not explore every scene of violence in his major films. Although
he treats each differently from the others, in this matter as in every matter, enough is enough.

* * *

As Richard Slotkin observes of *The Wild Bunch,* "The 'exaggerated' display
of bloodshed is in fact a truer representation of the real effects of violence
than the conventional and sanitized 'clutch your chest and fall' of the
Hollywood western and combat film. The mix of slow and regular motion
allows the audience to experience the subjective distortion of time experienced by those engaged in violent action."[21] Peckinpah films the
gunfight scenes from a variety of angles and camera speeds—24 frames
per second (normal speed) and 30, 60, 90, and 120 frames per second,
making the speed slow, slower, and still more slow—and he optically prints
frames three times to make the result more breathtakingly slow; he then
edits them together in a whirlwind-like, almost dizzying pattern.[22] The
editing of varying shots and speeds so compresses the action that one
result of the first gunfight scene, the Bunch's escape from the bank, is a
huge explosion, with lethal bullets spraying not only the combatants and
bystanders caught in the middle, but, seemingly, the spectators as well.
As Marshall Fine notes, the complex editing of many individual cuts gives
this film's "violent-action sequences an almost kaleidoscopic feel, without losing the sense of placing the viewer smack dab in the middle of the
action."[23] Peckinpah enhances his kaleidoscopic effects, which depict the
battles from myriad viewpoints rather than the customary few, by giving
each gun and rifle a distinctive sound and by amplifying some sounds.
In addition, the intercutting of normal with slow and slower speeds gives
the battles—notwithstanding the actual falls of bodies onto the ground,
the visual impact of bullets and hooves of horses hitting people, and
blood-spurtings—a beauty that, as mentioned, seems balletic. In close
collaboration with his editor, Louis Lombardo, Peckinpah has produced,
as David Weddle says, "the most creative use of montage since Sergei Eisen-
stein's *Potemkin*. [He] had forever changed the way movies would be
made."[24] Let us more closely examine this film's first gunfight, the escape
from the bank.

The rapid pace of a scene is a consequence partly of a variety of tempi
within it and partly of the pace of the scene immediately preceding it, that
scene itself employing different tempi. Immediately before the Bunch
escapes from the bank with the loot (not real money, it later learns), Peck-

inpah prepares the getaway. The preparatory scene, two minutes and twenty-nine seconds, begins with Angel spotting a gun on the roof and ends with Bishop throwing the chief clerk out the front door. It edits together 61 shots, averaging 2.44 seconds each, all in normal speed, none in slow motion.

The longer sequences receive emphasis and make what follow them seem more rapid. For example, after two one-second shots of Angel looking out a bank window and a view of what he sees, a roof with a rifle barrel sticking up, come two two-second shots: a return to Angel looking upward and calling, "Rifles!" and Abe, Buck (in a suit), and Bishop packing money bags into saddle bags and freezing when they hear him. Short as they are, the latter two shots are twice as long as those before, thus receiving dramatic emphasis and giving the two one-second shots that follow a quicker tempo. In cuts of one second each, Crazy Lee points his rifle at bank clerks and a female customer, asking, "I kill 'em now?"; the hostages face the camera; and Bishop responds, "No, hold them here as long as you can until after the shooting starts." The next cut, in which Crazy Lee says, "I'll hold 'em 'till hell freezes over or you say different," lasts five seconds, which is, by contrast, significantly longer than the previous cuts, and thereby registers the moment so that we will recall it when Sykes asks Bishop about Crazy Lee. Such instances can easily be multiplied.

Most individual shots are short, but other, longer shots provide, in addition to emphasis, a sense of the geography of the area: the location of the bounty hunters, the townspeople (the first shot of the parade of the South Texas Temperance Union down the main street lasts five seconds, as does the second, four shots later), and other members of the Bunch in the street, in uniform or in civilian dusters (when Tector, after noticing rifle barrels on the rooftop, in a one-second shot, unobtrusively moves between two horses to unleash them and remove a rifle from its saddle holster, his actions take five seconds). Thus, when the Bunch breaks out of the bank, the segments of the kaleidoscope are dazzling, not confusing, for the director enables us to follow the story of the escape. The duration of shots edited together suspensefully accelerates, and the last thirteen shots total twenty seconds.

In this preparatory sequence, the greatest number of shots and most of the two and a half minutes are inside the bank. Views of the inside from outside are framed by a window, and shots of the outside are from the viewpoint of those inside. Only after forty-eight seconds does Peckinpah move the action outside, to show the temperance union marching. He cuts back to the interior for nine seconds before he returns to the parade. When he cuts to the rooftop, where the threat to the Bunch lies, he does so one minute and thirty-three seconds after the preparatory sequence begins; and he alternates rooftop shots with shots of the parade. He returns to the bank interior thirty-three seconds after leaving it, and, except for a one-second cut to the parade, he remains there for twenty-three seconds. The general effect of the preparatory sequence is claustrophobic, depicting men who are trapped and anxious to break out. Therefore, when Bishop throws the chief clerk out the door and the Bunch bolts from the building, the result is an eruption of violence.

The director dramatizes the breakout and escape from alternating viewpoints of three groups of people, each with a clear goal and one or more obstacles. The Bunch aims to flee with the loot. The outlaws' obstacle is the bounty hunters shooting at them, an impediment to which they adjust by shooting back, avoiding the gunfire, and taking cover between or behind the townspeople, whom they use as shields. The bounty hunters aim to kill the Bunch. Their obstacles are twofold: since they have lost the edge of surprise (the Bunch begins firing at them the moment Bishop throws the chief clerk out the door), they must evade bullets rather than fire first at unsuspecting targets; and the townspeople block their view of these targets. By ducking or dodging the bullets, the bounty hunters try to adjust to the first obstacle; they try to adjust to the second by the accuracy of their aim, which, unfortunately for the civilians, is mostly poor. The townspeople try to avoid being shot by gunmen whose whereabouts they do not know, which constitutes an obstacle; their other hurdles are the Bunch's horses, which at times get in their way, and their fellow townspeople, who bump into them.

The battle sequence, consisting of the breakout and escape, lasts approximately three minutes and forty-eight seconds.[25] It begins when Bishop shoves the chief clerk out the door, which precipitates the gunfire; it concludes when Thornton, on the roof, tells the bounty hunters to stop firing, since the Bunch, except for the few gang members they killed, has escaped. This sequence contains 209 shots, averaging 1.09 seconds each, more than twice as fast as the average shot in the preparation. Not only are the pace and speed of action quicker in themselves, since the average time means that many shots are less than a second each, but their contrast with the preceding scene suggests greater speed, faster pace, further chaos, and more enormous mayhem than they otherwise would.

With so many more shots per minute, and from a wider variety of angles and duration than in the preparatory scene, the effect dazzles. By editing together at least seven viewpoints, using twelve cuts that last just under eight seconds, one as brief as a third of a second, Peckinpah creates a kaleidoscopically coherent effect. In a long, therefore seemingly objective shot of the front of the bank, the marching band observes the chief clerk starting to rise from the ground where he was thrown, stumble toward the porch, be shot again, and fall down. The director cuts to Buck, who shoots his rifle toward the roof, then to the left glass of the bank's bay window, hit by a bullet from above and starting to shatter, then to Abe, shooting, then to the center glass of the bank's bay window, which is hit by a bullet and starts to shatter. Peckinpah cuts back to Buck, shooting, then to the shot of the shattering left glass of the window, then to Abe, shooting, then to the shattering left glass window. He cuts to a new shot, upward toward the roof, showing bounty hunters firing downward, then to a new shot of Buck and Abe together, shooting upward, and next to a different angle of Abe, shooting.

Using different types of camera angles, speeds, and lengths for different takes, with one cut as short as a tenth of a second, Peckinpah achieves a dizzying variety that plunges us into the action. After a bounty hunter shoots downward, a man in a duster shoots upward, Tector does the same, the bounty hunter is hit, blood splattering as the bullet goes through him, and he begins to pitch forward. The director cuts to a medium, front view of the bounty hunter starting to fall from the roof in slow motion. He cuts to Lyle, running and shooting, then back to the bounty hunter falling. After different shots of members of the Bunch and the bounty hunters firing at each other, he cuts to a full view of the bounty hunter falling in profile in a somersault in slower motion than before, then to a close-up of Abe, then to another bounty hunter, hit, starting to fall in slower motion than the other man. From a medium shot of Angel, he returns to a full view of the first bounty hunter somersaulting down in slower motion, then to the second bounty hunter falling less slowly, then to a medium close-up of Thornton, after which he returns to a full view of the first bounty hunter hitting the ground in slower motion, and back to the second bounty hunter slowly, but faster than before, falling and hitting his head on the ledge of the roof.

Peckinpah combines different camera views, using slow and slower motions. For example, a man on horseback is shot and falls with his horse through a shop window, behind which are women's dresses on manikins and hats suspended from the ceiling. He alternates these shots with shots of Dutch, who falls when his horse is shot, as does the horse.

More forcefully still, Peckinpah organizes a twelve-second sequence of chaos that implicates the townspeople as casualties of the bounty hunters and the escaping Bunch, including cuts of Bishop's horse trampling on a fallen woman despite his attempt to turn the horse away. The cuts from and to the woman and the horse serve as focal points in a minuscule drama that gives unobtrusive focus to the chaos, which would seem incoherent were it to last longer than the twelve seconds Peckinpah allows it.

When a suited member of the Bunch is shot and falls in slow motion, the camera cuts from him to the townspeople, including children, and returns to him as his horse drags him on the ground. After he rises, in slow motion, a bounty hunter shoots him. He whirls and falls in normal speed which, contrasting with the previous slow motion, seems twice as fast and violent.

The film's first gunfight, a dazzling and dizzying sequence, has several effects. First, partly because of the preparatory sequence and partly because of the contrasts within it, the battle seems to erupt like a bomb and proceed at breakneck speed. Second, Peckinpah uses different cameras at different slow-motion speeds sparingly. Only twenty-seven of the 209 shots, slightly more than an eighth, are in various slow-motion speeds. Furthermore, he spaces them for dramatic effect. He uses only five such shots of the man falling from the roof, and they begin more than nineteen seconds after the first burst of gunfire. Over a minute after the last of these are five slow-motion shots of the man in the duster falling through the shop window. About a minute and a half later are seven other slow-motion shots that include a townsman shot and falling. Only sixteen seconds later, in accelerating tempo, there begins two slow-motion sequences of Dutch and a man on a buckboard falling—nine shots in all, the longest number of slow-motion takes in this sequence. The beauty of the slow-motion shots contrasts with and enhances the normal camera speed, which seems mercuric.

The bounty hunters—that is, the law—inflict deadlier havoc on the civilians than the Bunch does. Whereas the Bunch shoots upward, where there are no townspeople, the bounty hunters shoot downward, where the Bunch and the civilians mingle. The first townsman to be killed is shot by a bounty hunter, and juxtaposed shots suggest Harrigan killing a townsman. Despite Abe's using a townswoman as a shield, he thrusts her away to make his escape, at which point Thornton's bullet fells him. Except for the man on the buckboard, the Bunch does not kill townspeople even by accident: the woman on whom Bishop's horse stomps was shot by a bounty hunter.

To prevent the audience from overly sympathizing with the Bunch as victims, Peckinpah cuts from the exterior slaughter to the relatively calm but grotesquely deadly interior of the bank, where Crazy Lee holds hostage three clerks and a woman. Most of these interior shots, in which one of the Bunch is a victimizer, last longer than shots of the mayhem outside. After a minute and eighteen seconds, Peckinpah cuts to inside the bank, where a woman calls Crazy Lee "Trash!" (one second), then to Crazy Lee moving toward the hostages (three seconds). The next cut to the bank, twenty-three seconds later, is a relatively long single sequence of seven seconds, in which Crazy Lee, to the distaste of the female hostage, tongues her ear, tells her to hush, and giggles. After four seconds outside, the camera returns to the bank for four shots, lasting fifteen seconds, in which Crazy Lee terrorizes the hostages into singing "Shall We Gather at the River" and marching in time to it. After twenty-eight seconds outside, the director cuts to inside the bank again for a single, four-second shot, showing the hostages still marching. The effect of these alternations is partly contrast and variety; but mainly, they serve to link the Bunch to its abandoned member as victimizer and thereby to prevent excessive sympathy for them.

Apart from using photography and editing to achieve his effects, Peckinpah unobtrusively and ingeniously employs the device of the play-within-a-play to mirror and guide audience responses, and he does so thrice. First, a minute after the mayhem begins, Crazy Lee, inside the bank, becomes a spectator of the gunplay in the street, which he finds entertaining, and he exclaims, as audiences might, "Man, they're blowing this town all to hell!" Second, almost two minutes later, is a fifteen-second sequence involving a pair of tow-haired children who cling to each other in fear, the boy's arm protectively around the girl, as violence erupts around them. The children, in full height, are framed by trees as, in a blur, horses and townspeople rush back and forth. Thornton shoots a suited member of the Bunch on horseback, who carries a saddle bag with loot and falls, one foot in a stirrup, dragged by his horse. Peckinpah cuts to the children in close-up, the camera moving closer. They still huddle for protection but—a vital distinction—turn their faces to see the spectacle around them. The gang rides toward the camera, Dutch bending to retrieve the fallen saddle bag from the ground. From a different angle, the camera moving closer, the director cuts to a close-up of the girl and boy, who watch Dutch. Bounty hunters on the roof shoot and, in slow motion, a man is dragged by his horse, which begins to fall. The boy and girl observe this action. The horse continues to fall in slow motion and the man starts to rise. The camera moves closer to the boy and girl, watching. In this sequence, the children, like the theater audiences, try to but cannot avert their eyes from the slaughter, which engrosses them. Seven seconds later, Peckinpah varies this type of play-within-a-play: a Mexican boy and girl, the boy's head above the girl's, peeking safely behind the corner of a building, are absorbed by the violent action—as are audiences, from their safer position. Beginning with a medium close-up of the children, the camera gets closer in three successive shots and moves closer within the last two, until it shows only the girl's face, as at increasingly long intervals people ride, shoot, are shot, and die.

This quintet of spectators on screen, from one adult to two blond children to two Mexican children, reflects the audiences, who may be delighted by what occurs on the screen, as Crazy Lee is. They may be frightened by it, as the first pair of children are. They may, in safety, absorb the startling events, as the second pair of children do. And they may experience all three reactions.

* * *

The second gunfight, the film's finale, is considerably unlike the first. In the first shootout, Peckinpah stresses chaos, which he films from multiple viewpoints: members of the Bunch, the bounty hunters, and groups of townspeople. In the second, he emphasizes carnage, which he films from the viewpoint of the four surviving members of the Bunch. The ferocious destructiveness of this climax achieves what he claims to have aimed for: "a film that showed violence as it is, not as some goddamn Hollywood piece of shit."[26]

Like the first battle, the last is preceded by a preparatory sequence. Unlike that of the first, it is almost two minutes longer than the battle itself, which for this reason seems to explode faster than it does. It is more dizzying, kaleidoscopic, and violent than the first battle. Highlighting the frenetic slaughter of the fight between the Bunch and Mapache's federales, Peckinpah shoots and edits the preparatory sequence with slow restraint, the style conforming to the deliberation and preparation that are the subjects of the action, which begins when the Bunch awakens in Agua Verde in the morning. In three movements, the preparatory sequence uses a hundred shots that last slightly more than seven minutes and two seconds.

In the slow, first movement, the four gringos decide to retrieve Angel. Peckinpah cuts from the drunken, sleepy Mapache the previous evening to vivid sunlight the next morning, for two shots that last ten seconds. In the first, Dutch sits beside a building, idly whittling and waiting while, to his right and left, three federales kiss and leave a woman in front of another door to the building and a seated woman pats the head of a sleeping federale. In the second, closer shot of Dutch sitting by the building, a guitar plays softly and slowly.

The director cuts to the interior of the building, where Bishop is in a room with a young, pretty woman whose purity is suggested by a crucifix on a wall. He intercuts medium shots and close-ups, some three, four, and five seconds long, of the woman seated, calmly making a doll, and washing herself from a basin on a table; a four-second close-up, the camera moving closer, of her clean, neatly dressed baby, crying; and medium shots and close-ups of Bishop getting dressed and ruminating. Shots of Bishop last as many as seven and thirteen seconds. In an adjoining room, a woman argues in Spanish about money. After showing the curtain separating the rooms, Peckinpah cuts to the next room, where the Gorch brothers argue with a whore, older than Bishop's, her face less soft than his woman's, and not silent, as his madonna is. The director cuts back to Bishop who, in three shots that last eleven seconds, listens to her complaint, the crying baby, and the soft guitar. After he rises and enters the adjacent room, she stops speaking and the men look at each other. "Let's go," he says. Suddenly serious, Lyle looks at him, then at his brother. In several shots, the three men look at each other. "Why not!" exclaims Lyle at the end of a more than four-second shot. They do not have to exchange other words. They know what is on each other's mind, as does the audience. We saw Bishop reflecting and pondering; and we sense that what made him worried and pensive helped make the Gorch brothers dissatisfied and argumentative. Closing the curtains, Bishop returns to his room. The slow tempo radiates subtextual intensity. Bishop pays his woman, whom Peckinpah contrasts with the one in the other room. A close-up of over five seconds shows her observe the coins on the table, her lips forming what may be a placid smile, pick them up, and look at him. A medium close-up of almost five seconds has her observe the money in her hand and watch him calmly, slightly and shyly smiling, as she catches his eye. He exits via the next room, where Peckinpah stresses dissimilarity by having the other prostitute complain as the men leave. Before Peckinpah cuts to the exterior, he shoots an over five-second close-up, the camera moving closer, as it did to the baby of Bishop's woman, of a sparrow Tector fondled when arguing with his whore, now lying on its back on Tector's pallet bed, nearly dead, its heart throbbing—a deft foreshadowing of the extermination to come.

Outside the building, the three men stop and look at Dutch. Seeing their gunbelts, he recognizes that they have decided to do what was on his mind.

He puts down the stick he was whittling, rises—the camera rising with him—and smiles. At the end of this shot, the sound of the guitar stops.

The first movement of the preparatory sequence is exclusively from the viewpoint of the four members of the Bunch, who make a decision. The action lasts three minutes and thirty-five seconds, averaging almost four seconds per cut.

In the second movement, which is also from their viewpoint, they prepare to do what they have decided to do and go where they must do it. They walk to their horses and—in two medium shots lasting forty-three seconds—arm themselves with rifles, more pistols, grenades, and ammunition. Near the end of the second shot, they begin their trek to Mapache's headquarters. Peckinpah cuts to a long, twenty-eight-second shot of the four men, their backs to the camera, as they march. He cuts to a long shot as they move toward the camera, Mexican federales passing in different directions in the foreground; next cuts to a medium shot, the camera moving closer, of federales beside the road, noticing them as they pass; then cuts back to the quartet going toward the camera. He films their march through a long lens that, leveling or flattening the perspective, all but eradicates it, thereby appearing to eliminate the space between foreground and background, and making the gringos seem to walk slower, traverse less ground, and take longer to reach their destination. More important, the telephoto lens, by removing the planes on which the Bunch and the Mexicans walk, gives the impression that they are about to collide. The effect of impending collision enhances the suspense, which the music amplifies.

A moment after the quartet starts to walk, the distant sounds of barking dogs and talking people stop, as an encore of the serenade sung to the Bunch when they left Angel's village rises as a distorted chant (the Bunch's attempt to retrieve Angel links to his departure with the gang), and soon the sound of drums (the Bunch's theme) echoes the opening of the film, when the men pass boys and girls tormenting a scorpion and ants, audibly linking the massacre to come, identifying the Bunch and federales with the scorpion and ants, and foreshadowing mutual destruction. The drums become louder, drowning out the chant (the peaceful village theme). When the four men—their unified purpose stressed by every shot, showing all four—reach their destination, they stop, decisively; the sound of the drums stops with them, and Mapache sees them.

This second, suspenseful movement, in which the quartet prepares to do what it has decided upon, edits together sixteen shots and lasts two minutes and nineteen seconds. It decelerates to an average of 8.68 seconds per shot—more than two-thirds slower than the average in the first movement.

In the third, final movement of the preparatory sequence, they attempt to do what they have prepared to do: retrieve Angel. The action remains from their viewpoint. Mapache and his men respond to what the four outsiders initiate. The movement starts with Mapache's reaction: on a porch before a building on the other side of a courtyard, he notices them. "Ah, los gringos otra vez" (Ah, the gringos again), he says wearily. As the camera cuts to him, the ominous theme associated with him begins and grows louder. Zamorra (his second in command), Herrera (next in command), and the German officers, all at a table on the porch, notice them, as do federales and women near the porch. Since the audience is familiar with the geography of the area, only two brief shots reestablish it. Peckinpah cuts back to the four, who resume their march, the drum music returning as they do so. He cuts to Mapache, Mapache's theme blending into that of the Bunch—the ants engaging the scorpions, as it were. In alternating shots, Mapache theme and Bunch theme oscillate in intensity. When the four men stop again, more forcefully, the drums stop. "What you want?" asks Mapache. When Zamorra joins him, the ominous music ends. "We want Angel," says Bishop.

Placing his hand on his heart, Mapache declares with feigned geniality, "You want Angel, no? All right, I am going to give it to you." In Spanish, "give it to you" is the same as "give him to you," but because Mapache previously used the pronouns "him" and "he" for Angel, his use of the English neuter pronoun is sinister and is underscored by ominous music on the sound track that rises in intensity, increasing suspense; it reaches its climax thirty-seven seconds later, when Mapache slits Angel's throat. In a medium shot of slightly more than ten seconds, the members of the Bunch, in the foreground with backs to the camera, watch him push Angel forward toward them. Peckinpah cuts to a one-second medium shot in which the four men, facing the camera, see Mapache push Angel toward them. In a medium shot almost two seconds long, the camera moves to a medium close-up of Angel and Mapache, who readies his knife. A close-up shows Dutch, apprehensive; in a medium shot, the camera moves closer to Mapache and Angel; a close-up reveals that Bishop realizes what Mapache will do; in a medium shot, Mapache grabs Angel's hair, pulling him backward, and raises his knife to Angel's throat; the camera moves closer to Dutch, who opens his mouth in horror; and in a medium shot, Mapache slits Angel's throat and pushes him forward as the music rises to peak intensity. Amplifying the suspense, the duration of these last six cuts decreases to about half a second each.

In the third, climactic movement of the preparatory sequence, the four men make a decision and act on it, though with a repercussion on which they had not counted (being sure is his business, said Bishop, but as we have seen, he is not that good at his business). It edits twenty-nine shots and lasts sixty-six seconds, an average of 2.27 seconds per shot, almost 25 percent faster than the second movement. The tempo of this preparation has increased to a climax.

A fraction of a second after Mapache cuts Angel's throat, the second battle begins: Bishop draws his pistol and shoots Mapache. The sound of his shot obliterates that of the music, and during the battle only the sounds of pistols, rifles, machine guns, grenades, dynamite, screams, curses, and commands are heard. The fight ends, moments after the death of Bishop and Dutch, the last surviving members of the Bunch (albeit by less than a minute), when a pre-adolescent boy wearing the uniform of a federale, who has fatally shot Bishop, puts down his rifle, and an old, bearded man in a sombrero, who has done the same to Dutch, emerges from a shaded area. The fighting lasts five minutes and ten seconds, about two minutes shorter than the preparation. With 340 shots edited together, the average cut is nine-tenths of a second, which is shorter than that of the first gunfight, and the pace of the action is swifter. Indeed, it is so rapid, the fray so violent, the number of people so much greater, and the shots so many and from such a variety of angles and speeds, that, paradoxically, the clash may seem to last longer than it does.

Although the battle may appear to bewilder, because so much happens in giddily rapid intercutting, who does what to whom is clear. One reason for this clarity is that Peckinpah maintains the viewpoint of the four gringos. He dramatizes their enemies and observers only as they watch, try to kill, or are killed by the quartet. Despite the scope of this struggle and the means used, its unifying focus results not in chaos but in precise activities between four men and their adversaries. More so than the first clash, this battle is an explosion that, even as it blends small portions of time, elongates time.

This climactic fight divides into four dramatic movements—a less arbitrary term than "scenes"—the first ending in a surprising victory for the Bunch. Each of the next three is punctuated by shots of Thornton and the other bounty hunters, who watch the action or ride to it, and the third movement briefly cuts to the bounty hunters about halfway through, apparently the climactic high point for the Bunch's leader, Bishop; the third movement's end reveals the appearance as momentary, for he swiftly and dramatically falls to the ultimate low point, his death. The interrupting accents of Thornton and the bounty hunters have several effects. First, the carnage becomes a play within a play—a less important feature here than in the first battle—which the onlookers first witness through binoculars—large opera glasses, as it were—that magnify people as their images are magnified on the cinema screen. Second, and because of the first, Peckinpah achieves a (possibly Brechtian) distancing effect, both actually and symbolically, momentarily muting the battle's impact and the movie audience's total immersion in it; he permits a view of the warfare if not *sub specie aeternitatis,* then from a long remove, providing perspective. Third, by making the combatants smaller, the view through the binoculars connects the battle to the ants and scorpions devastating each other at the start of the film. To paraphrase *King Lear,* whose title character demands, "kill, kill, kill, kill, kill!" the warring Bunch and federales become to the gods, ironically those in the theater audience, what the scorpion and ants are to the children, creatures killed for sport. Fourth, Thornton and the bounty hunters remind the audience of the larger picture. The Bunch comes to Agua Verde to escape the danger outside, the bounty hunters, but ironically plunges itself into a more dangerous situation inside, against greater odds.

The first movement of the film's second major battle begins with the killing of Mapache, whose army is initially too stunned to act, and some raise their arms to surrender. For the moment, it seems that, miraculously and to their surprise, the Americans just might get away with their deed. Guns drawn or rifles aimed, they crouch, reducing their size as targets, waiting for the Mexicans to react with gunfire, which they do not do. Recognizing that this stalemate cannot last, Bishop acts on his terms, not theirs: he decides to kill Mohr, the German colonel whose plan to rob the train brought them to this impasse. His decision ends the first movement, the Bunch's impermanent victory, which edits together thirty-nine shots into forty-three seconds, an average of 1.1 seconds per shot.

In the rapid, initial action, shooting Mapache, no shot lasts a full second. Cuts range from two-tenths to nine-tenths of a second. In one particularly fast piece of intercutting, after a shot of Bishop's bullet going through Mapache, in profile, Dutch shoots him with his rifle. A medium shot of slightly over two-tenths of a second shows Mapache hit again, the direction of his fall changed by this bullet. In a two-tenths-of-a-second close-up, Colonel Mohr and Captain Ernst rise in reaction, after which a two-tenths-of-a-second medium shot shows Bishop shoot Mapache again.

After several reaction shots, Dutch in a three-second cut shoots Mapache in the back, blood spurting from the body.

A slow tempo follows. Peckinpah alternates among the four members of the Bunch, who serve as lodestars, and an equal number of antagonists or groups of antagonists: Zamorra, Herrera, a group of federale officers on the porch, and the group of federale troops in the courtyard. He cuts from Herrera (arms raised to surrender) to the Bunch (on the ready) to the officers (too stunned to move), back to the Bunch, then to the federales in the courtyard (stunned but rising), back to the Bunch, then to the troops, back to Lyle, and so forth, including a camera panning the federales to focus on one of them; and he uses a variety of shots from long to extreme close-up, the latter reserved for members of the Bunch. In addition to identifying different groups facing the four men, the cross-cutting fortifies the audience's knowledge of the site's geography. After twenty seconds of this intercutting, shots lasting between about half a second and two seconds, Peckinpah cuts to a four-second shot that culminates in a decision to commit another act: flanked by Tector and Dutch, Bishop and Lyle, crouching with guns on the ready, survey their antagonists; from a medium shot, the camera moves to an extreme close-up of Bishop, who straightens up, faces the camera, and decides on the object of his next action. Peckinpah cuts to a three-second clip, the camera moving from a medium shot to a close-up of Mohr, facing it; then to a one-second extreme close-up of Bishop who, watching Mohr, raises his pistol and pulls the trigger. The actions are straightforward, pursued one at a time, with clear-cut distinctions between those who instigate the deeds and those who react to them.

Colonel Mohr taking the bullet and falling starts the second movement and its accelerated, turbulent action, in which the Bunch battles the four opposing groups established in the first movement. The second movement contains a miniplot: the Bunch storms and takes the commanding combat position, the porch, which is shaded and on a higher level than the courtyard (thereby affording some protection from above); armed with a machine gun, the men overlook all sources of gunfire except those inside the building. This dramatic movement ends when Tector takes and fires the machine gun, and it is punctuated by two takes, lasting five seconds, of Thornton and the bounty hunters observing them from afar, behind rocks on a mountain. The second take, through Thornton's binoculars, framed by overlapping circles, shows the federales resembling ants, who are battling scorpions. Except for these two cuts, the second movement contains 106 shots, in one minute and nineteen seconds, an average of just under three-fourths of a second per shot, a speed that seems breakneck.

Not only does Peckinpah rapidly intercut many shots of different duration, he also varies the speed of shots among normal, moderately slow motion, slow motion, and slower motion; and he maintains the clarity of small narrative segments: one person fires on another or others, who are or are not hit. Dutch grins broadly as he sees (in the next shot) Herrera reaching for the gun in his holster. Bishop, his back partly to the camera, like the other gringos, shoots Herrera; Herrera turns as he falls in slow motion, as (in the next shot) Bishop watches. Interrupting a shot of federales in the courtyard, who duck to get their weapons, is a shot of Tector grinning as he watches Dutch and Herrera, but Peckinpah cuts back to the federales in the courtyard seizing rifles, then to Lyle turning his head and crouching when they do so. Peckinpah cuts back to Herrera, in slow motion, falling, spinning, and knocking down an officer behind him. He then cuts to the courtyard troops, who move forward and start to fire, then to a bullet hitting the wall behind Bishop, then back to the federales in the courtyard, knocking down tables for cover and shooting.

After a variety of shots, some showing women and children hiding under tables, comes a sequence that demonstrates a major, recurring aspect of Peckinpah's technique. A federale officer behind the machine gun tries to reach it and pull its trigger. In a medium, full body shot, Lyle shoots his rifle. In a slow-motion close-up, the officer's torso is hit, blood spurting from it. In a close-up from a different view, the officer falls, in normal speed. Because the penultimate shot is in slow motion, less than half a second, the last shot seems to occur twice as fast as the normal speed in which it is filmed.

Peckinpah continues to intercut mini-actions, each involving a different member of the Bunch. After Dutch, in profile, shoots his rifle, the director cuts to a federale, in a slow-motion medium close-up, taking the bullet, dropping his rifle, and falling. Next is a long shot of Bishop at the table, Lyle shooting and making his way to the porch, and Tector moving to an opening in the wall of the building. The ensuing three shots focus on Tector, who jumps through the opening in a rolling fall, the camera moving with him, a federale shooting at him, and Tector, hitting the floor and firing at the federale who shot at him. A federale, shot by Lyle, falls. In five cuts, Zamorra, facing the camera, shoots at Bishop; Bishop, hit, falls back against the wall; Dutch shoots Zamorra in the back; blood spurts from Zamorra's shoulder; Bishop falls but recovers, as Zamorra falls to Bishop's right. Next, Lyle jumps through the opening in the wall, joining Tector, back to the camera, as Tector fires into the courtyard. Peckinpah edits these mini-stories together, not always in one linear sequence at a time, but what happens in each is clear.

As the director intercuts different camera speeds, Bishop shoots a federale in the courtyard; the man falls in moderately slow motion; Tector emerges from the building to the porch; the federales in the courtyard move forward, shoot, and are shot, in a bit slower motion; Bishop shoots; while Lyle, in the background, shoots, these federales continue to move forward, shoot, and are shot, in a slower motion similar to that of the other group. As before, the perspective of the gringos integrates the variety of clips.

The third dramatic movement begins with the Bunch in a commanding position. As before, the action is from the gang's viewpoint. Tector fires the machine gun, mowing down federales in the courtyard below and on the roof of a wall with arches. Approximately midway through this movement, the fortunes of the Bunch reach their high point when Bishop kills a would-be assassin who is hiding in a room, behind a mirror, before the man can shoot him. Underscoring this dramatic peak is a cut to Thornton and Coffer observing the action and moving back to get their horses. The movement ends with the start of the Bunch's decline, when Bishop is shot in the back by the whore in the room, whom he spared. Emphasizing the close of this movement are two shots of the bounty hunters riding to the site of the conflagration, where they expect to arrive after the battle ends. Except for the last two shots, this movement contains 105 cuts that last a minute and twenty-seven seconds, averaging .83 of a second, a slight deceleration of the speed of the preceding movement.

The mayhem is more spectacular than before. Dutch throws a hand grenade that, in the next shot, explodes, killing some of the federales who climb steps leading to the porch. Tector fires the machine gun and, in the next shot, a federale on the ledge of the porch is hit in slow motion; in the next, in slow but less-slow motion, several federales climbing onto the porch are mowed down by machine gun bullets; then, the hit federale on the ledge pitches upward in slow motion; next, in less-slow motion, the climbing federales are shot and fall; then, in slow motion, the hit federale continues to pitch upward; then, in less-slow motion, the group of federales continues to fall; next, the sole hit man falls down in slow motion. The camera cuts to Tector firing the machine gun into the courtyard; the previously hit man falls headfirst over a ledge in slow motion. Dutch throws a grenade in a different direction. Peckinpah cuts to the federale falling in slow motion and crashing onto a barrel. More federales enter through arches, this time making headway, but Dutch's grenade explodes, killing some, including a man in the foreground whom it hurls upward. In the courtyard, an old woman and two boys hide under a table. Through the arches, in very slow motion, federales continue to fall and somersault to the ground as they are hit. The old woman and boys under the table shut their eyes at the sight of casualties, but they open them to watch the destruction. In slow motion, federales in the courtyard fall and roll over. In very slow motion, grenaded men coming through the arches fall, somersaulting. In slow motion, federales in the courtyard fall and roll over. As is Peckinpah's custom, each slow motion shot is brief, but its reappearance after one or several shots creates the impression that it lasts longer.

The movement's main narrative arc is a minidrama that involves the protagonist Bishop, a federale officer behind a mirror, and a prostitute. The shooting of Bishop is a distorted echo of a flashback, which also involves a full-length mirror, in which Bishop is shot by the husband of his beloved, who earlier in the flashback does not shoot him but slaps him.[27] This plotlet is interrupted by other sequences of killing, all intercut with each other and filmed in different speeds. In it, Bishop turns to look through a door into a room. A close-up shows what he sees, a woman's face, but the camera pulls back to reveal that the face is her reflection in a full-length mirror, and to emphasize the mirror as dramatic scenery. He enters the room, looks at her, but does not shoot her. Again we see a close-up of her face in the mirror, then a close-up of Bishop turning toward it, then her face in it again. In a medium shot, Bishop, his back to the camera, shoots the mirror displaying her full-length reflection. A close-up shows the mirror shattering. Peckinpah cuts to the previous shot to show a federale officer, who Bishop deduced was hiding behind the mirror; the officer falls to the side of the mirror, which jaggedly reflects the woman—a shrewd directorial hint of danger and of something else that may be hidden. Most of these shots last a second each. At the end of the third movement, spectators see what Peckinpah hinted. As Bishop stands outside the doorway, facing the camera in a medium shot, the whore, in the room in the background, removes a pistol she held behind her and shoots him in the back, his blood spurting as the bullet passes through his right chest. The camera cuts to a close-up from inside the room as Bishop turns, facing the camera, crying, "Bitch!" and shoots her, then to a close-up as she slides down the wall, dead, then back to Bishop, who throws his rifle away. These three shots last between about one and two seconds each.

In the final movement of this battle, the endgame, all four members of the Bunch are wounded but stubbornly refuse, for as long as possible, to give up the ghost. Partly because their antagonists, despite their sheer num-

ber, are less individualized than they are, the viewpoint is that of the gringos. The fourth movement begins after Bishop kills the woman who shot
him: he staggers to the table, which he overturns for cover. It relentlessly
chronicles the expiration of the Bunch, whose members require more than
a few bullets to die: Tector, then Lyle, then Bishop, and finally Dutch
(among the film's refreshingly unconventional aspects, the leading man
is not the last to expire). Upon the conclusion of this dramatic movement,
the scene dissolves to the bounty hunters riding toward the ruins. Although
Peckinpah edits eighty-six shots into one minute and thirty-four seconds,
averaging 1.09 seconds per shot, this movement's tempo is faster than the
statistic suggests because the intercutting of the last moments of Bishop
and Dutch has shots of four and five seconds each. Not only is this movement a winding-down of the pace, but within it, rapid tempo alternates
and finally concludes with slowly paced death, the protracted dying appearing more agonizing in contrast to what precedes it.

Twenty seconds after the movement starts, during which federales die
in normal speed, slow motion, and slower motion, Bishop and Dutch,
both shot, are on the floor behind the overturned table. "Come on, you
lazy bastard!" Bishop orders Dutch as he grabs the table to help himself
rise—repeating his words near the end of the first battle, after Dutch and
his horse fall to the ground. This time, the ritualistic command is ironic,
since in contrast to the first gunfight, from which they ride away safely,
the wounded men know they will not emerge safely from this battle.

Before the final moments of Bishop and Dutch, the pace is exhilarat-
ingly frenetic and breathtakingly violent. Despite the dispersal of shots
among different actors and reactors, from extreme close-ups to long shots,
in lengths as short as three and four-tenths of a second, and in speeds
between normal and very slow motion, Peckinpah's editing unifies the
carnage through the members of the Bunch: Bishop shoots several times,
followed by several consequences; a federale shoots, and Lyle is hit; federales advance, shooting, and Tector is hit again; Bishop shoots, and a
federale is hit. Particularly spectacular is Bishop's last act of destruction.
He fires the machine gun. The camera cuts to a medium shot of a table
and quickly moves closer to the top of the table, focusing on a box of
dynamite, which explodes—the movement to close-up making the flow
extremely fast and forceful—and cuts next to a long shot of the box of
dynamite exploding, killing federales who advance on both sides of it.
After a cut back to Bishop firing the machine gun, the film cuts to a medium shot of the exploding dynamite causing a box of dynamite beside
it to explode while some people try to take cover, then cuts back to an

extreme close-up of Bishop, then to a close-up of the dynamite exploding, and then to a medium shot of the explosion from a different point of view, with federales ducking or being hit, as are their horses, by the explosion.

Following this brief sequence, the film slows down as, in several alternating shots, a preadolescent boy shoots Bishop, a man in a sombrero shoots Dutch, Bishop's face contorts in pain, Dutch falls in slow motion, calling "Pike!" and each expires. The focus is on those shot, not the shooters. Among the film's ironies is that while spectators may bemoan the women and children killed by the dynamite, they see female soldiers attired as male soldiers and women wearing bandoliers, a woman shoot Bishop in the back, and a boy firing the bullet that finally kills him.

Keeping in mind that each dramatic movement has varied tempi, the pace of the four movements accelerates from an average of 1.1 seconds per shot to .74 seconds per shot, decelerates a bit to .83 of a second per shot, then gradually drops, as the chief characters gradually die, to an average of 1.09 seconds per shot, which is close to that of the first movement. The structure is almost classically symmetrical. Far from being an orgy of bloodletting, the sequence is sustained, carefully crafted, and masterfully modulated.

Part of its brilliance is that the style deftly harmonizes with the subject. The delirium of intercutting matches the delirium of battle, the slower moments match the occasions when characters catch their breath, and the excruciatingly slow deaths of members of the Bunch, to whom the camera repeatedly returns, match their refusal to let go and their determination to overcome their opponents. Inexorably, this battle becomes the "one last hit" that Bishop, after the failed bank robbery, said he wanted. Whereas he referred to a successful robbery, the hit that is true to his nature and that of the other members of the Bunch is a literal hit or series of hits by bullets. These men, who as Peckinpah says, "lived not only by violence but *for* it,"[28] appropriately die in an enormity of violence.

Whatever glory may attach to them resides in their choice to retrieve Angel, their battle against enormous odds, and the way they die. What prompts them to dare is their solidarity with each other. While they are not "good guys," they surely are better human beings than their antagonists, who torture for pleasure. In Angel's village, Bishop warns Angel not to dwell on revenge for an individual who was killed. The action of Bishop and his comrades at Agua Verde does not violate this dictum, for they seek rescue, not revenge. Bishop's killing Mapache may be reflexive, but after Mapache cuts Angel's throat, what other option has he? The murder of Angel not only represents defiance, it constitutes a threat. Were Bishop and his group to back off, Mapache's people would kill them. Bishop's only alternative, his only chance to live, which he perceives perhaps reflectively, is to strike first, despite the overwhelming odds.

Partly for these reasons, audiences tend to root for the Bunch. "My idea," said Peckinpah, "was that *The Wild Bunch* would have a cathartic effect."[29] *Catharsis?* Did Peckinpah's study of Greek tragedies and Aristotle make him go overboard in his claims for the film? Like the heroes of Greek tragedy, notably Oedipus (also a murderer) and Antigone, like Hamlet (another murderer, who kills without regret) and Lear, the four members of the Bunch who take on Mapache and the federales do not employ halfway measures but go all the way to accomplish their goals.

As chapter 2 has demonstrated, Peckinpah's films feature flawed heroes, a characteristic that is often postulated as an attribute of tragedy. The members of the Bunch, flawed as they are, also have stature and integrity, which often mark the heroes of Greek and Renaissance tragedies. These qualities are usually not among the attributes of the heroes of modern tragedies, indeed do not generally characterize protagonists of modern drama, tragic or nontragic, on stage or screen. Stature and integrity: whatever prophecies attach to or external constraints act upon tragic heroes (Oedipus is usually a prototype), those figures have the stature to choose their actions (Oedipus kills Laius, who he does not know is his father, because of the type of man Oedipus is) and the integrity to mete out a large measure of their fate or punishment (Oedipus, not a god or oracle, elects to blind himself). The action the tragic hero pursues, however painful or deadly it may be to himself or herself, has grandeur in it. Grandeur is what the final action of the Wild Bunch exemplifies, and the qualities discussed in this paragraph inhere in *The Wild Bunch*.

According to Aristotle's *Poetics, hamartia,* which is a mistake or error (chapter 13), brings about *catharsis,* which consists of pitiful and fearful acts that purge these emotions (chapter 6). In *The Wild Bunch,* the mistake or error of judgment may consist of the group's belief either that it could get away with keeping a box of weapons and ammunition from Mapache and giving them to the peasants who fight him for their freedom or—closer to the climax—that it could buy back its comrade, whom Mapache tortured. Those who commit *hamartia* and who, of their own volition, perform actions that involve pity and fear, or commit pitiful and fearful actions, create a catharsis of these emotions. They are neither entirely virtuous nor entirely villainous (chapter 13). They may be flawed human beings, but their flaw does not precipitate their destruction; the term "tragic flaw," which may be appropriate to Shakespeare's tragic heroes, appears nowhere in the *Poetics*. Although the members of the Bunch are thieves and killers, they are better human beings than Harrigan, the railroad representative, who is cavalier about causing the slaughter of civilians, and better than Mapache, who tortures for pleasure. Their desire to retrieve their comrade, despite the odds against doing so and despite the danger to themselves, which they recognize (else why arm themselves so fully?), is noble. One can also argue that their action is heroic on a positive, not merely relative scale of values. As Michael Bliss recognizes, "despite all of the talk about loyalty and faithfulness, the Bunch gains our respect only when they finally act on their assertions."[30] In Robert Culp's words, Peckinpah "has created a tragedy" of vital importance not only in itself but also in that "it is terribly important for us to know that the creation of an artificial (Theatrical) Tragic Event is still possible." The four members of the Bunch who take on an army discover "the difference between Right and Wrong" and realize that this discovery "will cost you everything."[31]

In the *Poetics,* says Aristotle, pity is stimulated by undeserved misfortune, fear by the adversities of people like us (chapter 13). Whatever else the members of the Bunch do, their high-minded goal makes them more kin to us, or more like us in our best moments, than any aim or action of their adversaries. In the *Rhetoric,* Aristotle is clearer about pity and fear: pity creates anguish and pain, especially if one might expect good to have arisen from the source of that anguish and pain (book 2, chapter 8); and fear is imminent pain or injury from those who have the anger, hatred, and power to create destruction or to give pain or harm (book 2, chapter 5). In one meaning of *catharsis,* the commission of a pitiful and fearful deed or act purges those who commit it of these emotions.[32] After Mapache, who has agreed to give Angel to the gringos, slits his throat and gives them his corpse, their actions accomplish this purgation. The traditional meaning of *catharsis* is that the pitiful and fearful acts purge the spectators. If so, this is one source of the film's power. Both interpretations help to account for the elation that we, or many of us, feel at the conclusion of this masterful film.

* * *

The scope of carnage and violence at the end of *The Wild Bunch* is massive and widespread, with hundreds of people, including most of the principles, dying. The devastation at the end of *Straw Dogs* involves just nine individuals, one-third of whom, including the two principals, survive.

Whereas most of those who die in the ferocious finale of *The Wild Bunch* are anonymous, no one in the brutal conclusion of *Straw Dogs* is unknown. Whereas the scale of *The Wild Bunch's* finale is awesome, the much longer finale of *Straw Dogs* is extraordinary in its sustained intensity. Whereas the slaughter in both major sequences of violence in *The Wild Bunch* occurs outside in bright daylight, the most violent sequence in *Straw Dogs* occurs chiefly indoors, and when the camera moves outside, the time is not only night, but the atmosphere begins foggy and becomes foggier. This confinement, enhanced by the editing, helps to create the impression that the violence in *Straw Dogs* is more compressed, therefore more conventionally dramatic, and therefore perhaps more brutal, frenzied, and disturbing than it is in *The Wild Bunch*.

The confined locale of the battle that concludes *Straw Dogs* is like the culmination of a stage play: besieged people trapped in a house. In Peckinpah's hands, cinematic directorial means enforce dramatic methods. He intensifies suspense by increasingly raising the stakes, by making each attack more threatening and dramatically consequential to the potential victims than the previous assault, and by having each side employ greater violence at every successive stage. He does so without making the onslaughts schematic by punctuating the end of each phase, and he starts a new incursion before the last incursion ends. In writing and editing the film, he progressively confines the locale to inside the Sumner home, then to more restricted parts of the interior, and his cuts to exteriors are fewer in number and duration, with longer intervals between them, until there are none at all. Thus, he compresses in place what he condenses in time. He enhances the sequence's nightmare-like atmosphere by having the camera increasingly shoot its subjects from angles. His manner of direction corresponds to the matter: as the fighting continues, he creates more pressure on the protagonist.[33] For this reason, perhaps, he is restrained in his use of slow motion. To be otherwise would call attention to directorial mannerism, thereby detracting from the subject. In filming mayhem, he is immensely disciplined. If he were not, the film would be less effective than it is.

The climactic war against the House of Sumner, so to speak, occupies more than a fourth of the film, lasting thirty minutes and forty-four seconds, with an aftermath of two minutes and thirty-seven seconds, a total of just over thirty-three minutes.[34] Each phase of the siege is a minidrama, with a beginning and end, and a conflict different from those of the phases before and after. Peckinpah avoids stressing what I have described, probably because to do so would make the battle seem too schematic. Instead, he emphasizes the flow between phases. Nevertheless, conflict and resolution help to generate dramatic excitement. Let me briefly list the major thrust of each phase of battle and the aftermath.

Phase 1: Tom Hedden and his four young allies arrive at Trencher's Farm to abduct Henry Niles. Since the four "know the American," they believe, they can enter without Tom and easily take Niles. Despite threats to and minor violence against David by Venner and Scutt, David firmly refuses to surrender Niles and persuades them that since Niles is in too weak a position to hurt anyone, they should leave him there until the doctor and police arrive. When Amy emphasizes the imminent approach of the law, they go. Once Tom learns that they have failed to take Niles, he is furious.

Phase 2: David locks the doors. Tom cries for blood, and Cawsey, the rat catcher, throws a rat through the window. Conflict surfaces between David and Amy, who unlike David wants to surrender Niles. Whereas phase 1 ends with a victory for David, phase 2 ends with a defeat. The Sumners do not realize that the stakes are increasing, for Cawsey suggests that they need not leave after they have grabbed Niles, since with David defeated, Amy can be theirs.

Phase 3: Major Scott, who is the law, enters the house and sees the destructiveness of Tom and his gang. He goes outside to make them leave. As he tries to wrest Tom's shotgun, it goes off, killing him. This homicide, as the perpetrators recognize, increases the stakes. "Accessories, we are," says Scutt. Phase 3 ends with a serious setback for David, the death of his most formidable ally.

Phase 4: With renewed impact, the return to the interior of the house stresses the siege. Internal conflict intensifies as Amy, ready to give up when Major Scott is killed, refuses to help David prepare to ward off the attackers. When, at Venner's invitation, she prepares to defect to the opposing side, the conflict heightens. To stop her, David hits her and grabs her by the hair, insisting that if the aggressors gain entry, they will kill both of them as well as Niles, since they have gone too far to back down. When she nods in comprehension, resolving the conflict in his favor, he gently thanks her and enjoins her to stay put until she recovers, while he secures the house against the invaders. Whereas the last two phases end with defeats for David, phase 4 ends with victory for him.

Phase 5: As Scutt tries to open the inside latch of a window to enter, David traps him by tying his hands around the latch with a wire, with Scutt's head inside, surrounded by broken glass. Phase 5 ends with victory, albeit short-lived, for David against one of his antagonists.

Phase 6: As a relief from the conflicts of the previous phases, the besieged husband and wife unite to protect their home. They remove the man trap from above the fireplace and set it on the floor for easier access.

Phase 7: A new problem arises when Henry Niles bursts out of the lavatory into the bedroom, where Amy has gone. While the increasingly beleaguered David rushes upstairs to protect her and get Niles out of the way, Cawsey, who has freed Scutt, sets fire to a pair of window curtains, which creates another problem.

Phase 8: David throws boiling oil on Tom and Charlie as they try to enter and, with Amy's help, puts out the fire. Phase 8 ends with victory for David, who uses more violence against his antagonists.

Phase 9: In the wake of the violence of the last phase, as their enemies mount a new siege from a different direction, the couple barricades the living room from the kitchen, creating a smaller area to defend.

Phase 10: Using his wits and a fire poker, David hits the barrel of Tom's shotgun as Tom tries to enter through the window, so that Tom shoots himself in the foot. Phase 10 ends with another victory for David, who uses more violence against his enemies.

Phase 11: David picks up the shotgun Tom dropped. When Riddaway enters, he tries to shoot, but the gun fails to fire. David again picks up the fire poker, which he had put down, and he knocks out Riddaway with it. Victorious by employing greater violence, he incapacitates an intruder before the man can make headway.

Phase 12: As Scutt begins a flanking movement by climbing upstairs, Cawsey enters the living room through a window and, with knives, battles David, who knocks him senseless, perhaps killing him, with a fire poker. In phase 12, an intruder gets further into the house than the last one did, but David wins through more violence in a harder battle.

Phase 13: Charlie, David's sexual rival, appears, holding Tom's shotgun, which David says is not loaded. Before Charlie can verify the claim, they hear, from the bedroom upstairs, the screams of Amy, whom Scutt is trying to rape, and rush to her. Pushing David aside, Charlie points the shotgun at Scutt, reversing the situation in the rape scene, in which Scutt dispossessed Charlie with a shotgun. Scutt pulls a knife on him. When Charlie pulls the trigger, the shotgun fires, killing Scutt. David's proxy when he raped Amy, who fleetingly (revealed in flash cuts) identified him with her husband, Charlie becomes David's proxy again, defending Amy by killing Scutt, who to her extreme displeasure sodomized her while his shotgun prevented Charlie from stopping him.[35]

Phase 14: After Charlie kills Scutt, David tackles him, grappling as they move into the hallway, and making him drop his weapon. They roll downstairs. David scampers to the living room, where he strikes Charlie with the man trap, which closes around Charlie's neck, piercing his throat with its teeth. Using the most savage weapon so far, David wins against what he and we think is his last antagonist.[36]

Phase 15: He and we are mistaken. Riddaway, whom David had knocked out but not killed, revives and uses his foot to try to break David's back. David pleads with Amy to shoot Riddaway with Tom's shotgun, and she does. Through his ally, he defeats the final opponent.

Aftermath: After David and Amy reconcile, he takes Niles to town. The aftermath ends when the credits begin to roll up the screen.

Note the duration of each phase and the amount of time consumed by exterior shots. During the last, climactic three phases, which occupy a fifth of the battle, there are no exterior shots.

Phase 1: four minutes and thirty-four seconds, which include fifty-five seconds (20 percent) of exterior shots, mostly in the first minute.

Phase 2: four minutes and twenty-four seconds, which include one minute and ten seconds (slightly over a fourth) of exterior shots, mostly midway through.

Phase 3: two minutes and forty-six and a half seconds, most of which (one minute and thirty-three and a half seconds) are exterior shots.

Phase 4: five minutes and thirty-seven seconds, which include one minute and twelve and two-thirds seconds (over a fifth) of exterior shots, mostly midway through.

Phase 5: one minute and twenty-one and a half seconds, which include nineteen seconds (a bit less than a fourth) of exteriors, all brief cutaways.

Phase 6: thirty-nine seconds, of which only two one-second shots (a fraction over 5 percent) are cutaways to the exterior.

Phase 7: forty-seven seconds, of which only eight seconds (17 percent) are cutaways to exteriors.

Phase 8: one minute, which includes ten seconds (13 percent) of exterior shots, all brief cutaways.

Phase 9: twenty-nine and a half seconds, none an exterior.

Phase 10: one minute and forty-four and a half seconds, which include thirty-four seconds (a third) of exterior shots.

Phase 11: twenty-one and a half seconds, which include five seconds (slightly under a fourth) of exterior shots.

Phase 12: fifty seconds, of which only four seconds (8 percent) are exterior shots.

Phase 13: one minute, thirty-eight and a half seconds, none an exterior.

Phase 14: two minutes and 24.4 seconds, none an exterior.

Phase 15: a bit over one minute and forty-nine and a half seconds, none an exterior.

Aftermath: two minutes and thirty-seven seconds, of which the last fifty-three seconds are exterior shots.

* * *

The thrust of the sequence is the defense of the Sumners' home. Only one part of the battle takes place outside (the death of Major Scott). Thereafter, Peckinpah shows as much exterior as is necessary for dramatic contrast and variety. As the intruders gain entry, he shows less and less of the exterior. When the threat is entirely inside, he shuts off the outside, compressing the drama. During the almost six minutes of phases 13, 14, and 15 (about 20 percent of the battle), there is no outside. Therefore, when David and Henry Niles leave at the end of the aftermath, the effect is of release, freedom from oppression.

Let us now examine Peckinpah's dramatic stratagems in more detail.

Preparing the half hour of violence that concludes *Straw Dogs* is a sequence over six minutes long, in which Tom Hedden, at the church social, learns that his daughter Janice, last seen with Henry Niles, is missing; he, his son, and his young cronies search in vain for them; and David, taking his distraught wife home, accidentally hits Niles with his car and takes him to their house. At home, David phones the doctor and the constable, but no one answers. He then rings the pub and leaves a message for the doctor and Major Scott that Niles is with him. The publican conveys this information to Tom Hedden and his young allies, who have gone to the pub from the church meeting hall. Chiefly because to analyze this preparatory sequence would belabor the obvious, there is no need to do so in detail. A few broad strokes should suffice: while David and Amy tend to the injured man, the village ruffians, frustrated at not finding him or Janice, stir themselves to a frenzy, ready to do violence to Henry Niles, whose brother they rough up; once they learn where he is, Tom grabs his shotgun and everyone reaches for booze, as they leave to seize Henry. Anxiety and drink prepare them for violence.

Phase 1, an introductory minidrama, encapsulates the entire sequence. Helped by Amy, David prevents the village louts from removing Niles from their home. The pace is leisurely but varied, with eight- and nine-second cuts alternating with one- to six-second cuts, none less than a second.

David hears a knock at the door and opens it. Peckinpah films this five-second shot at an angle, a hint that something is awry and that David's world will turn into a nightmare. After David grabs Scutt's wrist to pull him away from Niles, Scutt flings him back and threateningly circles him. Repeatedly, Charlie pokes David in the chest, forcing him to retreat, and intimidates him verbally: "We've come to get this bloody freak. We're going to get him. With your cooperation or without it." This speech is part of an eleven-second sequence of five shots, in which three different views of Charlie's action alternate with two close-ups, between the sentences, of David reacting to the blows as he moves backward. Ironically, Amy tells her husband, who is being victimized, rather than his victimizers, two of whom raped her, to desist. She perceives him as vulnerable now as she was earlier. Cawsey giggles, but the others stare at her. As Charlie starts to back off, Peckinpah shows but does not dwell on David observing eye contact between him and Amy.

David asks Niles whether he saw Janice Hedden at the church social, then moves Niles's limp head back and forth. After a cutaway to Tom and Riddaway drinking whisky outside, Peckinpah returns to David, who pleads that Niles is "helpless. I mean, look at him. He couldn't hurt a fly." He suggests their time would be better spent searching for Janice, whom, he does not know, Niles has accidentally killed. Charlie agrees to leave to find Janice while David goes to find the doctor. The camera reflects the tension and David's shaky resolve. In a medium shot from above, at an angle, David, beside the sofa on which Niles lies, faces Charlie, then Amy, then Charlie again. "I'm not leaving him with my wife," he says. Cawsey and Scutt badger him: "I thought you said he was helpless." "Yeah. You wouldn't leave him alone with your wife or your kid, if you had one. Oh, that's different, huh?" Peckinpah cuts back to the angled shot from above. David's resolve to keep Niles until the doctor and police arrive strengthens. "He's my responsibility." "Your responsibility?" asks Scutt, incredulously. In a close-up from below, David looks at Scutt, Amy in the background: "That's right." This shot, the first to show David from below, suggests strength or stature. Peckinpah holds it for a fraction over one second, and he neither repeats it nor uses it climactically to make David's antagonists back down. Subtly, it suggests David's qualities, which the situation begins to tap, and foreshadows his ability to rise to the occasion. When Scutt asks, "Why?" David does not reply until five shots and nine seconds later, "This is my house," in a medium shot looking down on him and Niles at an angle, coupling them as victims. With a one-second cut to the exterior, Peckinpah underscores the danger David's stand entails: Tom crisply cracks his shotgun. Eight camera shots and thirteen seconds later, Amy bluffs the intruders that the police will soon arrive. They leave. Phase 1 winds down, preparing for phase 2.

The thrust of this minidrama, with an inciting incident, climaxes, and resolution, adumbrates the movement of the entire sequence: intruders threaten, but David, with Amy's help, defeats them. As later, his victory is short-lived and is immediately followed by another threat. In phase 1, Peckinpah edits ninety-eight shots in four minutes and thirty-four seconds, averaging 2.79 seconds per shot. Not flashy editing of short cuts, but skillful editing of a variety of cuts, many relatively long, enhances the tensions of the dramatic conflict.

Whereas the skirmish in phase 1 is between outsiders and insiders, the conflict in phase 2, another minidrama, is between the insiders. When a frightened Amy, who believes David cannot cope with the attackers, tries to pressure him to give up Niles, phase 2's dramatic action begins. Despite physical and verbal attacks from without and her verbal pressure from within, David becomes more resolute than before, concluding this minidrama.

Phase 2 begins with two interior shots, Niles in extreme close-up and David in medium close-up, as Tom's and Riddaway's voices from outside bombard them. When Tom knocks the foyer door open with the butt of his shotgun, Amy pleads with David to stop them. To reassure her, he ensures the door is locked, hits it to prove it is solid, and threatens the outsiders that unless they stop he will press charges against them. Swiftly and without warning, terror invades what is no longer their sanctuary. Largely because Peckinpah did not earlier rapidly intercut shots of half a second or less and juxtapose slow motion and normal speed, his use of these techniques now startles if not frightens the audience, as it does Amy. In five cuts, each between four-tenths and six-tenths of a second, he edits together a medium shot of a window with Cawsey's voice giggling as something crashes toward the camera in slow motion; a close-up of David looking up at it; a return to the window, its glass breaking as the something, revealed to be a rat, continues its movement in slow motion; a close-up of Amy, frightened; and a return to the glass breaking in slow motion. Apart from the intrinsically audible and visual impact of breaking windows, on both David and the audience, Peckinpah has, in the first half of the film, shot so many sequences of David observing and being observed through windows—of a pub, his house, and his car—that here, the director enhances the effect of violence against David's very self. Next, Peckinpah intercuts shots of Amy watching and moving away from the rat as it scurries past her, David moving and observing the rat and Amy, and Cawsey outside the window. He moves the action outside, partly to reveal what the invaders are planning and partly to prevent viewers from seeing more of Amy, so that when they see her again they will apply knowledge of what is happening outside to internal pressures she experiences, thereby justifying her.

Outside, Cawsey giggles, rides a child's tricycle, and honks its horn while Scutt and Charlie drink whisky and Riddaway works himself up to righteous anger, which Scutt hypocritically encourages. Mirroring the strife inside the house, Charlie tries to persuade his comrades to back off, but he is ineffective. As Riddaway and Scutt work themselves up, Riddaway roughly lifts Cawsey from the tricycle because he is treating the event as a game. To the enraged Tom, there is no playfulness about their goal to seize Niles. Cawsey persuades the others to make a diversionary row so that, unobserved by the Sumners, he can enter through a window and abduct Niles.

Inside, David reacts to the row, Cawsey's throwing another rat into the house, Tom's threats, and the rocks Scutt throws at the window. Charlie tries to work on David's reason, "It's just that Niles we're after, Mr. Sumner," but failing to do so, he threatens, "Look, you stupid Yank, let's have Niles before someone gets hurt." Meanwhile, Niles's need to go to the lavatory complicates matters. To Amy's protests, David helps the limping man to the toilet upstairs, off the bedroom.

This view of Amy is the first after one minute and ten seconds of pressure by men outside and inside the house (she fears Niles near the bedroom), which magnifies her beleaguerment, vulnerability, and panic. When she reiterates her demand that David surrender Niles to them, terror informs her moral defection. David, who throughout the film she insisted should take a clear, principled stand, can hardly believe her words.

> *David:* They'll beat him to death.
> *Amy:* I don't care. *(He stares at her silently.)* Get him out!
> *David:* You really don't care, do you?
> *Amy:* No, I don't.

After a three-second medium-long shot of both on the steps, Peckinpah cuts, as if punching David, to a dramatically long, thirty-three-second close-up of him as he reacts to Amy's verbal blows. David looks at her, descends a step, turns to her, walks up that step (regaining relinquished territory), looks away, then at her, and reasserts his ethical stance: "No. I care. This is where I live. This is me. I will not allow violence against this house." Peckinpah cuts back to a medium-long shot of both, as if pulling back to take in David's decision. Telling her to go to bed, David descends to deal with the invaders. The long take that culminates this phase focuses on character, not action.

In phase 2, 103 shots occupy four minutes and twenty-four seconds, an average of 2.56 seconds per shot, slightly faster than the average shot in phase 1. Since the duration of shots varies from less than half a second to thirty-three seconds, the average may mislead. The succession of short takes creates a rapid tempo and gives dramatic emphasis to the longer takes, which focus on character.

The minidrama of phase 3 has a point of attack, a turning point, a denouement, and a discussion of the implications of the resolution. Photography and editing enhance drama: suspenseful action, with shots at angles; slow build-up; rapid intercutting, including slow-motion shots, as action accelerates to an exciting denouement, and deceleration after the climactic resolution. Although more than half of phase 3 (one minute and thirty-three and a half seconds) occurs outside, mostly during the second half, the exterior is so foggy that the claustrophobic atmosphere is varied, not relaxed. The thrust of this phase is the killing of the one outsider—Major Scott, representing the law—who might help the besieged and whose murder raises the stakes for all.

His arrival begins the dramatic action. "I see you finally got through the enemy lines," is David's greeting. Less than half a minute after Scott is inside, Cawsey throws another rat into the house; Amy screams; Cawsey calls, "I don't just kill 'em, you know. I breed 'em as well"; and the rat scampers past Amy, who continues to scream. "I'll deal with them," declares Major Scott, who goes outside to confront the attackers.

During Scott's initial encounter with them, Peckinpah emphasizes dramatic action, not conspicuous editing, with shots no faster than two seconds and some as slow as 5.3 and 7.5 seconds. Major Scott orders Tom to surrender his weapon. When Tom refuses, he grabs the barrel and they grapple with the shotgun. As the action accelerates, so does the duration of the shots. Peckinpah intercuts takes of the shotgun barrel, the killing, and reactions to the murder. A close-up of the major trying to wrest the shotgun from Tom is followed by a close-up of Charlie observing. The director cuts back to a close-up of the major, then to a medium shot of him and Tom grappling. In a dramatic and cinematic climax, the camera cuts to a tenth-of-a-second extreme close-up of a blaze of flame as a shell passes through the shotgun barrel; then to a half-second medium shot, in slow motion, that shows the blaze continuing as Major Scott takes the blast and is hurled upward by its impact; back to an extreme close-up of the shotgun barrel, lasting two-tenths of a second, with a blaze of flame as a second shell is fired; a return to a half-second shot of Major Scott falling backward in slow motion. As if punching, Peckinpah cuts to the interior: in close-up, David and Amy pull back in shock (half a second); he cuts again to Major Scott falling backward in slow motion (three-tenths of a second); then to a close-up reaction of Charlie, startled (almost a second); and back to Major Scott, who falls to the ground in slow motion. The tempo decelerates to cuts of three seconds and longer. David and Amy recognize they are unprotected. From her command to him to telephone someone, Peckinpah cuts to Scutt leaving the group around the major's body. "Phone!" demands Amy. Scutt cuts the telephone wire. David tries to call, but the phone is dead. Scutt returns: "No calls tonight." David moves to ensure that the outside door is locked and orders his stunned wife, "Get the lights." In an eight-second take, the men stand around the body. "I didn't reckon on nobody getting killed, Norman," Riddaway says. "Ta," responds Scutt, "well, that's too bad: we're all in it now." Peckinpah cuts to a medium close-up of the corpse from above; then to the previous shot, Scutt adding, "Accessories, we are"; then to Cawsey and Charlie, who confirms, "That's the law."

In phase 3, eighty-five shots last two minutes and forty-six and a half seconds, averaging 1.95 seconds per shot, more than half a second faster than the average in phase 2. In phase 3, the editing spellbindingly enhances the speedy escalation of the drama to major violence. The action seems more rapid than it is because of the slower tempo that precedes it and the intercutting between slow motion and normal speed when Major Scott is shot. The two gunshots, the first in the film, are shocking in themselves and in that they increase David's and Amy's vulnerability.

From conflict outside the house, Peckinpah moves to conflict inside the house. Phase 4's minidrama, more than twice as long as phase 3's, contains a crucial dramatic issue on which David's success hangs, the allegiance of his wife, who sets the conflict in motion by urging him to surrender Niles. When he rejects her demand, she refuses to help him ward off the attackers. When she responds affirmatively to Charlie's request that she desert her husband and their helpless charge, to join him, the conflict reaches a turning point. David uses physical force to prevent her from leaving but, more important, he uses reason to make her understand why she must stay inside with him, thereby resolving the conflict and retrieving her allegiance.

Aurally and visually, Peckinpah stresses the magnitude of her upsetting the apple cart. After Tom cries, "Henry Niles!" Amy (facing the camera) moves forward from a medium shot to a close-up, instructing David to give them Niles. A rock thrown by Charlie crashes through a window, underscoring her fear. David picks it up, accepting the gauntlet. Also aurally and visually, directorial technique emphasizes a beleaguered David rejecting her demand and taking a firm stand. Peckinpah cuts from Riddaway banging a door with a tire iron to David in a corner, literally and symbolically, reaffirming his decision to keep their foes out. Stressing the import of his determination, Peckinpah cuts to shattering glass as a rock goes through a window.

Deftly, he suggests David's small chances by showing him in diminished stature (a close-up from above as David removes his jacket), Amy's strength (a close-up from below), and the prize (Niles in the lavatory, frightened). As David bends to unplug the lamp, Amy retreats. In a medium shot from below, underscoring destructive force, glass shatters as a rock smashes a window. Accenting the danger and the apparent hopelessness of David's position, Peckinpah cuts to Charlie throwing another rock. "David, how are you going to keep them out?" asks Amy. Peckinpah punctuates her question with a cut to Riddaway banging a door with his tire iron. Dialogue moves the conflict further.

> *David:* I can keep them out.
> *Amy:* How? Five men out there!
> *David (picking up a fire poker):* I know that.
> *Amy:* They have a gun.
> *David:* I know they have.

By rapid editing, camera shots, and sound effects, Peckinpah heightens the drama: in close-up, a rock crashes through the window to Amy's left; in medium close-up from below, David turns from her; in an exterior, medium shot, Charlie throws a rock through a window; in a close-up of Amy, she hears the rock go through the window; in an exterior, medium shot, several men throw rocks through the window. "God damn you, David," says Amy in a close-up, "if you don't give them Niles"—and the director cuts to a medium close-up of David from below, enhancing his stature as Amy finishes her sentence—"I will," and he instantly responds, "Oh, no, you won't."

Visually intensifying their verbal duel, Cawsey throws a rat toward the window, glass cracks as the rat goes through it, a pole lamp (hit by the rat) falls in front of David, and Amy is terrified—all in two seconds. Peckinpah cuts to a seven-second close-up of David, angrily lashing at the window with his fire poker, then turning to Amy, whom he orders to go upstairs and turn on the lights. The director cuts to a medium-long shot of Amy to the left of the window and David to its right, hitting the sill with his poker; then to a close-up of David, as if punching him in the face, for his explanation, "They won't be able to see me, but I'll be able to see them," and his frantic demand that she act. In dramatic contrast, her reaction is calm: "No. No, I won't." "Go!" he erupts in dramatic opposition. "God damn you, move!"

Niles interrupts their dispute with a cry from above. The director intercuts their reactions: Niles pounds on the lavatory door and a rat faces the camera in close-up, both unnerving Amy more, but David clambers up the steps. Relieving the intensity through grotesque comedy, Peckinpah cuts to Cawsey outside, riding a child's tricycle, honking its horn and giggling. He cuts to David in the bedroom, an outside view of the house as a light goes on in the bedroom window, a downstairs window breaking as something goes through it, and Charlie throwing a rock, which so panics Amy that she rushes upstairs. After a quick cut to Cawsey swinging to and fro on the greenhouse door frame, he returns to the bedroom. As rocks smash the window, David (in long takes) puts on his sneakers, calmly preparing to act against the intruders, while Amy (in a long cut) refuses to help him.

After David closes the lavatory door behind Niles, Peckinpah moves outside, where violence continues. Scutt and Riddaway throw rocks at the greenhouse windows, but while this action, a foil to the violence against the home, serves as a relief to the perpetrators, its drunken, giddy senselessness increases their threat to the Sumners. Peckinpah alternates takes of rock-throwing at the greenhouse and Cawsey riding on a tricycle with shots of Niles in the lavatory, frightened, and David preparing to cope with the invaders—he turns on the stovetop's gas burners, puts a pot on the floor, pours two bottles of oil into it, puts it on the stovetop, and gets wire from the cupboard. The director cuts to a twenty-second shot of the drunken villagers in the fog: Cawsey knocks down Riddaway with his tricycle, which falls over, knocking Cawsey himself off. Riddaway rises, grabs the tricycle, and chases Cawsey, until they are out of sight. After a pause, they return, each riding a tricycle, honking, giggling, and laughing as Riddaway threatens to wrap the bike around Cawsey's neck. This breakaway, relieving and heightening tension inside by violence outside, serves another dramatic function: it is a separation scene between David's acts of preparation, suggesting enough time for the oil to boil, David to unwind enough wire to tie window handles together, and Amy to become more hysterical.

As David prepares to secure another downstairs window with wire, a turning point occurs. Moving in the dark living room, Amy hits a knee on a table. She hears Charlie cry, "Amy!" Peckinpah cuts to David returning to the living room. As the camera moves closer to him, he hears Charlie repeat her name. The director cuts to a close-up of the window, Charlie outside, still calling her. A bit from below, the camera shows her rise and look at the window as Charlie implores, "Open the door and let's have Niles." A close-up of the window shows Charlie reach through it and part the curtains. As Amy turns to David, Charlie continues, "I won't let them hurt you." A close-up shows David, pained. He turns away as he hears Charlie add, "Please, love." The camera moves with Amy as she rushes past the window to the kitchen: "Wait there. I'm coming, Charlie." Her decision marks a crucial forward thrust in the minidrama of phase 4, a change of allegiance.

As she begins to open the kitchen door, Charlie stops Tom from kicking the other side of it, to allow Amy to open it. When the door opens, Tom starts to enter, shotgun first. Seeing what is about to happen, David pulls Amy from the door, through which the shotgun pokes, and grabs the barrel. As Tom and Charlie pull the gun, David lets go, thrusting them backward and giving him time to close the door. They listen to Amy's and David's altercation. Peckinpah intercuts takes of them and of Amy and David. Although David initially agrees to let her go, he yanks her from the door when she begins to do so and bolts it, starts to slap her, his hand connecting in a slow-motion shot, and, also in slow motion, rebolts the door. His willingness to act brutally is magnified by camera shots at angles and in slow motion. As Peckinpah intercuts Amy in pain, David's hand closing another bolt, and the outsiders listening, David threatens, "Stay there, and do what you're told. If you don't, I'll break your neck." His actions and statement mark a turning point in this phase, for they suggest the lengths to which he will go to achieve his goal.

Tom, quick to react, fires his shotgun, a literally shattering reminder of the lengths to which he has gone to achieve his own. An extreme close-up of two-tenths of a second shows flame coming from one barrel as a shell goes through. In a close-up of the door at an angle, the blast splinters the wood above the knob. In another close-up, David yanks Amy from the door and a close-up of the door from inside shows the same shell smashing the wood near the knob as, in the foreground, David moves her into the kitchen. A two-tenths-of-a-second extreme close-up shows flame coming from the other barrel as a shell goes through. The director cuts to a close-up of more wood by the knob splitting as the shotgun shell hits the door, then to a medium close-up of David and Amy, who hear Tom shout,

"I've got cartridges enough for all." Peckinpah intercuts shots of the men outside; David and Amy inside; Tom firing at the door, the shotgun barrel flaming again as a shell goes through and hits the door, shattering wood; then David and Amy; then the other shotgun barrel as a second shell goes through. The intense violence and speed of the short cuts (shells blasting) contrasts with longer reaction cuts of Tom and of David and Amy.

Having turned his conflict with Amy in his favor by force, David resolves it by reason. "Listen to me," he quietly tells her, his voice contrasting with Tom's yelling in the preceding shot. Peckinpah accentuates David's statement by intercutting it with a shot, at an angle and in slow motion, of a kitchen window's glass shattering as Riddaway pokes his tire iron through it. David continues: "Do you know what happens if they get in, then? They'll kill us all." In three shots that last about one second, Riddaway goes to a vestibule window, he smashes it with his tire iron, and David and Amy hear the shattering glass. In a contrasting six-second shot, David quietly explains, "They've gone too far to back down now." Italicizing his statement, Peckinpah cuts to a close-up of Riddaway's tire iron smashing a glass window, which opens as plants fall. "You understand now?" asks David. She nods. For emphasis, Peckinpah cuts to David in close-up: "We're dead if they get in." He highlights the words with a slow motion shot of another window smashed, glass spattering and plants falling. He returns to David, who in two shots calmingly tells Amy, "Thank you, sweetheart. Stay," then leaves to cope with the next threat.

Phase 4, which lasts five minutes and thirty-seven seconds, contains 184 shots, averaging 1.83 seconds per shot, slightly faster than the average shot of phase 3. In phase 4, Peckinpah varies the tempo of his editing, including spare use of slow-motion insets, to heighten suspense and to underscore the drama with contrasts, builds, climaxes, reversals, and resolutions.

In phase 5, David traps Scutt by wiring his hands tightly around window handles he tries to open to enter the house. Although David's victory proves short-lived, it buys time to prepare more defenses. Less than 25 percent shorter than phase 4, phase 5 is an action sequence. Peckinpah uses no slow-motion insets but employs different types of close-ups for intensity and varies the duration of takes, using longer cuts to dramatize David's methodical procedures.

While Cawsey, who collects not only dead rats but live ones (he breeds them, he boasted earlier in the siege), distracts the Sumners by throwing another rat into the house, Scutt breaks a glass window and reaches inside for the handle. Peckinpah alternates close-ups, extreme close-ups, and medium close-ups as David, who in phase 4 wired the handles together, loops more wire around Scutt's hand and the other window latch; Scutt cries in pain; David, placing a knife at his neck, quietly warns, "Make one move, you son of a bitch, and I'll slit your throat"; and he demands the other hand. In an eleven-second close-up, Scutt gives him the other hand, which he ties with wire. While he completes this operation, Scutt with hypocritical servility tries to placate him: "It wasn't any of my doing, sir. It was Venner and Hedden. Been after your wife, he has." "Am I hurting you, Mr. Scutt?" asks David, mocking him with politeness, as Scutt had mocked David earlier in the film. "My neck's on the glass," says Scutt. "Good," says David, calmly. "I hope you slit your throat."

Phase 5, which lasts only one minute and twenty-one and a half seconds, edits together forty-three shots, an average of 1.895 seconds per shot, a hairsbreadth slower than the average of phase 4. Focusing on dramatic action, the editing shows David calmly and methodically coping with the enemy.

Phase 6, less than half as long as phase 5, is an interlude in which, while hostilities continue, David's previous victory is undone (Cawsey frees Scutt), a distraction comes from upstairs (Niles in the toilet), and the Sumners gingerly remove the lethal man trap and set it on the floor. David then orders Amy to deal with Niles while he completes setting the trap.

The thirty-nine seconds of phase 6 use twenty-three shots, averaging 1.695 seconds per shot, slightly faster than the average shot in phase 5. Emphasized more than the rat or the rock, Scutt's imminent escape, or Niles's fears, is the restored alliance of David and Amy, who act in concert to defend themselves.

Phase 7, a bit longer than phase 6, is another interlude in which David saves his wife from Niles, who bursts out of the toilet, and efficiently gets him out of the way so that he can cope with the threat below. Tension rises as, with few exterior shots, the atmosphere becomes more claustrophobic.

Producing the effect of bombardment, the director's editing merges threats from two sources. Niles's feet kick the lavatory door open. Niles enters the bedroom, the camera moving with him, as he sees Amy by the bed. Outside, Riddaway hits the window jamb with his tire iron, trying to enter. Inside, David swings the fire poker. Riddaway starts to enter as David's poker misses and hits the jamb. Upstairs, Amy tries to free herself from Niles. David swings the poker again and hits Riddaway, knocking him out. Niles and Amy grapple, the camera at an angle and moving closer, as she calls, "David!" He runs up the steps. Alternating shots of the different threats increase the frenzy and danger, and further establish David as a man of action.

In the bedroom, David pulls Niles off Amy and punches him in the face. He reels back. Instantly, David grabs his head, pulls him upright, and shakes his own head, quietly and efficiently ordering him to stop. When Niles calms down, David releases his head, tells Amy to open the attic door, and leads him there. Peckinpah films these actions in three shots that last seventeen seconds, the slow tempo contrasting with the fast tempo of David's previous actions. The director intercuts David locking Niles in the attic with Cawsey reaching inside a window to set fire to the curtains, a preparation for the action of phase 8.

David has two successes in phase 7, whose forty-seven seconds have twenty-one shots, averaging almost 2.24 seconds per shot, more than half a second slower than the previous phase. Peckinpah varies the tempi downstairs and upstairs, the latter containing longer takes, contrasting David's violence with his protectiveness, and underscoring the difference between his treatment of Niles and that of the villagers. David's blow is necessary and therapeutic, not gratuitous and vindictive.

In phase 8, David puts up an obstruction to prevent Tom and Charlie from entering, but although the barrier does not last, it gives him time to position himself to throw boiling oil on them. As they recover, he and Amy join to put out the fire. This phase is the same length as the previous one, with only ten seconds of exteriors. Peckinpah uses two slow-motion in-sets, providing emphasis and aesthetic balance to the more violent shots.

While Cawsey calls Tom's attention to the fire, Tom and Charlie go to the window and Tom prepares to enter. David carries two pots from the stove to the living room. "Open the door," Tom demands, aiming his shotgun, "or I'll blow you to pieces." "Okay," says David, who surveys the situation, decides what to do, and crouches to put the pots on the floor. Taking advantage of the blaze, which prevents Tom from getting a good aim on him, he rises and lifts the table upright as a barrier against the window. In two camera shots, each less than half a second, Tom aims his shotgun and two shots rip through the table. David swings out of the way and bends to pick up the pots as the table, under the impact of the shells, starts to fall, in slightly slow motion. Peckinpah intercuts Tom lowering his shotgun, a close-up of the table continuing to fall, Tom and others outside, and David, who picks up the pots. After a cutaway to Tom and Charlie trying to see through flames into the house, Peckinpah goes to David, who in slight slow motion throws boiling oil through the window, then to a medium close-up of the oil hitting their faces. While Tom and Charlie cry in pain, David and Amy put out the fire.

Phase 8, which ends in success for David and Amy, has forty-one camera shots in one minute, an average of 1.46 seconds per shot, almost one second faster than shots in phase 7. As the action increases, the tempo speeds up. Two moderately slow-motion insets provide variety, emphasis, and stylized poise that strengthen the impact. The slow speed of David throwing the oil (half a second), followed by the normal speed with which it hits Tom and Charlie (one second), heightens the violence, since the latter take seems to occur more quickly than its normal speed.

Phase 9 ends with another success for David and Amy, who barricade the living room against the intruders, giving themselves more protection and less space to defend. The antagonists burst into the kitchen, but before they can enter the living room, David and Amy block the door with a tall, sturdy breakfront. After Tom fires a bullet through it, they move a short but strong cabinet in front of the breakfront for additional support. "It'll hold," David concludes, and, preparing for the next onslaught, asks Amy for the fire poker.

In phase 9, a twenty-nine-and-a-half-second interlude, nineteen shots average 1.55 seconds per shot, slightly slower than the previous phase. Preparation against violence takes longer than the violence itself.

A battle between exterior and interior is the conflict of phase 10. Tom, who killed Major Scott, tries but fails to invade the house to kill David. Contrasting outside and inside, where Tom wants to go, about a third of the shots are exteriors. Phase 10 is the most violent so far, but David uses his mind to strike at the right moment, making Tom put himself out of action.

While Riddaway batters and smashes windows and frames with his tire iron, trying to enter and to distract David and Amy from Tom, David strives to cow the trespassers by playing Scottish bagpipe music on his record player. Tom is so heavy that to go through the window, the young men must lift him and push him in. Unseen by them, David positions himself by the window, fire poker in hand. By repeatedly switching medium shots and close-ups, by progressing to shorter cuts, and by rapid intercutting at the most violent moment, Peckinpah creates what W. S. Gilbert calls "a short sharp shock" (*The Mikado*). He cuts from a medium shot of David by the window as the men behind Tom push him in and Tom, a foot inside, lowers his shotgun; to a close-up of David, waiting for the right moment; to a medium shot of Tom getting further inside, his shotgun pointing further down; to a close-up of David, ready; and to a medium shot of David swinging the poker to hit Tom's shotgun. In a two-tenths-of-a-second close-up from above, the poker hits the barrel of Tom's shotgun, knocking it downward. An extreme close-up of one-tenth of a

second shows the shotgun barrel blaze as the blow makes Tom accidentally fire it. A three-tenths-of-a-second close-up from above shows Tom's
right foot hit by a bullet. An extreme close-up from above, a tenth of a
second, views Tom's right foot, shoe blown apart, red with blood. In a two-
thirds-of-a-second close-up, David recoils at the sight. In a two-thirds-of-
a-second close-up, Tom looks down and screams. The shots lengthen to
show reactions: David recoils (half a second), Tom looks down (a shade
over one second), he drops his shotgun as Riddaway and Charlie pull him
out (one second). Peckinpah intercuts shots of Riddaway and Charlie
pulling Tom outside, laying him on the ground, David backing away from
the window, several shots of Tom directing Riddaway and Charlie to look
at his foot, and a shot, from their point of view, of the top of Tom's shoe
with a bullet hole, the shoe blown apart, bloodied.

Phase 10, lasting one minute and forty-four and a half seconds, uses fifty-
eight shots, an average of 1.8 seconds per shot, somewhat faster than the
average length of phase 9. As the action accelerates, so does the tempo.
On the principle that less is more, Peckinpah does not dwell on takes of
violence or gore, but focuses on preparation for them and reactions to
them.

In phase 11, David picks up Tom's shotgun to face Riddaway who, furi-
ously shouting, "You're dead," enters to kill him. After Riddaway wildly
rips off window frames and throws them into the house, the director intercuts Riddaway and David in visual as well as verbal collision. "You don't
come in here," warns David, pointing the shotgun at him. David clicks
the trigger, but the weapon fails to fire. Riddaway lurches forward as David
picks up the fire poker, with which he hits Riddaway, knocking him down.

Phase 11 has eighteen shots in only twenty-one and a half seconds,
averaging about 1.2 seconds per shot, which is faster than the average in
phase 10. Peckinpah alternates relatively long takes (2.1 seconds is the
longest) with short takes (three-tenths of a second is the shortest). This
phase demonstrates the alacrity with which a resilient David seizes upon
a new means when a prepared method fails him.

In phase 12, as Scutt begins a flanking movement by climbing to enter
the bedroom window, this phase's only exterior shots (two, totaling four
seconds), Cawsey enters the living room through a window and traps
David, whom he attacks with knives as David defends himself with the
fire poker. They parry, and when the violence occurs, it is swift. For example, in two shots that occur in one minute, Cawsey throws a knife at
David, who ducks, and the knife hits and becomes embedded in a wood-
en wall. Cawsey flashes another knife, with which he duels David, who

wields his poker. When David strikes, Peckinpah elongates the blow and the physical pain it inflicts. He cuts from David swinging toward Cawsey's feet (half a second) to Cawsey's face in pain as he starts to sink (seven tenths of a second) to David's arms completing the swing, the camera rising with them (half a second), to Cawsey falling in close-up (half a second) to Cawsey falling in a medium shot (half a second). When David sees Cawsey unconscious, perhaps dead, he slowly, sadly, drops the poker.

The fifty seconds of phase 12 use thirty-one shots, averaging 1.6 seconds per shot. Since the first nine shots last twenty seconds and the final shot, just described, seven seconds, the average is deceptive, for when destructiveness occurs, after stealthy maneuvering, it is swift, the rapidity conveying great violence, and the director slows the survivor's winding-down. Peckinpah's adroit blocking and editing make the violence of this phase different from that of the previous phases.

By phase 13, with all of David's and Amy's antagonists in the house, every shot in it and the next two phases is an interior, which condenses the pressure, making it more explosive. In phase 13, Charlie appears, pointing at David the shotgun he threw away. Interrupted by the screams of Amy, whom Scutt is trying to rape, they race upstairs, but Charlie pushes David out of the way and points the shotgun at Scutt, who directs the knife with which he threatened Amy at him. Phase 13 ends with David's success: instead of killing one of his two surviving antagonists, both rivals for his wife, he lets one kill the other.

At the start of phase 13, a ten-second, angled medium close-up shows David, sofa behind him, drop his poker on the floor and survey the unconscious or dead rat-catcher. In the background, Charlie enters with Tom's shotgun. The record of the bagpipe music ends. Charlie advances on David. In a six-second shot, David turns toward him, his face desolate at the carnage for which he was responsible. In a three-second shot, he completes his turn. "The gun's empty," says David in a five-second close-up. "Is it, now?" asks the skeptical Charlie in an angled, two-second close-up. A six-second close-up follows: "Why don't you pull it and kill me?" In a four-second close-up, Charlie begins to speak but is interrupted, the camera shifting to David in close-up, by Amy's screams from upstairs. Peckinpah cuts to the bedroom, where, in a series of seven shots of about one second each, Scutt and Amy struggle on the bed. He cuts to the men below, editing in two close-ups Charlie looking upstairs and moving toward the stairway, and David moving to the steps.

In the bedroom, Amy (her head at the bottom of the screen, which expressionistically distorts her situation) pulls Scutt's hair to pull him off her, while he, one hand on her neck, the other holding a knife to her forehead, tries to overcome her. David reaches him and, grabbing his feet, pulls him off Amy. Charlie gets between them and brutally shoves David backward with the shotgun, which he points at Scutt, who jolts upright and points his knife at Charlie. The two men have made David irrelevant.

In this intensely dramatic encounter, Peckinpah edits together shots of each of the four characters, of whom only David does not know about Amy's rape and sodomization. Each regards the shotgun differently. Since David thinks it is empty, he readies himself for whatever the men do. Charlie is uncertain whether the shotgun is loaded. With no reason to believe it is empty, Amy is tormented by Charlie's not shooting Scutt immediately. To Scutt, the threat of the gun is real. As he and Charlie face off, Peckinpah reverses the image of the rape scene, in which Scutt held a shotgun on Charlie, forcing him to dismount from Amy and not interfere while he sodomized her. Scutt brashly commands, "Take him [David] downstairs, Charlie. You put him to sleep." Reversing the order of their previous rape of Amy, he adds, "I'll call you when I'm ready." Charlie hesitates. Like the spectators in the audience, Amy is in suspense, waiting for him to fire.

Peckinpah edits the climax with dizzyingly furious speed, each cut ranging from one-tenth to three-tenths of a second. In an extreme close-up, one barrel of the shotgun flames as a shell goes through. In an extreme close-up at an angle, Charlie blinks and recoils as he fires. A medium shot shows Scutt taking the bullet. A medium close-up shows him continuing to take it. In a close-up from above, Amy screams. A medium shot shows Scutt hurled backward. In a close-up, David watches him. A medium shot reveals him dropping down. The eight cuts last two seconds.

Peckinpah's pacing of phase 13, which lasts one minute and thirty-eight and a half seconds, is exceptional. The average length of each shot (1.86 seconds) is less consequential than the pacing. He begins slowly, a suspenseful face-off between David and Charlie. He speeds the tempo when Amy cries from above, retards it during the face-off between Charlie and Scutt, but not as slowly as in the previous face-off, and accelerates it rapidly at the climax. When the dramatic tension is internal, the takes are relatively long, for the director concentrates on the battle of wills between characters; when tension erupts into action, his editing is lightning-fast, for the tempest is thunderous.

In phase 14, which like phase 13 has only interior shots, David kills, in the film's most savagely violent way, the man he thinks is his last surviving antagonist, also the major rival for his wife. It ends with apparently complete victory, after which the pace relaxes, in harmony with his relief.

Initially, the tempo is rapid, using cuts of a second and less. Instantly following the death of Scutt, Amy screams while David grabs a desk lamp to hit Charlie, who recoils but falls. Peckinpah edits three takes in one second: David starts to grab Charlie, Amy retreats while hiding her eyes with a blouse, and David grabs Charlie around the neck, pushing him from the bedroom. Moving through the hall to the staircase, they wrestle, kick, and punch each other. As the battle becomes hallucinatory, Peckinpah uses longer takes and more frequent angle shots, and he employs slow and slower speeds more extensively than before, enhancing their effect with slow musical chords. Unlike his previous use of slow motion as insets, four successive takes, totaling seven seconds, are in slow motion. In a medium close-up from below, David's back is to the camera as he and Charlie struggle and turn, Charlie's hands around his throat; the camera follows them as he tries to clutch the banister (now in close-up) but falls down the steps. A medium shot shows him (back to the camera) fall down the steps to the landing before the stairs angle to the floor below, grabbing the banister to break his fall. In a medium close-up, David (facing the camera) starts to hurl himself at Charlie. A medium shot from a different point of view focuses on Charlie (facing the camera), as David hits Charlie's stomach headfirst, grabbing his waist; they turn, grappling. After two shots—one at an angle, the other from above—they fight in normal speed. In three slower-motion shots intercut with the battle in normal speed and Amy observing it, they somersault down the steps—the slow motion and the way they descend increasing the spectral quality of their combat.

Ten shots of Amy at the head of the stairs, all but one close-ups from below, watching her rivals fight, intercut with the continuing battle. These insets total less than fourteen seconds, but they are crucial in making her a spectator of a combat that, like the duel between Hamlet and Laertes, resembles a play within a play. Her horrified reaction prompts and mirrors that of the audience, particularly at the climax of the fight, when in an angled medium close-up from above, David grabs the man trap as Charlie comes toward him. In an angled close-up from below, Amy screams. A medium close-up from below, also at an angle, shows Charlie jolt upward, his head caught in the trap; his head jerking and the sound of the trap snapping shut make it appear that we see it close, but it encircles his neck at the start of the shot. The camera returns to the angled close-up from below of Amy, horrified, screaming. It cuts to an angled medium close-up of David holding the handle of the man trap, which Charlie unsuccessfully tries to loosen from his neck, the camera moving back and forth as Charlie jerks right and left. It cuts back to a close-up of Amy, who averts her head so as not to see more. After alternating shots of Charlie falling and David starting to rise, the camera cuts to Amy who, like the tow-haired boy and his sister in the first battle of *The Wild Bunch,* turns her head to watch death at work. Twice more, the camera shows her observing Charlie's death, after which, still looking down, she shudders and, the ordeal over, begins to calm down, which cues and mirrors the audience to react similarly.

In a series of seven shots, each a long take of four or more seconds, the camera dwells on the ostensible end of the siege: Charlie's and Cawsey's bodies, David's replacement of a fallen chair, and his and Amy's survey of the scene. Concluding phase 14, a very long twenty-seven-second shot shows David pass through the wreckage, squinting to see the scene (his glasses fell off during the scuffle with Charlie), moving toward the camera from a medium close-up to close-up, and sighing with relief that he defeated all his opponents. He smiles at his accomplishment.

Phase 14 lasts two minutes and 24.4 seconds, its fifty-six shots averaging 2.578 seconds per cut, almost three-fourths of a second longer than the average shot in phase 13. The tempo of phase 14 differs from that of phase 13, which has long takes at the start, rapid editing at the end, and no slow motion. Phase 14 has a few short takes edited together at the start, then employs longer takes than the previous phase—some in slow, others in slower motion, in cuts that are longer than the different slow-motion insets of *The Wild Bunch* and that enhance the hallucinatory effect of the fight. This phase also utilizes the technique of a play within a play, with Amy as spectator, watching the struggle between her husband and the man who shot the man who had sodomized her earlier and tried to rape her moments before. Reflecting and cuing the emotions of the audience, she expresses horror and, like the child spectators in *The Wild Bunch,* wants to stop watching the violence but cannot help herself from looking at it.

In phase 15, which like 13 and 14 has only claustrophobically interior shots, the brutal Riddaway, who David thought was out of the way, returns to kill him. Unable to save himself, he pleads with Amy to help, which she does by shooting Riddaway. Although shaken by her deed, which defeats the last antagonist, she reaffirms her alliance with her husband.

Nearly thirty years after *Straw Dogs,* the return of a villainous antagonist who the hero thought was dead is a cliché, but in 1971, when *Straw*

Dogs opened, this plot twist was so novel, or infrequently utilized, as to shock audiences; in this film, it still does. In the opening shot of this phase, Riddaway lurches through the doorway behind David, viciously knocks him against the wall, and hurls him across the room. David tries to climb the stairs, but Riddaway clutches him. As he pleads with his terrified wife to get the gun dropped on the upstairs landing, Riddaway tries to pull him down the steps. He grasps a stair baluster, which breaks in his hand when Riddaway yanks him down, and in one of the many angled shots in this phase, he hits Riddaway with the broken baluster, breaking Riddaway's grip and knocking him downstairs. Riddaway knocks down David, who grasps another baluster, and puts one of his feet on the small of David's back, trying to break it. By this time, Amy, still frightened, has picked up the shotgun.

Accelerating the suspense, Peckinpah intercuts Riddaway's left foot on the small of David's back (from above); Amy, with the shotgun, going to the top of the landing (from below); Riddaway's foot on David's back, trying to break it (medium shot); a different view of his foot on David's back (close-up from above); David looking up (close-up), the camera moving from Amy's scared face to the shotgun in her hands, her finger on the trigger, then back to her face (close-up at an angle); and back and forth between her and the men. Finally, she raises the shotgun and fires.[37] In a three-tenths-of-a-second medium close-up at an angle, a shell goes through Riddaway's lower back. In a close-up of the same duration, Amy recoils. In a three-second close-up from above and at a different angle, Riddaway is thrust against the wall; as he slides down, the camera following him, he leaves bloodstains on it. Still shaken, Amy drops the shotgun. The tempo decelerates. In a close-up from above, David, left hand on the railing, rises; he looks at Amy reprovingly, for having taken so long to save him. After this last shot, which lasts 7.3 seconds, Peckinpah intercuts a 7.6-second shot of a still-shaken Amy and a 6.2-second shot of a still-resentful David. He ends the phase with a more than eighteen-second shot of Amy leaning against the wall, David climbing the steps, each looking at the other; when he reaches her, he pats her left cheek and strokes her hair, which are affectionate acts of gratitude, suggesting that he has controlled or expelled his resentment.

In the one minute and 49.6 seconds of phase 15, fifty-five shots average about two seconds per shot, over half a second faster than the average in phase 14. Craftily, Peckinpah alternates short and long takes. After Riddaway grabs David, hits his head against the wall, and hurls him across the room, most of the shots in phase 15 are short (one or two seconds).

Later, the cuts are longer, for suspense, and those of David's and Amy's reaction after she shoots Riddaway are still longer. However violent this phase is, and it is, the director emphasizes brutality less than he does the relationship between David and Amy, who cements her bond with her husband unmistakably, by killing the man who would murder him. Perhaps for this reason, he uses no slow motion and edits few takes that are less than a minute. He focuses on characters, not on directorial self-display.

After more than half an hour of accelerating violence—from Scutt tossing David from the sofa as if he were no more obstacle than a pillow, and Charlie jabbing him in the chest, forcing him backward, through assaults with rats, shotgun shells, boiling oil, knives, a fire poker, a man trap, and a foot on the small of the back—the tempo of the aftermath is, with emotional and artistic justification, slow: the twenty-one shots in its two minutes and thirty-seven seconds average a long 7.47 seconds. After the storm, Peckinpah dramatizes release, relief, calm. David unlocks the attic and takes Niles downstairs. Exhausted, sad, and perhaps afraid that the inanimate Cawsey may not be dead after all, Amy looks at the carnage below. "You're okay?" asks David before leaving with Niles. Three shots and ten seconds later, she nods. His terse question and her silent answer reaffirm their marriage.

Once David and Henry leave, the last fifty-three seconds of the aftermath are exteriors. Outside is freedom and the takes are suitably long, the penultimate shot lasting nineteen seconds. Unlike lesser directors, Peckinpah does not pad time with people opening and closing the doors of houses or cars, since these actions are not dramatic. He cuts from a close-up of Amy, who despite her relief is about to cry as she looks at the carnage, to an exterior long shot of darkness, which is brightened by the headlights of a car driving toward screen left. He intercuts medium close-ups and close-ups of David and Henry in the car with long shots of the car. "I don't know my way home," says Henry, beginning the final, frequently quoted exchange. "That's okay," replies David, turning to him, then back to the road as he thinks, smiles, and says, "I don't, either." The aftermath ends when credits roll up the screen.

Through great variety in photography and editing, Peckinpah artfully makes this more than half-hour siege immensely exciting. After a long nightmare, viewers are relieved. They are elated that the worm has turned, that David has defeated five Goliaths who have murdered a man representing the law, and that David has done so with the participation of his wife, whose loyalty he secured after it seemed lost. Their union to defeat common enemies may improve their relationship. At a critical point,

David has found his manhood by doing what Amy castigated him for not having done: taking a stand. He wins not only by using violence, since his wits play an equally vital role, but by a willingness to do so when no other alternative exists, even though (his reactions make clear) the violence shocks, dismays, and saddens him. She achieves a similar victory when confronted with a choice, which is more than violence or nonviolence: it is to save her husband or let him be killed. She takes her stand as he takes his. Only the first sentence of this paragraph concerns the director's technique, on which previous paragraphs, analyzing the phases of the siege, have dwelt. As the conclusion of this sequence stresses, Peckinpah's primary concerns are drama and character. *Straw Dogs* is not "about" mindless savagery. Its subjects include finding one's identity and allegiance; the complexity of human beings, some of whom act for affection (Charlie does not want to harm Amy, and Tom's main concern is justice, based on his love for his daughter); commitment (David's to the man in his care, whom he injured, Amy's to her husband); manhood (which involves gentleness—David toward Henry, for instance—as well as action); and marriage. Corpses notwithstanding—again note the small body count compared to that of *The Wild Bunch*—*Straw Dogs* ends dramatically on a note of gentle and tentative affirmation.

* * *

Drawing upon a familiar theme of Peckinpah, *Junior Bonner* focuses on men who may have outlived their time and whose ways of life may be obsolescent, but the two principal characters, Junior and Ace Bonner, are dynamic personages who fight vigorously for their identities and ways of life. They represent what is not yet past but is still vital and may survive. No one in *Junior Bonner* tries to kill or seriously injure anyone. In its first major sequence of violence after the opening credits, bulldozers demolish Ace Bonner's abandoned, decrepit house. However, cuts to antiquated photographs inside, picturing him in his prime, and to his son, Junior, watching the wreckage, personalize the destruction; and Junior's engagement with an agent of it renders the devastation more moving. This dramatic sequence, which lasts four minutes and about thirty-three and a half seconds, divides into three phases.

Lasting two minutes and ten and a half seconds, phase 1 shows the past in the present. In the opening shot, a bit over five seconds, Junior drives his dented, dirty white car and horse-trailer past wreckage in the foreground—wood from a broken shed lying on the ground and an old, junked car (possibly Ace's) without a hood—while in the far background is land that has been terraced for construction. The next three shots reveal Ace's abandoned, dilapidated house, an empty corral to its left, a broken fence in front of it, an open front door, and a rusting rural mailbox with "Ace Bonner" painted on it in capital letters, its lid open. Junior observes the desolate home of his father, who he thinks is there, then looks back to see the present destroy the past: a bulldozer dumps a load of earth.

Walking from his car through the gate posts, whose gate has fallen off, he calls, "Ace! Ho, Ace!" Receiving no reply, he enters and surveys the sparsely furnished house: an old, perhaps no longer functional radio sits atop a dusty chest of drawers; a dirty towel hangs on the side door, which is ajar; a chair lies before a battered, broken stove; old newspapers are on the floor; tacked on a wall, beside a crutch leaning on it (suggestive of injuries to a different part of Junior's body, seen in the opening credits), is a torn, old, black-and-white photo of Ace on horseback in a rodeo during his glory days, surrounded by a crowd (contrasting with the solitary figure of a defeated Junior in the credits); a table and chair are upturned (like the other fallen chair, a possible allusion to Junior thrown by the bull Sunshine during the credits); pictures and posters, some peeling, hang crookedly by nails on another wall; a cheap, timeworn bed is unmade; half a curtain partly frames one side of a window, through which is a bleak view. "Together," as Michael Bliss says, "these images create a depressing sense of abandonment."[38] In shots lasting over fourteen seconds, Junior picks up a framed picture lying flat on top of the chest of drawers, shakes the broken glass off it, takes a long look at it, props it upright against the radio, and says to the empty room, "Sorry I missed you, Ace," which more fully identifies the house with the man. Peckinpah cuts to a close-up of the picture, possibly clipped from a magazine (printed words are beneath the photo): Ace in action at a rodeo, jumping off a horse to down a roped calf.

As Junior leaves the house, the director shows what he observes. Starting with an extreme long shot, the camera moves to a closer long shot of a mobile home development (his brother Curly's, we later learn). The shot provides a glimpse of the conformist, unindividualized future at work in the present to replace the individualistic past, including Ace's house on a prairie that is less open than it used to be, but that still exists, if only for moments longer. As Junior surveys bulldozing and other construction activity, he drives past the abandoned house, a bicycle wheel propped against it (a relic of youth), the camera lingering on the decaying abode.

Although Junior leaves this emblem of the past, the past does not leave Junior. The first phase, lasting almost two minutes and eleven seconds, employs twenty-seven shots, an average of about five seconds per shot.

Many shots are long—two last more than fourteen seconds each—as befits a reexamination of the past.

Whereas phase 1 dramatizes the past in the present, phase 2, which lasts two minutes and 12.6 seconds, slightly longer than phase 1, dramatizes a pastless or past-destroying present. With much bulldozing activity in the area, loud noise saturates the sound track as Junior drives to the construction site. The dramatic thrust of this phase consists of Junior's futile effort to find his father, during which he has a showdown with a bulldozer driver while other bulldozers destroy Ace's house.

As Junior's car drives by, the camera pans land-clearing machines, conveyor belts, and steam pipes. A soil-sifter piles mounds of earth so high that, in another shot, they eclipse the car and show only the top of the horse-trailer attached to it. He pulls up alongside a man in a hard hat, wearing a dark visor and an air-filter to protect his nose and mouth from the dust. He whistles, barely audibly above the din, to gain the worker's attention. Peckinpah cross-cuts medium close-ups of the two, who shout above the noise: "Have you seen Ace Bonner?" "Who?" "Ace Bonner!" "Never heard of him!" Junior nods and salutes him in thanks. A cylindrical machine turns and churns, bulldozers with rocky soil in their scoops commute, and Junior drives to find another man who might know his father's whereabouts.

Moving to the climax of this phase, the destruction of the house and the showdown, Peckinpah intercuts a bulldozer, its scoop loaded with soil, Junior noticing something else, and what he sees: a bulldozer passes in front of Ace's house, and Ace's mailbox, in the foreground, is knocked down by its scoop. He turns to the front of his car to see a scoop coming toward him (which identifies him with the mailbox) and behind it a man in a hard hat and sunglasses. Peckinpah cuts from Junior's car, from the viewpoint of the bulldozer in the foreground, moving toward it, to the scoop from Junior's viewpoint, moving toward him. The bulldozer stops.

The dramatic showdown commences, the threat to Junior paralleling the destruction of what symbolizes his father. Junior rises to let the driver know he is in the car. The driver, the glare of the sun behind him making it impossible to see the features of his face, leans forward, elbows on the wheel. Peckinpah cuts to a close-up inside Ace's house of the roof caving in, as a bulldozer knocks down the beams; then to Junior calling to the driver of the bulldozer in front of him, his voice inaudible because of the roar of the machines; next to the driver, looking impassively at Junior; then to a bulldozer destroying Ace's house, the roof continuing to cave in and the front of the house collapsing; then to the driver facing

Junior, shifting a gear, which suggests a threat. Junior sits, backing down. The bulldozer moves forward. Junior backs up his car. Directly, Peckinpah cuts to two shots of bulldozers demolishing Ace's house, then to Junior backing off at the onslaught of his bulldozing opponent. Dramatic conflict intensifies. Within two and a half seconds, the director intercuts a close-up of the impassive driver of the vehicle facing Junior, a medium close-up of Ace's house collapsing, a close-up of a bulldozer continuing to destroy the house, and a close-up of the house capsizing. He next cuts to Junior's car backing up as the bulldozer before it empties rocks from its scoop, then intercuts a medium shot of another bulldozer attacking the house from the rear, scooping up its remains from the bottom, which makes the house fall, and counterpointing the fall, a close-up of the scoop that faces Junior, which rises to obscure the unemotional face of its driver. Peckinpah continues to intercut the bulldozer that threatens Junior with the bulldozers that raze Ace's house. When Junior is at a safe distance from his antagonist, he observes the debris of the house. In the last shot of phase 2, a bulldozer drives over what was Ace's home.

The present consists of destruction and the threat of destruction. The director edits sixty-six shots into the two minutes and 12.6 seconds of phase 2, averaging two seconds per shot, which is 40 percent faster than the average shot in phase 1. In the present, destruction is swift and ruthless, and individuals are indistinct and not allowed to stand in the way of the future.

In a ten-and-a-third-second recapitulation of the first two phases, phase 3 shows the past and present in tension. In the most rapid intercutting so far, Peckinpah has Junior look at the remains of Ace's house (present); its roof collapse at the assault of a bulldozer (immediate past); the black-and-white picture, propped against the radio, of Ace in action at the rodeo (recent past); another view of the house collapsing (immediate past); the house intact, before destruction (further past); the house continuing to collapse (immediate past); and a view of the house intact, before destruction (further past). In a moment, Peckinpah cuts to a more distant past, Ace on a horse, using a lasso, at a rodeo, then to the house being destroyed in the immediate past, next back to the more distant past, Ace in action at a rodeo, before, finally, a bulldozer knocking down Ace's mailbox. Over the last three shots—four-tenths of a second, half a second, and 1.43 seconds, respectively—Ace's voice insists, "Only costs five thousand dollars, Curly!" His voice, in the present, states a brutal reality, price in dollars. In this brief, ten-second phase, seven of the thirteen shots last half a second or less. In phase 3, Peckinpah's signature method of editing—short takes cut together to create a striking impression, but without slow-motion insets—time fragments, collapses, and regathers into a unified whole. The past and present before Junior's eyes reflect the tension of past and present in his existence, which he is about to put on the line at the rodeo. In phase 3, the average shot is .79 seconds, less than 40 percent shorter than the average in phase 2, itself 40 percent shorter than that of phase 1. The tempo of the sequence accelerates, implying with thematic aptness that time may be running out for Junior.

Following this sequence of destruction are two shots: the exterior of Scott Community Hospital in Prescott, Arizona; and a room in the hospital, with Ace in bed, a bandage on his head (a coupling of injuries to the man and his house), and his other son, Curly, in the foreground. In both, Ace concludes the speech begun at the end of the sequence just analyzed: "I don't need a penny more, and I wouldn't take it if you dropped it playing solitaire." Whereas the start of the speech emphasizes cost, which is the present, its continuation emphasizes the past, which is independence. Their tension is unresolved until the end of the movie. Unlike Ace's house and mailbox, and like Junior, Ace has not been destroyed, merely injured. Although he is temporarily down (he is in the hospital, not the morgue), he is not out, and like Junior he vigorously fights for his future.

The destruction of Ace's house, with Junior Bonner's prudent backing-off in a showdown with a representative of the force that destroys it, is violent but not lethal. This violence devastates property, which symbolizes its (former) owner, and threatens to wreck the spirit of him and his older son. A remarkably well made sequence, it is emblematic of major themes in this expertly directed film.

* * *

Although the first hour and a half or so of *Junior Bonner* is a preparation of the sequence in which Junior rides the bull Sunshine for the second time, a three-minute-and-twelve-second sequence immediately precedes the dramatic eight-second ride, which lasts forty seconds of real time. The preparatory sequence is almost five times longer than the turbulent, climactic ride. Unlike the violent climaxes of *The Wild Bunch* and *Straw Dogs*, no one is injured or killed in the high point of *Junior Bonner*, although the possibility of injury exists. Unlike the violent denouement of *The Wild Bunch* and like that of *Straw Dogs*, that of *Junior Bonner* ends in triumph for the protagonist. After its bull-riding climax is a one-minute-and-three-second epilogue that depicts the waning violence of the ride, which does not end after eight (or forty) seconds, and makes the title character's success resoundingly joyous. The subject of *Junior Bonner* and the nature of its violence result in directorial treatment that differs from the handling of violence in these other movies.

The preparatory sequence divides into three phases, each of the last two faster in tempo than the previous. Phase 1 begins with Junior preparing for the ride by stretching his rope to maximum tautness, while Buck's voice orders the raising of the bull pen. Ending with Charmagne watching Junior just before he climbs to the top of the starting gate, it edits twenty-seven shots into one minute and twenty-nine seconds, averaging 3.296 seconds per shot. Peckinpah primarily alternates shots of Junior stretching his rope while watching Sunshine as the bull moves down the narrow chute, ferociously kicking it to free himself, to the starting pen, labeled "1," which indicates his championship status (no cowboy has ridden him for eight seconds, and in the opening credits he throws Junior). Peckinpah intercuts Sunshine in the pen, butting himself against its iron gates; Junior watching him as a voice orders, "Let's go, J.R."; and cowboys lassoing a calf, a reminder that the rodeo is on. As Junior adjusts a spur and looks up at Buck, who warns him, seriously but affably, "Better pull your hat down today, pard," suspense increases. Few shots are as short as one second, and the shot of Buck walking to the chute, Junior pulling his hat down tighter on his head, and heading to the starting pen lasts fourteen seconds.

Phase 2 starts with Junior climbing the starting gate to position himself to mount Sunshine and ends with a long shot of spectators just before the first bull charges from the gate into the arena. It edits eleven shots into twenty-four seconds, averaging 2.18 seconds per shot, a tempo over a third faster than that of phase 1. The camera intercuts Junior's preparations with shots of Sunshine, one an extreme close-up of each of his threatening eyes as he turns his head; shots of riders preparing themselves; and shots of spectators. Two shots are one second each, the rest two and three seconds each. Tension accumulates.

Phase 3 of the preparation commences when the first bull, rider upon him, bolts from the pen into the rodeo ring and ends with Junior, on Sunshine, nodding a signal for the gate to open. It edits forty-two shots into fifty-nine seconds, averaging 1.4 seconds per shot, over twice as fast as that of phase 2. Violent images begin the third phase: six shots of four riders on bulls who charge out of the gate, bucking as they do so. Peckinpah cuts to Junior above Sunshine, then to a close-up of him tightening his rope around the bull, then to fourteen shots of different riders fiercely, bruisingly bounced on bucking bulls, all in slow motion, which create a tension between the physical danger of the riders and the aesthetic beauty of their springing up and down. He intercuts these slow-motion scenes with such shots as Junior blowing into his glove to inflate it and cushion his hand when he holds the rope that is around the bull, Sunshine's threatening eyes, Junior's face, and his tightening the rope to get a firmer grip. He cuts to a slow-motion shot of the full body of a bucking bull who has thrown his rider—the strength, power, and triumph of this bull increasing the suspense. He intercuts shots of the crowd, Buck, and Charmagne with shots of Junior's preparation; then a slower-motion grainy shot of Junior's memory of the rodeo in the credit sequence in which, thrown by Sunshine, he holds onto the rope as the bucking bull whirls him around before he lands on the ground; next, cuts to two shots of Junior in the present, a return to the flashback, and cuts to Junior again in time present, giving the signal to open the gate.[39]

In the climax, Junior rides Sunshine for eight seconds, which Peckinpah, as noted, elongates. He intercuts simultaneous action shots; cross-cuts the ride, a stopwatch held by a rodeo official's hand, and spectator reactions (groups of the anonymous audience in the stands, Buck, Charmagne, Red Terwilliger, and rodeo hands we have seen); places two slow-motion scenes of Sunshine bucking Junior (two seconds and 1.7 seconds) between normal-speed scenes not of Junior on the bull but of Buck, Charmagne, and a stopwatch. He oscillates between close-ups of Junior's face while Sunshine bucks and a two-second flashback, in slower motion than time present, of Sunshine whirling him in the previous rodeo. At the climax, he intercuts 1.5-, 1.4-, and 3.3-second slow-motion shots of J.R. successfully riding the bucking bull with shots of spectators, Buck, Junior's face, and the stopwatch going from seven and a half to eight seconds, confirming Junior's success. He cuts to a shot that begins, in real time as well as dramatic time, at the final moment of the last movement of the stopwatch: a three-tenths-of-a-second shot of the blasting horn that indicates the end of eight seconds.

Peckinpah deftly uses the stopwatch for suspense. Eight-tenths of a second after he shows Sunshine charging from the pen, but dramatically simultaneously with this shot, the second hand moves from zero to half a second. In a shot of the second hand going from two to three seconds—starting in close up, the camera moving closer—the real time goes from 17.7 seconds after the ride has started to 18.9 seconds. In extreme close-up, the second hand is at three and a half seconds, real time twenty-three and a half seconds. In very extreme close-up, the second hand moves from six to six and a half seconds, real time from 32.1 to 32.8 seconds. The final shot of the stopwatch ends at eight, really 39.7 seconds.

In this sequence, the director edits thirty-five shots into forty seconds, averaging 1.14 seconds per shot, a slightly faster tempo than the last phase of the preparation.

The epilogue—which starts immediately after the horn blows and ends with the rodeo cowboys congratulating, cheering, and surrounding Junior and Charmagne, who has descended from the stands into the arena and holds hands with him, obliterating them from view—edits twenty-eight shots into one minute and three seconds, averaging 2.25 seconds per shot, rapidly decelerating the tempo, as befits the triumphant aftermath. Amid shots of cheering spectators rising in acclamation, and of Buck, Charmagne, and Red, Peckinpah intercuts slow-motion shots of Junior wheeling atop the still-bucking bull before being thrown off. The violence of his hitting the ground, a nine-second shot in normal speed, which makes the fall seem unusually hard, is tempered by Junior's hands breaking his fall, a broad grin on his face, his painless rise in triumph, and the rodeo announcer's voice, "J.R. has done it! The first man ever to ride old Sunshine, and what a dandy ride it was!" Physically, emotionally, and thematically, Junior's rise is underscored by the cheers of the spectators and by the announcer's statement, which continues in subsequent shots, confirming Junior's victory and paying tribute, "This is some way to end the Eighty-fourth Frontier Days rodeo. I think you'll agree with me that after eighty-four years they still make cowboys as tough as they ever did." The congratulations of J.R.'s peers unmistakably mark Junior's triumph, which reverberates as a success over the bulldozers that razed his father's home earlier, an achievement over the supposed progress they and his brother Curly represent, and an affirmation of the way of life he and his father symbolize, in which an individual reveals his mettle. Unlike Peckinpah's previous dramatizations of violence, his depiction of the violence in this rodeo contest conveys jubilation, not terror or desperation; and his use of camera and editing techniques, as well as dramatic tempo, enhances the effect.

* * *

Peckinpah dramatizes the violent deaths of the title characters of *Pat Garrett and Billy the Kid* unlike his other dramatizations of violence. This section analyzes the shootings of Garrett and Billy, and the reprise of the former after the latter. While these dramatizations also differ from each other, stylistic and thematic bonds connect them. In both, the title characters take the fatal bullets and fall in slow motion, in contrast to the surrounding scenes, which are in normal speed. In both, largely through the graceful beauty of slow motion, the violence of their murders seems less brutal than other violence—the shooting of chickens in the first sequence, the beating of Poe in the second. Although Billy has been dead more than two dozen years when Garrett is killed, the director's editing connects him with Garrett's death; and although Garrett has over two dozen years to live when he kills Billy, the director suggests that in shooting Billy, Garrett destroys a bit of himself. Partly through pacing, partly through the movement of the actors, and partly through slow guitar music, the tempo of events leading to Billy's death is languorous, which suits the elegiac aura the film exudes. As is customary with Peckinpah, the manner reflects the matter.

In the first part of the opening title sequence of the director's restored version of *Pat Garrett and Billy the Kid,* but not in the mutilated version the studio originally released, Garrett is killed by forces we later learn were responsible for his killing Billy. In charge of Garrett's ambush is Poe, who served as deputy of the governor and big landowners when they demanded the Kid be killed, and who was with Garrett when Garrett killed Billy. Lasting three minutes and forty seconds, intercutting seventy-one shots, averaging more than three seconds per shot, this sequence starts the movie and ends with an entrapped chicken's final death spasms a second and a half after the trapped Garrett's final death spasms. The tempo begins slowly, the first cut lasting 21.9 seconds; accelerates as Garrett and chickens are shot; decelerates when Garrett, in a flashback, joins Billy; and increases when the director intercuts the killing of Garrett and chickens.

The sequence begins with a long shot of a semiarid landscape, cacti in the foreground. In the background, a wagon (with Garrett and a driver), beside several men on horseback (one of them Poe), moves toward the camera. Startlingly, the film lacks color. It looks not like a sparkling black-and-white print but like a movie that is ashen or blanched—as if life, like color, had been drained from it. Accenting this quality by contrast, a legend appears in bright red: "Near Las Cruces, New Mexico 1909." In a few subsequent shots, the sky seems wanly blue and Garrett's face has a slightly pallid complexion.

In the first long cut, and in the eight that follow, the latter totaling about thirty-five seconds, Garrett and Poe argue while a man with a rifle, lying in ambush, enshadowed by an immense cactus, inches forward and the driver of Garrett's wagon, on the pretext of fixing the harness, stops and descends.

Garrett: I thought I told you not to run them sheep on my land.

Poe: It's my land, Garrett. It became mine when we signed that lease.

Driver: He's right, Mr. Garrett.

Garrett (to the driver): I'm paying you off when we get back, *(to Poe)* and I'm breaking that goddamned lease.

Poe: I don't allow the law would agree to that.

Garrett: What law is that? Santa Fe Ring law? Shit! The goddamned law is ruinin' the country.

"Ain't you still a part of that law?" asks Poe. "I believe they elected you and paid you good wages fer killin' the Kid." "You rotten son of a bitch!" exclaims Garrett. This opening dialogue adumbrates contradictions inherent in one title character—a man who is part of the law intends to break a legal document and condemns the law—and it throws the audience off balance by indicating that he killed the other title character.

Three seconds after the man by the cactus rises and aims his rifle at Garret, the movie cuts to a shot, in color, of walls with an open gate, behind which are adobe buildings, horses, and people. Another legend, also in bright red, appears: "Old Fort Sumner, New Mexico, 1881." The film cuts to a five-second close-up of a chicken buried up to its neck in a mound of earth, then to a five-second medium-long shot of a group of men, Billy the Kid among them but indistinguishable from them. Peckinpah intercuts shots of a row of chickens buried to their necks and a medium shot of the men, notably Billy. Billy now stands out from the others partly because he is in center screen and partly because, unlike the others, dressed as cowboys, he wears a black hat, black jacket, and black string tie—a garb that, like Hamlet's inky cloak, suggests death.

In a virtuoso montage, Peckinpah intercuts 1881 color shots with 1909 uncolored shots, visually implying a connection, creating tensions, and raising dramatic questions the film must resolve. For example, after Billy, in 1881, aims his pistol at a chicken, the man with the rifle, in 1909, aims at Garrett; in slow motion, Garrett reaches for his rifle, whereupon Billy shoots, smoke issuing from the pistol; then, in slow motion, Garrett is shot in the heart. After the man with the rifle shoots toward screen right, smoke coming from the barrel as the bullet passes through, an 1881 chicken is blown to bits by a bullet, its feathers flying amid dust. Since post hoc (chronological progression) suggests propter hoc (causality), the 1881 Billy, in color, and the 1909 man with the rifle, colorless, seem to shoot each other's target, Billy hitting Garrett, the rifleman killing the chicken. Going further, Peckinpah suggests through montage that Garrett is caught in crossfire between the 1909 gunmen—the rifleman shooting toward screen right, the driver shooting a pistol toward screen left, and Poe shooting a pistol toward the audience—and the 1881 Billy, shooting toward screen left. The bullet hitting Garrett directly follows the shot from Billy's pistol, which is followed by the rifleman's shot. More montages sustain these visual impressions: a shot of Garrett taking the driver's bullet is followed by a shot of another chicken exploded by a bullet; after Billy shoots, Garrett falls from the wagon; after Garrett tries to rise from the ground, dust settles on chickens; one of Billy's gang shoots and Garrett takes a bullet. Although we know we are witnessing cinematic slight-of-hand, we also know that dramatic linkages are established and we expect them to become clearer. Such linkages and expectations increase when a freeze-frame after Garrett's head starts to fall backward has a voiceover by one of Billy's gang, "That got him damn near perfect," which refers to a chicken but which, in the different visual context, seems to refer to Garrett. We see Garrett caught in crossfire between what the 1909 rifleman, driver, and Poe represent (the law and the Santa Fe Ring, which had Garrett kill Billy) and what Billy represents, and we anticipate answers to dramatic questions that Peckinpah's cinematic montage raises.

Directly after the 1909 freeze-frame and 1881 voiceover, the director cuts to 1881, when a younger Garrett rides into old Fort Sumner with Deputy Bell, sees the gang sporting at target practice, dismounts, and aims his rifle. After several cuts between Garrett aiming and a rear view of Billy and Beaver, as if they were his target, Garrett shoots. Billy and the gang turn in surprise and fear, only to discover that Garrett, like them, is shooting chickens. Peckinpah juxtaposes 1909 Garrett in his final death spasm (in slow motion), 1881 Garrett lowering his rifle, and the body of a decapitated chicken in its death throes, smoke rising from its body as Garrett says in a voiceover, "Hello, Bill," the montage continuing to imply that Garrett, like the chickens, is trapped. He also reveals that Garrett and Billy are friends. They shake hands in fellowship and adjourn for a drink and chat, during which Garrett reveals that in five days he will officially become sheriff and be obliged to capture or kill Billy, whom he urges to leave the territory before this happens.

As mentioned, the sight of helpless chickens blown apart by bullets creates a more violent impact than the slow-motion death of the ambushed man, partly because the former is repeated and executed with loud gunfire on the soundtrack, partly because of the aesthetic beauty that relatively long slow-motion shots impart to Garrett's expiration, and partly because the frames of other slow-motion shots of it freeze for seven and even eleven seconds while credits appear, enabling us to enjoy the artistic composition. Furthermore, the use of Garrett's death as a framework to tell a story that happened twenty-eight years earlier establishes a remove, whether one considers it aesthetic distance or Brechtian alienation, between the audience and the major story of 1881. Either way, we become, as Michael Bliss observes, "more distant from the characters" and are thereby "prevented from totally identifying with them."[40]

* * *

Reviewing the restored director's print of *Pat Garrett and Billy the Kid* in 1989, J. Hoberman accurately calls its unique flavor "elegiac" and "terminally autumnal."[41] The lassitude and almost sorrowful somnambulism with which Peckinpah endows the sequence in which the Kid is ambushed and shot distinguish no other feature film by Peckinpah. In dramatizing the Kid's entrapment and death, he devotes more than twelve minutes of the fourteen-minutes-and-fifteen-second sequence to the slowly paced, stealthy ambush, and he emphasizes the tempo by wistful guitar music. The sequence divides into four phases.

Phase 1, in which Garrett prepares the ambush with Poe and Sheriff McKinney, begins when they ride from Rupert's saloon-whorehouse to Fort Sumner and ends when they position themselves for the kill while Billy beds down with Maria in old Pete Maxwell's house. This phase lasts five minutes and twenty-six seconds and employs forty-five shots, averaging 7.24 seconds per shot. One shot of the men riding takes over twenty-two seconds; a shot of Alias telling Billy that Garrett is on his way lasts almost twelve seconds; and three shots in which Eno and Beaver watch Billy, Alias joins them, and Billy ruminates, consume seventeen and a half seconds.

As the trackers move mournfully but inexorably toward what is inevitable, the tracked waits patiently. When the pursuers arrive at a spot overlooking Fort Sumner, they seem uneager to do what they came to do, their attitude resonating the reluctance with which Billy and Alamosa Bill, who meet by chance, fight each other. In two shots lasting twenty-one seconds, the trio appears to sleepwalk a few steps, then stops, as if loath to go forward.

McKinney: I'd just as soon ride in, get it over with.
Poe: He ain't gonna be there anyway.
McKinney: Hell, I don't have nothing against the Kid. Saving, maybe, he killed J. W. Bell.
Garrett: Yep.
McKinney: Sure did like J.W.

Poe seems to seek an excuse not to go to where the Kid is, McKinney's second statement belies his first, and Garrett utters his monosyllable so sadly as almost to nullify its affirmation.

When Billy and Maria enter Maxwell's house to copulate, the old man's weariness, the director's unhurried pace, the slow guitar accompaniment in the background, and the subject of Maxwell's memory provide ironic discords to a life-affirming act. After giving them permission to use his bunk, the old man meanderingly reminisces about a sneaky murder, during which, as Peckinpah intercuts shots of him with Billy and Maria, they leave him, walk down the hall, and enter a bedroom. He recalls a cattle drive that is apposite to the antagonism of Garrett and the Kid. "Recollect the time Toddy Sparks got his horse stole. Jace Summer stole it. Just up and stole it." As Billy and Maria leave and enter the bedroom, the old man continues. "Was up by Del Rio. Old Toddy got even, though. He sure did. Put a rattler in Jace's blanket. Bit him through the neck. Buried him in a thunderstorm. Summer of '71." Peckinpah intercuts shots of Billy and Maria undressing with shots of the trackers. Two takes lasting ten seconds each show Poe and McKinney carefully and fearfully walking through the night, like avengers (paralleling Toddy Sparks) stalking out of shadows, toward Maxwell's place.

In the second phase, Garrett, Poe, and McKinney move in for the kill. It lasts six minutes and thirty-six seconds and has eighty-five shots, an average of 4.66 seconds per shot, a bit more than 2.5 seconds faster than the average shot in phase 1, thereby increasing the tempo.

Phase 2 opens with a twenty-five-second minidrama that reveals Poe's cowardice and brutality. Outside a bedroom, a net barely concealing it from the hallway, Poe sees the naked back of a man embracing a whore, his lower body covered by a blanket. Thinking the man is Billy, Poe enters apprehensively. When the man—Luke, one of Billy's gang—turns, castigates him for voyeurism, shrewdly suspects he may be looking for Billy, and moves for his gun, Poe pistol-whips him unconscious, then recoils, frightened by what Luke almost did, what he just did, and perhaps what lies ahead.

Outside, McKinney and Garrett move stealthily in the dark, like rattlesnakes slowly and silently positioning themselves to strike, their movements intercut with Billy and Maria continuing to undress and getting under the blankets. Garrett encounters a coffinmaker, Will, beside a small coffin, as if for a child—perhaps a surrogate (like Will's name) for the Kid. Will insults Garrett, "I thought you'd be out pickin' shit with the chickens, cuttin' yourself a tin bill [a tin, star-shaped sheriff's badge]," and calls him a "chicken-shit, badge-wearing son of a bitch," which as Bliss notes, invokes the opening credit sequence that intercuts the killing of chickens and of Garrett.[42] Between Will's insults is a sound admonition, "When are you goin' to learn you can't trust anybody, not even yourself, Garrett," advice that, we have seen, Garrett does not take in 1909.

Ignoring Will, Garrett goes to the gate of Maxwell's house. In a thirteen-second shot that conveys caution and reluctance, he stands by the gate, opens it, pauses, and slowly enters. As he walks on the porch toward a rocker, he hears Billy and Maria make love. "Jesus," says Billy, twice. Peckinpah cuts to the couple kissing, then back to Garrett, who (his motive is ambiguous) steadies himself on the rocker or prevents it from making noise when he sits on it, and quietly rocks as he listens, allowing his friend not a last supper but a final sexual banquet before death. When Garrett hears Billy tell Maria, after coitus, that he is hungry and will go to the porch cooler for food, Garrett leaves to enter the house by another door. What emerges from this episode, which intercuts Billy's lovemaking with Garrett's sad, hypnotized face, is Garrett's affection for the man he must kill, his disinclination to shoot him in the back, and possibly his hope that one of his companions will do the job instead.

In a five-second shot, as Poe sits on the porch and McKinney on a bench, McKinney is startled by the sound of Billy opening the cooler door; in an eight-second shot, McKinney, who could draw his gun and shoot Billy, whose back is to them, fearfully whispers, "I think it's the Kid. Right there. Go on, shoot 'im"; Poe nervously rises. Peckinpah cuts to a two-second shot of the three men, then to a three-second close-up of Poe, who is obviously scared. After intercutting shots of Garrett watching Maria in bed, the director returns to the men outside. "Go on, shoot 'im," McKinney urges Poe, again in a whisper. "Who the hell are you?" asks old Maxwell when Garrett enters the parlor. Drawing his gun, Billy asks the two men on the porch, "Quién es?"—his question paralleling Maxwell's question to Garrett, which ironically, and therefore without triteness, translates Billy's phrase before he utters it. "Easy," the terrified Poe cautions Billy, recognizing that he has lost his moment, "we come to see Pete Maxwell." Reverberating Will's denunciation of Garrett, McKinney whispers to Poe, "You chicken-shit bastard."

In phase 3, Pat Garrett kills Billy the Kid. Employing twenty-five shots in forty-two and two-thirds seconds, it averages 1.7 seconds per shot, a rapid escalation of tempo from the 4.66 average of phase 2, the contrast giving an impression of extraordinary speed (actually, it is almost two times slower than the final shoot-out of *The Wild Bunch*).

The phase begins with Billy backing into the house to ask Maxwell who is outside. Once he turns, he sees Garrett and smiles, perhaps recognizing he should have guessed that the men on the porch were associated with Garrett, perhaps relieved that the inevitable is about to occur. Peckinpah cuts to Garrett shooting him, flame bursting from the barrel of his pistol as the bullet passes through (whereas in the opening credit sequence in which Garrett and chickens are killed, smoke, not fire, bursts from pistols and rifles). The flame of the bullet that kills Billy intensifies the dramatic climax. In a three-quarter-second shot, in slow motion, Billy takes the bullet, but neither bullet hole nor blood is visible on Billy's naked torso, which adds to the aesthetic beauty of the elongated moment and minimizes its violence. The film intercuts reaction shots of Poe and McKinney, Maria, and Garrett with slow-motion cuts of Billy falling backward through the door and onto the porch. Garrett looks dazed by what he has done. When he sees himself in a mirror, gun in hand, he aims the pistol at his reflection. In the next shot, he fires, flame again emerging from his gun barrel. In the following shot, from a different angle, the mirror cracks. Peckinpah cuts to a two-second close-up of Billy's head hitting the porch floor in slow motion, to Garrett holding his gun, to Billy's lifeless head on the floor, and back to Garrett, who moves to screen right, revealing his reflection in the cracked mirror. As he moves, the bullet hole in the mirror passes from the left chest to the right, which reflects the real man's left, where his heart is. It is meaningful that Garrett shoots his reflection, for he and Billy mirror each other; but his movement that places the wound in his heart is more significant, for in dramatizing his recognition that he has killed part of himself, he visually compels the mirror to reflect this realization. Phase 3 ends with a shot of Billy's lifeless head on the floor.

The tempo decelerates in phase 4, an aftermath that lasts one minute and twenty-eight and a third seconds. It uses fourteen shots, an average of 6.3 seconds per shot, over four and a half seconds slower than the average shot in phase 3.

Both actions and reactions in the aftermath are surprising. Members of Billy's gang gather at the edge of the porch, but unlike *The Wild Bunch*, in which Mapache's followers shoot at those who are responsible for killing their leader, Billy's followers do not. They stare at Garrett in numbed silence, some disbelieving, others accusatory. Not quite believing he has committed the deed he tried to avoid, he looks down at Billy, saying, "I shot him. I shot the Kid." His statement validates his dreamlike, often dazed movements and actions. With a sadistic exhilaration that betrays his cowardice, Poe removes a knife from his pocket, brutally pulls Maria off Billy's body and thrusts her away, and prepares to cut off Billy's trigger finger. Garrett screams a drawn-out "No!" and stops Poe by twice hitting him on the head with his pistol and repeatedly kicking him. The impact of Garrett's treatment of Poe is more violent than his killing Billy, which parallels the opening sequence, wherein the killing of the chickens is more violent than killing Garrett. Furthermore, the ferocious attack on Poe indicates not only a response to an attempted desecration of the body of Garrett's friend, but a recognition of Poe, deputy of the governor and the landowners, as his true enemy. Garrett's action, which gives Poe a personal reason to hate him, connects his killing the Kid with Poe's killing him at the start of the film. As Poe cowers beneath him, Garrett states slowly and emphatically, "What you want and what you get are two different things." The thematic statement resonates virtually the entire film. Garrett wanted the Kid to leave the territory so he would not have to kill him. His slow, circuitous pursuit gave Billy, as Billy acknowledges, more than enough time to leave. What Garrett got was killing the Kid. We return to producer Gordon Carroll's phrase, quoted in chapter 2, "a man who doesn't want to run is being pursued by a man who doesn't want to catch him."

* * *

Whereas most of the film, notably the ambush and killing of Billy, is autumnal, winter arrives at the end of the film, with metaphoric suitability, when, following a coda, a white-haired Garrett is killed in an abbreviated reprise of its opening sequence. The coda and reprise last two minutes and twenty-eight seconds, have twenty-seven shots, and average 5.48 seconds per shot, almost two seconds slower than the aftermath to the death of Billy. As befits the conclusion of the film, the tempo decelerates.

The coda begins the next morning, immediately following the last shot of the previous sequence. The sequence ends when the final credits roll up a freeze-frame.

Why does Peckinpah film it? The movie could (and the print originally released did) end without the reprise, for the story concludes with Garrett's departure, in the coda, after he kills Billy. As indicated in this and the last chapter, *Pat Garrett and Billy the Kid* is "about" more than the plot. The connections between these men, and with the forces responsible for both deaths, need tying together, a resolution that Peckinpah provides.

At the start of the coda, a Mexican man, women, and children watch Garrett on the porch rocker, with (a later shot reveals) Billy's corpse laid out on a nearby table. These onlookers are not combatants and their gaze is quietly condemnatory. By killing the Kid, Garrett and the law more clearly become their enemy, and Billy, friend of Paco and the other Mexicans, one of their own. The sides are more clearly drawn. As if to affirm this, four shots lasting twenty-five seconds show Garrett taking his sheriff's badge, Alias watching him, Garrett putting on the badge, and Eno and Beaver observing him. He dons the symbol of, thereby becoming, the enemy. Poe, his face black and blue, looks resentfully at him, Poe's gaze relating to film-time earlier, chronological-time later, when he leads an ambush that kills Garrett. Their sides too are more clearly drawn.

As Garrett rides away, a Mexican boy—a kid, thereby analogous to the Kid—throws rocks at him. His action creates a symbolic rebirth that resolves the discord created by self-deception. Garrett is no longer the kid's or the Kid's friend, and Garrett must live with the knowledge that in killing the Kid he has killed a part of himself that made him different from and better than the other hired guns of the wealthy landowners.

The shot of Garrett riding away in 1881 slowly dissolves to one of the 1909 rifleman crawling along the shadow of a cactus and rising while Garrett's driver pretends to adjust a horse's harness. The reprise of this and eight other 1909 shots is a dialogueless condensation of more and longer 1909 shots at the film's start. As Bliss notes, one difference is that "the opening title's views of Garrett reacting to being shot are all, save one, eliminated."[43] In addition, since the number of these shots is three, a third of the shots in the reprise, they become more important than they were earlier, and since they are in slow motion, they more clearly than before link to the slow-motion death of Billy the Kid, seen only a few minutes before. Another difference, increasing this clarity and forming a different, single focus, the killing of Garrett, is that the reprise contains no shots of exploding chickens.

Moreover, the sequence of shots is different. A shot of Billy firing a pistol in 1884 was followed by Garrett taking a bullet in 1909, then by the rifleman shooting Garrett, but this time only the rifleman shoots, smoke coming from the barrel of his weapon, before Garrett is hit. Peckinpah cuts to the driver firing a pistol, smoke coming from the barrel, whereupon Garrett takes that bullet. Next, Poe aims his pistol at Garrett, but Peckinpah stops this shot after a third of a second, before Poe fires, suggesting that Poe, like the Santa Fe Ring he represents, has others do his killing, and underscoring the view depicted in the ambush and killing of the Kid, that

Poe is a coward. In fact, in the opening sequence, Poe shoots Garrett after his henchmen do, when Garrett cannot fight back. After the flash cut of Poe aiming at Garrett comes another flash cut, also a third of a second long, of the 1881 Billy aiming at a chicken, followed by a slow-motion shot of Garrett falling off the wagon, stopping when the frame freezes and final credits roll up.

The effect of the Poe/Billy flash cuts are twofold. As Bliss says, they repeat "the suggestion in the prologue about Poe succeeding to Billy's place as Garrett's traveling companion."[44] More important, the shot of free, spirited Billy may suggest Garrett's brief flash of lucidity, just before he expires, that in destroying Billy he obliterated his own independent spirit. What remains is what the opening credit sequence dramatizes, an unhappy old man, who we now see contrasts with contented old Pete Maxwell, and who instead of reminiscing as Maxwell did, grumbles churlishly and impotently against the law that opposed Billy and now opposes him. In the reprise, the independent spirit of Billy symbolically destroys the dependent, emotionally drained man that Garrett, by killing him, has become. The reprise solidifies and expands the dramatic and thematic questions raised in the prologue credit sequence and resolved in the aftermath to the slaying of Billy; and its tempi resemble the dramatic tempo of each, in reverse order, as the film ends cyclically, with the ambush and execution of Pat Garrett.

* * *

The members of Corporal, then Sergeant, Steiner's platoon, in *Cross of Iron,* are not a wild bunch but are well-organized and highly disciplined, although like Pike Bishop's band they are an efficient team of killers. Emphasizing these qualities, their first encounter with the enemy at the start of the film resembles neither the failed robbery that opens *The Wild Bunch* nor the carnage that concludes it, but the technically proficient, successful train robbery that is the centerpiece of the earlier movie. In both, violence is less important than professional expertise. To adapt the title of and a phrase in the film Peckinpah made just before *Cross of Iron,* Steiner and his men are elite killers who plan properly and perform proficiently.

The treatment of violence in *Cross of Iron* derives from its subject, World War II, which differs from the director's other dramatizations of violence not only because the battles are modern warfare, but also because war has no personal attachments or conflicts between combatants and because its focus is unconfined. The scale of killings in *Straw Dogs* and *Pat Garrett and Billy the Kid* is small, the conflicts highly personalized. Although the slaughter that concludes *The Wild Bunch* is massive, since one side consists of a small army, the other side has only four men. While the bulldozers that raze Ace Bonner's house are impersonal, the scale of devastation is minuscule and the house's destruction is shown from the viewpoint of Ace's son, which subjectivizes it. The attack by Steiner's platoon on a Russian cannon position, mentioned in the last paragraph, is a small, tightly focused skirmish. The machine-gunning of his men by fellow German soldiers at the film's end is extremely personal (Stransky wants Triebig to kill Steiner) and has a limited scope. Narrow in scale, the tank attack is personalized, for it focuses on the retreat of a small group of men we know.

For these reasons, the two violent scenes in *Cross of Iron* on which this section focuses are those of war in which shells and bullets are aimed at a base camp and whoever may be there, not at particular individuals, and both attack and counterattack hope to destroy as many as possible, whoever they may be. The stake of the German soldiers, the side on which the director focuses, is survival, which while personal to each of them, is impersonal to spectators because they see not only a few characters with whom, to a greater or lesser extent, they have become emotionally involved, but also many characters whom they have not seen before. The first of these scenes is the brief bombardment of the camp while Captain Stransky is on his way from the command bunker to his own bunker. The second is the first major Russian attack and German counterattack some forty minutes into the film.

The preparation of the short bombardment of the base camp, which lasts thirty seconds, begins when Captain Stransky reports to Colonel Brandt in the command bunker. The Russian army's shelling, which aims to soften the target before the major offensive, gets closer to the command post. When Stransky relates that his former commander, approving his transfer to the eastern front, called him a "'heroic horse's ass,'" Peckinpah cuts to a bomb exploding outside, then back to the bunker, where no one reacts except Stransky, who is new to the front. After a brief display of apprehension, Stransky laughs, seemingly at the epithet but really to dispel his nervousness and maintain a good facade before his commanding officer. He repeats the phrase and laughs again with false bravado. Peckinpah cuts to another bomb, which is closer, and Stransky reacts again, trying with greater effort to hide his anxiety and give the appearance of strength. After another, larger explosion, still closer to the bunker, and another nervous effort at bravado, Stransky leaves. Brandt asks his adjutant, Captain Kiesel, what he thinks of the new officer. "I feel he thinks he's on some kind of special mission," replies Kiesel, "that is, to achieve spiritual domination of his battalion, thereby symbolizing the purity of the great German Wehrmacht itself." As he speaks, he stands and sardonically concludes his words with his right arm raised in a "Heil Hitler" salute. A bomb punctuates it, shaking the bunker.

This bomb, which falls very close to the bunker and whose explosion Peckinpah continues to film outside, begins Stransky's first, direct experience of war beyond the relative safety of the command bunker. The sequence ends when he becomes aware that the bombardment has ceased, but he is not the focus and we do not experience it from his point of view. While the slaughter of war is random and the viewpoints of the shelling are varied, the director coherently organizes war's chaos, editing twenty-three shots into a twenty-seven-second sequence, an average of 1.17 seconds per shot. Framing this sequence with Stransky, to whom he returns after the shelling ends, he juxtaposes explosions, often less than a second long and usually emitting a flame or blinding flash upon impact, with different soldiers, to whom he also returns, and he mixes slow motion with normal speed. The bombs may strike randomly, but the intercutting among men who are hit or almost hit gives coherence to what might seem haphazard.

The sequence begins with a blinding explosion, not quite a second long, between barbed wire fences. Peckinpah cuts to Triebig and Stransky's driver dropping to the ground for cover while Stransky, in the background, walks toward the car; he then cuts to the interior of the command bunker, where Brandt ducks for cover. He cuts to another bomb, also with a blinding flash and also less than a second long, then to the bunker again, this time a shelf with a photograph of Hitler propped against the wall, which the explosion's impact sends falling between shelf and wall, stopping at a point that gives the appearance of the shelf severing the head at the neck, a striking symbol of impending defeat.

In the sequence's last twenty-three seconds, the director intercuts six individuals, groups, or sites with each other, and returns once to the bunker. In slow motion, a bomb explodes, throwing a soldier upward, heels over head, toward barbed wire in the foreground, the camera moving closer to him. Peckinpah cuts to Triebig on the ground before Stransky's car as, in normal speed, a bomb explodes with a flash behind it, killing a soldier and making Stransky duck as he continues forward, the camera moving with him. Peckinpah cuts to the bunker, where Kiesel, his hand still raised, continues to cry above the din, "as it [the German Wehrmacht] all goes down in defeat"; back to the soldier, who continues to fall in slow motion, feet upward, the camera moving still closer to him, as his body hits the barbed wire; then to a second soldier, his back to the camera, who runs, in normal speed, as a bomb explodes with a blinding flash, just to his right, knocking him down and killing him. He cuts to a third soldier, beside barbed wire, as a bomb explodes behind him with a flash, in slow motion, raising a heap of dust and hurling him against the wire. He cuts to outside a bunker, sandbags in the foreground, where in slow motion a bomb explodes with a flame atop the bunker, smashing and scattering the sandbags. He goes back to the third soldier, who in slow motion hits the barbed wire, knocking down the wooden fence to which it is attached. Peckinpah cuts to the car, behind which Stransky continues to walk as a bomb explodes with a flash, in slow but less-slow motion, throwing the door of another car into the air and Stransky to the ground; he then cuts to a different point of view, showing a truck upside down behind and screen right of Stransky, who hits the muddy ground in normal (but seemingly faster) speed, his helmet falling off. Peckinpah cuts to the third soldier who, in slow motion, continues his backward fall against the barbed wire fence, knocking it down beneath him; then to a bomb hitting a machine gun emplacement in slow motion, with a flame and deafening sound, hurling one of the gunners to the side and another forward and upside down over sandbags; then back to the first soldier, who continues to fall backward, in slow motion, arms on the ground, feet against the barbed wire; next to outside the bunker again, where in slow motion sandbags explode as another bomb hits them; then to the first soldier crashing through the barbed wire, debris falling upon him, this time in normal speed, which gives his hitting the ground greater impact; and finally to the machine gunners, who in slow motion continue to fall as debris drops and the smoke settles.

Peckinpah organizes his six exterior shots by returning at least once to all but one of them (the second soldier) and cutting to the interior of the command bunker once. He shows the Stransky site three times, the first soldier four times, the third soldier thrice, the sandbags twice, and the machine gun twice. Because he does not intercut them schematically, he preserves the effect of chaos; because he returns to them soon enough for the audience to recognize them, he organizes the chaos, creating the effect of bombardment, in which all hell seems to break loose, yet defining the effect artistically. This bombardment foreshadows the longer, more complex pandemonium of the major Russian offensive.

The aftermath begins with a different view of Stransky in the mud, aware that the bombing has stopped. It edits seven shots into twenty-one seconds, an average of three seconds per shot, less than half as fast as the bombardment. When the fury of war ends, the tempo immediately slackens, a relief to the spectators as well as to the participants. From Stransky in the mud, Peckinpah switches to Kiesel: "If they're the last of us, Stransky and Steiner, then God help us!"—a statement that anticipates the film's conclusion, in which these men join to become virtually "the last" to leave. In this aftermath, the focus is on Stransky, who dons his helmet and rises; but seven seconds after it starts is an almost five-second shot of the unmanned machine gun slowly turning in normal speed. The absence of the two gunners is an effective visual image of the slaughter.

* * *

The second sequence is the first major Russian offensive. It begins with the first kill, which is arbitrary (in battle, anyone might be first to die): Steiner frees the Russian boy he took prisoner, permitting him to rejoin his people, but a Russian soldier on his way to the German lines sees him and kills him. The sequence ends with another arbitrary hit: Steiner is struck by a shell while trying to save a German soldier who is fighting amid a small group of Russians. There is no linear progression or causality between the two. In terms of structure, these ironic events, each designed to save a life but each resulting in death or injury (the man Steiner drags to safety apparently dies and Steiner suffers a concussion), frame the sequence. Whereas the bullets that kill the boy begin the battle, the shell that hits Steiner and the man he tries to save does not conclude it. The sequence's end, like its beginning, is arbitrary. It ends when we learn all we need to learn about the fate of the protagonist.

The battle lacks the type of focus typical of Peckinpah's other films. The Russian onslaught seems to come from everywhere; its targets are everyone in the German camp; its resisters may be anywhere. The sequence makes audiences feel that they are in the midst of combat, experiencing the confusion, bewilderment, disorientation, and chaos of battle, ordeals that are augmented by smoke, the relentless din of different types of weapons, and the sight of familiar and unfamiliar men fighting, dying, and being wounded.

Particularly important, Peckinpah does not clarify the action by starting it with an establishing shot of the base camp. Unlike both the bank robbery and the final bloodbath of *The Wild Bunch,* the camp's geography is imprecise. One forested hill resembles another, and one machine gun fortification, bunker exterior, trench, or unfamiliar face in uniform is like another. Nor did the director provide an establishing shot of the base camp prior to this sequence. He is deliberately unspecific. We know that Steiner's men occupy a position on the camp's perimeter, but how far it is from other sites is unclear. We infer that a second field post, with Lieutenant Meyer in charge, is some distance behind Steiner's position, but we do not know how far; that Captain Stransky's bunker, a first field spot, is behind this post; and that command headquarters, Colonel Brandt's bunker, is in a more protected area deeper inside the lines.

The sequence is not structured as an attack followed by a counterattack. As in war, they merge. Peckinpah artistically binds the sequence by intercutting shots of the attack with shots of defense and counterattack, and by intercutting both with characters we know. We recognize Brandt, Stransky, Meyer, Steiner, and the members of his platoon by face, costume, makeup, or name: Kruger wears a woolen cap, not a helmet; Anselm and Kern wear no head covering; Schnurrbart has a large moustache; Maag is called by name. Contrasts also weld the sequence, chiefly one between Stransky and Meyer, a dissimilarity important to the plot: Meyer, without prompting, leads the counterattack, but Stransky is bewildered and must be ordered from his bunker to lead it, and whereas Meyer is killed, Stransky fears that a minor scratch is a major wound.

The sequence, six minutes and twenty-four seconds long, has 288 shots, an average of 1.33 seconds per shot. Its eight phases vary from each other subtly. The chief sources of variety are characters, weapons, sites, and tempi within each phase. Types of moving and fighting are slower or faster than each other, but phases in which bombs fall, men shoot, and soldiers kill or die are faster than sequences involving Stransky in his bunker, because a major contrast is his inaction (slow tempo) and the action of the men under his command (faster tempi).

In phase 1, which edits twenty-six shots into almost thirty-one seconds, an average of 1.19 seconds per shot, the offensive begins. Freed by Steiner, the Russian boy descends a hill in the forest. Steiner, alert, hears a sound. Peckinpah edits together shots of Russian soldiers, the boy, and Steiner watching and listening, most of which are at least a second long (one lasts three and a half seconds). When a Russian soldier sees the boy, mistakes him for the enemy, and shoots him, the pace accelerates with cross-cuts of the soldier firing his automatic rifle, the boy receiving the bullets and dying in both normal and slow motion, and Steiner perceiving what is happening. For example: the Russian fires, flame coming from the barrel of his weapon (less than half a second); the boy moves upward, taking the bullet (two-tenths of a second); he falls backward in slow motion (half a second); the soldier fires again, hitting him again (three-tenths of a second); Steiner reacts (four-tenths of a second); the boy continues to fall backward in slow motion (half a second); the Russian moves away (seven-tenths of a second); and the boy hits the ground in slow motion (two seconds). Phase 1 ends as Steiner screams in agony and runs back to his position, his awareness that the attack has commenced superseding his personal grief.

Beginning and ending with shots of advancing Russian troops, the thrust of phase 2 is their attack on German positions, of which we see Steiner's. Its twenty-seven seconds contain nineteen shots, averaging 1.42 seconds per shot. Peckinpah intercuts Russians advancing and firing with Steiner's men, in their camouflaged machine gun position, firing back. Throughout, bombs explode in or by defense positions. Only two shots, near the beginning, are in slow motion: both of Steiner running through a barbed wire path to reach his men's position. In the context of the bombardment, he seems to take an excruciatingly long time, although the two shots actually last about three and a half seconds and are intercut with a one-second shot of Russian soldiers advancing down a hill.

In marked contrast to the fighting is phase 3, the reaction of Stransky in his bunker. Although its twenty-one shots last about forty-three seconds, averaging slightly more than two seconds per shot, the average may be somewhat misleading, since shots of Stransky contrast with shorter shots of bombs falling on German machine gun positions, Russians advancing, and Steiner ordering his men to fall back. In phase 3, which begins and ends with Stransky, the focus is on him and shots of him last three to five seconds. At the start, he answers Brandt's phone call. A shot of Brandt asking, "Is it a probe, Stransky?" cuts to a shot of Russian soldiers moving down a hill from behind trees toward German positions, then cuts to Stransky confirming what we have seen: "A probe, sir? It's an attack." A bomb explodes outside his bunker and he ducks for cover; then another, knocking him down. Between cuts to Colonel Brandt and Russians advancing, Stransky—beneath a small table—continues, "It's not a probe, sir. It's an attack in force," and pleads, "Sir, counterfire is needed at once." Brandt's bunker is hit, and a bomb shatters a wooden beam, behind which is the photo of Hitler, repropped upright on the shelf. Peckinpah cuts to the Russian attack and Steiner's retreat before returning to three shots, lasting nine seconds, of Stransky and Brandt, most of the time focusing on Stransky. Trying to disengage himself from the table, he asks for help. "Be calm, Stransky, you are not alone," says Brandt. Pulling the table off, the unprotected Stransky insists, "What do you mean, I'm not alone, sir? I am alone. I am alone." His fear of abandonment and helplessness ends this phase.

In swift counterpoint, phase 4 films the fury of attack, framed by shots of advancing Russians. The quick cuts—sixteen shots in 20.4 seconds, averaging 1.275 seconds per shot—match the ferocity of the onslaught. As shells explode, Russians overrun Steiner's position, he and his men retreat (one wounded in the arm), and other Germans die. Yet the battle is not one-sided. A striking medium close-up of the hands of a German soldier passing a shell, the camera moving with them, to another German soldier, who drops it into a mortar, which fires, and a shot of its explosion among advancing Russians, are intercut with shots of Russians moving toward German positions and Germans firing and reloading machine guns and rifles.

In similarly rapid counterpoint, phase 5 returns to Stransky. This phase lasts slightly more than a minute and fifty-three seconds and uses seventy-seven shots, an average of just under a second and a half per shot. Although Peckinpah frames phase 5 with shots of Stransky, he intercuts Stransky inside and just outside his bunker with Meyers's position, into which Steiner's men retreat, and advancing Russians beyond it. As bombs and shells explode, and as machine guns and rifles fire, the attack, retreat, and counterattack mix dizzyingly. Actions of soldiers who know and do their job contrast with Stransky's successive inactivity, impotent activity, and retreat to safety.

During the first ten seconds, Stransky pleads that he does not know where Steiner or Triebig is, he becomes disoriented when a man who may be wounded or dead is brought in, and Brandt orders him to the central section. The next four and a half seconds intercut Russians advancing with Germans firing and being hit. Peckinpah cuts back to Stransky's bunker, where, in five seconds, Brandt orders him to prepare a counterattack quickly; then to a half-second shot of a bomb exploding in a blaze outside Stransky's bunker; back to a two-second shot of Brandt wearily starting to hang up the phone; next to seven seconds that show Meyer rallying troops for the counterattack while bombs fall, Russians advance, and Germans fire machine guns; and next to a three-second shot of Stransky trying to find his automatic rifle. Meyer's purposeful, rapid activity contrasts with the confused movements of the dazed Stransky, who does not even know where his weapon is, let alone how to prepare a counterattack.

Peckinpah intercuts Russians advancing, Steiner and his men running amidst falling shells, and Germans counterattacking, with a half-second insert of Stransky still in his bunker. He edits a swift montage of medium shots, all in normal speed, of the German counterattack: from below, a Russian soldier, hit by an exploding shell, is hurled upward (half a second); from the rear, another is hit and hurled upward (eight-tenths of a second); the first, moving upward, drops his rifle (four-tenths of a second); the second starts to fall (six-tenths of a second); the first starts to fall (half a second); another Russian runs quickly toward screen right (three-tenths of a second); the second continues to fall and hits the ground (one second); and more Russians race toward screen right (half a second). The montage combines the counterattack's effectiveness with the threat of the Russian advance, both conveying war's deadly fury.

Directly, Peckinpah returns to Stransky's bunker, where in a more than two-second shot Stransky takes a weapon. Not only has he not left the bunker, he seems to take a long time to perform a simple action. The director cuts to Russians advancing, then to other Russians jumping over Meyer's trench, then to Meyer exhorting his soldiers to return to their positions. He intercuts shots of Steiner's platoon shooting at Russians, Russians being hit, and Kern pressing Germans to go to their posts. He then contrasts Stransky's delay—rifle in hand, in the bunker, he orders his telegrapher, "Get that [broken] pole fixed" (2.3 seconds)—with Meyer acting: as a Russian leaps onto a German in the trench, Meyer stops other Germans from fleeing, pushing and ordering them back (1.9 seconds). The next two shots underscore the contrast: after Stransky begins to move out of the bunker, Meyer is in a hand-to-hand struggle with a Russian. A continuing montage further stresses Stransky's ineptitude in contrast with skilled soldiers: Russians attack; Stransky calls to no one in particular, "Take your positions!"; a German throws a Russian over his shoulder; Stransky yells to anyone in general and no one in particular, "Everybody, keep firing!"; Russians advance; Meyer shoots a Russian as the enemy jumps into the trench; and Stransky shouts, "Forward, men!" as they ignore him and retreat. Germans drop shells into a mortar, landing and exploding amid Russians; Russians advance and Germans are hit by bombs. The phase ends with Stransky retreating into his bunker, crying, "We are winning! We are winning!"—ironically, because while he may be right, he played no role in the victory.

Also ironically, phase 6, intercutting attack, retreat, and counterattack, films the war's increasing fury and dramatizes the death of the man responsible for the counterattack's success, Meyer. Its fifty-four shots consume a bit more than fifty-six seconds, an average of slightly over one second per shot.

Following Stransky's triumphant cry at the end of phase 5 is a montage of battle at the start of phase 6. In the seven-second montage, Peckinpah edits eleven shots of a group of Russians advancing down a hill, some hit by bullets (slow motion); a close-up of the barrel of a machine gun, shooting (normal speed); a bomb exploding while other Russians advance, hitting some of them (slow motion); Steiner and his men running and shooting (normal speed); the first group of Russians advancing and falling as they are hit (slow motion); the other Russians continuing to fall (slow motion); a close-up of the machine-gun barrel, firing (normal speed); the first group of Russians continuing to fall (slow motion); Steiner and his men still on the move (normal speed); the second group of Russians continuing to fall (slow motion); and the first group continuing to fall (slow motion). Next, the director moves inside the bunker, where Stransky, on the phone, pleads for air cover and tanks.

Peckinpah returns outside to dramatize battle frenzy, counterpointing violence and aesthetic beauty. Apart from slow motion alternating with normal speed and different slow-motion shots oscillating with each other, the same shot may combine downward and upward movements, such as one in which a Russian jumps into Meyer's trench, knocking him down, while another Russian, whom Meyer knocked down, rises. For a bit over twelve and a half seconds, eleven shots individualize a depersonalized war as Steiner arrives too late to save Meyer but soon enough to kill the man who kills him: a Russian, bayonet fixed to his rifle, moves to screen right (normal speed); Steiner and Schnurrbart move toward Meyer (slow motion); after knocking down one Russian soldier, Meyer turns to face the soldier with the bayonet, who starts to stab him in the stomach (normal speed); the bayonet enters his belly (close-up at normal speed); Steiner sees Meyer being killed (slow motion); bayoneted, Meyer falls (slow motion); Steiner starts to draw his revolver (slow motion); Meyer continues to fall, pushed by the man holding the rifle (slow motion); the rifle with the bayonet in Meyer shoots him, flame coming from the barrel (close-up at normal speed); as Meyer's feet go up and he falls backward, Steiner moves forward and shoots the Russian in the back (slow motion); releasing the rifle as Meyer continues to fall backward, the shot Russian lurches backward in the opposite direction (normal speed).

In phase 7, which starts with Russians advancing and ends with them retreating, Steiner's platoon counterattacks with apparent success while a bewildered Stransky bluffs. In slightly more than one minute and twenty-five seconds, Peckinpah edits sixty-six shots, averaging just under 1.3 seconds per shot. Again, the average is deceptive, since within the phase the battle outside alternates with Stransky inside, the latter shots lasting longer than the former.

After advance and counterattack fluctuate, with anonymous Germans hit by Russian bullets and shells, and Kruger and Kern efficiently slaying advancing Russians, Peckinpah cuts to the bunker, where in takes of 1.3 seconds to 2.1 seconds, Stransky, on the phone, tries to respond to Brandt's question, "Where is your counterattack?" In three shots using two camera set-ups, Stransky replies, one sentence per shot, "We are attacking. We are defending. We are counterattacking." The different shots from separate viewpoints mirror Stransky's disorientation. Outside, while Kern and Kruger continue fighting, Meyer, in an almost three-second, slow-motion shot, leans against a wall, drops his hands from his wound, and gradually expires.

Inside, Stransky remains on the phone with Brandt. In four oscillating shots between them, Stransky feels his left temple, looks at his hand, and with one line per shot (a voiceover when the camera is on Brandt), tells him, "I'm wounded, sir. Shall I continue? I know my duty, sir, don't worry. But I need more ammunition." The quickly shifting shots for each line reflect his disorientation and fear.

Outside, the counterattack seems successful. Shots of Anselm firing his automatic rifle alternate with shots of advancing Russians being hit. Intercut with them, Dietz notices that Meyer is dead, Stransky feels his temple again, and a German rushes from the trench to pursue a group of fleeing Russians. When Steiner witnesses the man's rash action, he leaps from the trench to bring him back. Schnurrbart reaches for a machine gun and Maag runs forward to feed it a clip of bullets to cover Steiner, who in slow motion shoots the Russians fighting the German, who is wounded, and picks him up, dragging him uphill on his back as Russian soldiers flee.

Phase 8, the final phase, contains nine shots in nine seconds. The beauty with which Peckinpah films this episode, in which Sergeant Steiner is hit by a shell, displaces the violence. In a slow-motion medium shot, a flame flares when a shell hits the ground, followed by flying dust; when it clears, we see that Steiner, hauling the German soldier, is hit, for he drops him, moving upward toward screen left while his burden falls downward toward screen right; another shell explodes in flame behind them and another in front, the flame from the latter obliterating them from sight; after they reappear, continuing their movements, another light bursts from another shell, obscuring them. In a medium close-up in very slow motion, the light turns blue as Steiner, at screen right, falls and looks up as he is hurled up again; with another hit, the light turns white hot, then red, blocking him from sight and showing shell fragments shattering. In very slow motion, the light fades as Steiner, in close-up at screen left, looks up and falls backward. A medium close-up in normal speed of Kiesel on the phone dissolves to an explosion, in normal speed, which causes a light to appear at lower screen left, soaking up the screen and blotting out Kiesel's face. The light dissolves to an extreme close-up, in very slow motion, of Steiner at screen right, looking toward screen left and falling. A cut to a medium close-up of Brandt in normal speed dissolves as the light of an explosion, at the bottom of the screen, obliterates his face. The light dissolves to an extreme close-up, in very slow motion, of Steiner, at screen left, falling down. Phase 8 ends when a hospital door opens, showing that phase 8 combines Steiner hit by one or more shells with his memory of the event.

The entire sequence, the first major Russian offensive, has no linear progress. Its vague plot (attack followed by counterattack) is less prominent or clear than the chaotic, disorienting violence of war. Peckinpah organizes the dramatic sequence not by linearity but by points of reference (characters and sites to which he returns), contrasts (chiefly, Stransky and Meyer), and ironic circularity (at the start, Steiner unwittingly causes the death of a Russian boy he tries to save; at the end, he is hit while trying to save a German man). Unlike *The Wild Bunch,* this film has nothing resembling catharsis. Whereas one might complain, as some critics have, that in making us like the members of the Bunch, Peckinpah has, willy-nilly, glorified violence, one can raise no such objection to this or any other sequence in *Cross of Iron,* which despite artistic beauty, utterly deglamorizes war, which Peckinpah shows to be inglorious.

* * *

Peckinpah dramatizes and films violence artistically, and he does so differently in separate films and in individual sequences of the same film. In both turbulent shootouts of *The Wild Bunch,* the conflicting forces have distinct objectives and obstacles, and the progress of battle proceeds in a clear, linear fashion, with the end of the second providing a catharsis. Similarly straightforward and sharply delineated, although not cathartic, is the exceptionally lengthy violent climax to *Straw Dogs,* in which the stakes rise, a potential defector becomes an ally, and the brutality steadily escalates as a real David defeats a group of symbolic Goliaths. In *Junior Bonner,* the destruction of a house becomes a surrogate for the destruction of a man, yet while property is razed, the man himself is merely bruised, thus may rise again, phoenixlike. In the same film, a man's triumph over a powerful animal who earlier defeated him affirms his purity, skill, manhood, and way of life. Symbolism more than savagery is created by the editing of the death of Pat Garrett at the start of *Pat Garrett and Billy the*

Kid, whose impact is less barbaric than the killing of chickens during this sequence; the symbolism is consonant with the linkage of the title characters and their opposition to the powers that hire Garrett to kill the Kid. A somnambulistic languor characterizes the dramatization of killing the Kid, which is consistent with the film's theme and the killer, who does not want to murder the man his job obliges him to slay. Unlike this film, in which character relations dominate, *Cross of Iron* is dominated by war, whose random, chaotic, and devastating slaughter is captured in both short and long scenes of combat. Although Peckinpah films none of these sequences as he films the others, all are unmistakably his. Style and attitude toward character and violence connect the artistry in which this director would, and does, give us some and more than some violence, a theme to which he is faithful.

Straw Dogs. The village louts, in the Sumner home, try to make David surrender Henry Niles. Scutt (Ken Hutchison), seated; David (Dustin Hoffman); Cawsey, the rat catcher (Jim Norton); Charlie Venner, Amy's former boyfriend (Del Henney).

Straw Dogs. After Cawsey has set the curtains on fire, Tom Hedden tries to aim his shotgun through the window at David (Dustin Hoffman), who raises the table as a barrier.

Straw Dogs. Between Scutt (Ken Hutchison), with a knife, and Charlie Venner (Del Henney), with a shotgun, are David Sumner (Dustin Hoffman) and his wife, Amy (Susan George).

Junior Bonner. At the Frontier Days parade, Junior Bonner (Steve McQueen) reminds his father, Ace (Robert Preston), that Ace is riding his horse.

Junior Bonner. Ace Bonner (Robert Preston) tells his wife, Ellie (Ida Lupino), that he is going to Australia.

Junior Bonner. At the rodeo, Ace Bonner (Robert Preston) and his son Junior (Steve McQueen) are in a wild cow-milking contest.

The Getaway. Just after the bank robbery, Doc McCoy (Steve McQueen) makes his getaway before diversionary explosives go off.

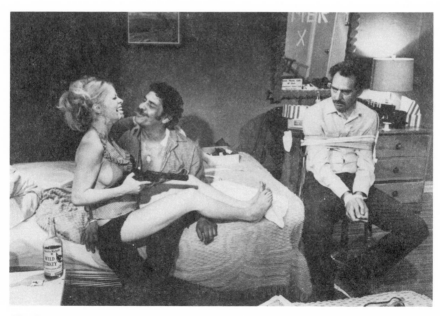

The Getaway. Fran Clinton (Sally Struthers) cavorts with Rudy (Al Lettieri) as her helpless husband, Harold (Jack Dodson), watches.

The Getaway. Doc McCoy (Steve McQueen) battles Beynon's men in the hotel.

Pat Garrett and Billy the Kid. After lunch, Alamosa Bill (Jack Elam) and Billy the Kid (Kris Kristofferson) prepare to duel. In the background are Horrell (Gene Evans) and his family.

Pat Garrett and Billy the Kid. One of Chisum's men whips Paco (Emilio Fernandez) while another prepares to rape Paco's daughter.

Pat Garrett and Billy the Kid. Pete Maxwell (Paul Fix) observes as Pat Garrett (James Coburn) kicks Poe (John Beck) after Poe has tried to sever Billy the Kid's trigger finger.

Bring Me the Head of Alfredo Garcia. Sappensly (Robert Webber) grieves over the body of Quill (Gig Young), killed by Alfredo Garcia's relatives.

Bring Me the Head of Alfredo Garcia. El Jefe's henchmen frisk Bennie (Warren Oates) before permitting him to drive into the compound.

The Killer Elite. After being wounded by his partner, Locken (James Caan) retrains himself for his profession.

Cross of Iron. After Sergeant Steiner (James Coburn) frees him, the Russian boy (Slavco Stimac), reciprocating Steiner's friendliness, returns Steiner's harmonica to him. In the film, he throws it to Steiner from a distance.

Cross of Iron. Sergeant Steiner (James Coburn) and Kern (Vadim Glowna) pass through their own lines disguised as Russian prisoners.

Cross of Iron. Captain Stransky (Maximilian Schell), accepting the leadership of Sergeant Steiner (James Coburn), agrees to be his entire platoon.

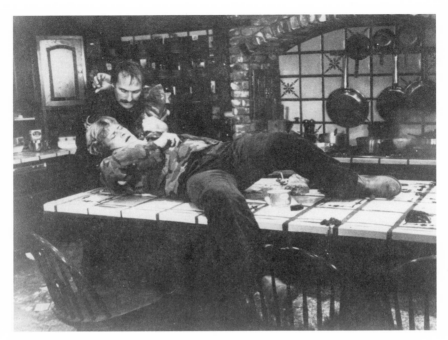

The Osterman Weekend. Bernard Osterman (Craig T. Nelson), trying to learn what is behind the events of the weekend, gains the upper hand in his fight with John Tanner (Rutger Hauer).

The Osterman Weekend. Maxwell Danforth (Burt Lancaster), head of the CIA, has presidential ambitions.

4

Continuing Companions

In his interviews, Sam Peckinpah gives the impression that *The Deadly Companions,* his first feature film, was an artistic disaster and an experience he wished had not occurred. When he refers to it, he either tersely dismisses it or else blames the scriptwriter and, chiefly, the producer, Charles FitzSimons, who tried to prevent him from changing the script.[1] Although Peckinpah regarded A. S. Fleischman's screenplay as "an unmanageable story" that was "all based on gimmicks," he nevertheless tried to manage it. "I offered my services as scriptwriter, which [FitzSimons] promptly refused."[2] Brian Keith, the leading actor (Yellowleg), with whom Peckinpah had worked on television, "knew we were in trouble, so between us we tried to give the thing some dramatic sense."[3] They "worked it out in such a way that we would be able to alter lines on the spot without letting anyone know and managed to get about twenty percent of the most awful bullshit out of the film."[4] But as FitzSimons forbade Peckinpah from even talking to Maureen O'Hara, the leading actress (Kit), "all of [Keith's] scenes worked, while all of hers were dead." After Peckinpah completed the first cut, FitzSimons assumed control of the editing and recut the film to make it seem that Turk (Chill Wills), not Yellowleg, shoots Billy (Steve Cochran).[5] But Peckinpah meticulously avoids blaming anyone except the writer and producer. When an interviewer calls Maureen O'Hara's performance "terrible," the director defends her: "I don't think her performance was terrible—she had a very difficult script to work with." When the same interviewer applauds the music, the director refuses to accept praise, since the score was part of the post-shooting phase from which the producer had excluded him: "I didn't like it. . . . I had nothing to do with that."[6]

Although the movie received mixed reviews, as Garner Simmons observes, "Peckinpah's notices were frequently better than the picture's." Simmons quotes the *Hollywood Reporter's* assessment that "he displays a genuine feel for drama and film" (6 June 1961) and *Variety's*, "an auspicious debut as a director" (7 June 1961).[7]

For the most part,[8] authors of books also give him more credit than he gives himself. Jim Kitses calls Peckinpah's dismissal of the picture as unworkable "surprisingly cavalier given how much of himself he got into the film," which Kitses labels "an astonishing first film, Peckinpah wholly dominating the material and overcoming the considerable problems," including peculiar psychology, poor dialogue, and "a shortage of physical action." The last item is surprising, since the movie includes a near-hanging, a bank robbery, an attempted rape, rampaging Indians, a solitary brave who stalks and tries to kill the protagonist, (a mere?) four fatal shootings, a final gunfight between the antagonists, and an aborted scalping. Calling the film "a fine work," Kitses concludes that "whatever Peckinpah may say, *The Deadly Companions* could not but have involved him imaginatively given its movement of a journey into the past, its theme of the interior struggle with the temptations of savagery."[9]

Terence Butler too tries to make a case for the film. Can one grant his contention that Turk and Billy "are less unpleasant than the citizens of the townships through which they and Yellowleg ride"? It is difficult to admire these killers, one of whom (Turk) had tried to scalp Yellowleg at the battle of Chickamauga, on the grounds that their cruelty is "at least not coldly rational" and that "unlike the men in the saloon at the beginning of the movie, they would not string a man up and then calmly sit around and play cards as he suffers." Although Butler concedes that Billy tries to rape Kit, he still sympathizes with Billy, because Billy "is incapable of the cynical indifference that the citizens of Gila City show to her when they let her go alone into Indian country to bury her dead son by her husband's grave." Oddly, Butler praises the director for lack of success: "Considering the circumstances under which the movie was made, Peckinpah's greatest achievement in *The Deadly Companions* is possibly his failure to integrate his themes: called upon to tell a love story that recalls the relationship of [John] Ford's Wyatt Earp and Clementine, Peckinpah just cannot bring himself to do it."[10]

"Amazingly, the film does have life to it," says Paul Seydor. "Whether by sheer good luck . . . or divine intervention," he adds, "the script, for all its intractable elements, contained enough material to energize his abilities, engage his imagination, and enlist his sympathies."[11]

While recognizing that the circumstances in which *The Deadly Companions* was made resulted in a film that is not really Peckinpah's, critics also recognize, paradoxically, themes or motifs that are distinctively Peckinpah's. I contend that many of the themes or motifs, even a number of gimmicks, in *The Deadly Companions* recur in different combinations and with varying emphases in Peckinpah's later films, emerging as individualizing preoccupations that characterize this director's work. What is particularly noteworthy, as well as surprising, is that virtually all of them derive from Fleischman's work.

Philip French points out that children are important in the director's first as well as his subsequent films,[12] but he goes no further into the subject. Several aspects about children in this picture foreshadow Peckinpah's later films. First, Kit's son is an innocent boy who naively tells his mother that if heaven is populated with the type of people who deride her, he does not want to go there. As Peckinpah said in an interview, "I believe in the complete innocence of children. They have no idea of good and evil. It's an acquired taste."[13] Second, the boy is killed in crossfire. While the movie is unclear whether he is in a vulnerable position because he is curious about the bank robbery taking place, it is clear that he is a curious lad: when Yellowleg and his entourage arrive in Gila City, he inches close to them to discover who these strangers are, and he eagerly offers to take care of Yellowleg's and Billy's horses. Less consequential, though of some importance in relationship to Peckinpah's *Cross of Iron,* is that the protagonist picks up the dead boy's harmonica—a touch that is not in the novel or, presumably, in the screenplay either, since the novel otherwise conforms to it.[14]

While French also declares, credibly, that Peckinpah's westerns imply prostitutes are more honest than other women, he cites no specific film.[15] Butler observes that Kit is performed (and, he does not state, written) as if she "were one of Ford's noble prostitute figures," such as Dallas in *Stagecoach,* "clearly a woman who is basically ashamed of what she is and yearns to be like so-called decent folk—exactly the kind of woman . . . who would be a hypocrite in the Sam Peckinpah canon." Whereas other Peckinpah heroines express physical delight in themselves during the act of bathing, "a moonlight bathe by O'Hara serves to be merely decorative."[16] Seydor relates Kit to specific Peckinpah heroines. Had the director received sufficient latitude to rewrite her role, he says, she might have become "the film progenitor of his later whores-as-heroines": Hildy in *The Ballad of Cable Hogue* and Elita in *Bring Me the Head of Alfredo Garcia*. Without such freedom, Peckinpah treats Kit as little more than "the standard western euphemism [then] allowed for prostitutes—a barroom or dance hall girl—leaving unexplored both her shame (briefly alluded to in the script) for what has become of her life after her husband died and the contradictions in her attitudes": contempt for the self-righteous Gila City residents and a desperate need to reach Siringo, where she claims her husband is buried, to prove her son's legitimacy. Mostly, Seydor justifiably concludes, Kit is "a collection of possibilities."[17]

A related theme is the contrast between the outcast and the respectable world. What Peckinpah acknowledged in 1963 holds for his later films as well: "most of my work has been concerned one way or the other with outsiders, losers, loners, misfits, rounders—individuals looking for something beside security."[18] Such figures, dramatically revealing their status as contrast to upright citizens who exclude or ostracize them, are habitual in Tennessee Williams's plays, with which Peckinpah was familiar.[19] Butler notes the irony at the end of *The Deadly Companions,* the surprising arrival of men from Gila City at the ghost town of Siringo: "Although none of them would accompany Kit on her trek [because they feared Apaches], they have now ridden out as a posse to retrieve their stolen money; even the parson is among them. 'You know how people are, as long as it's their money, the gates of hell wouldn't stop them,' the sheriff comments."[20] Although Butler does not say so, this view of bourgeois respectability typifies Peckinpah's oeuvre.

Furthermore, Seydor points out, the revenge theme, which is the linchpin of *The Deadly Companions,* recurs in *The Ballad of Cable Hogue* and *Bring Me the Head of Alfredo Garcia* (it also becomes a prominent feature of *The Osterman Weekend*), and in *The Ballad of Cable Hogue,* as in *The Deadly Companions,* a prostitute tries to dissuade the protagonist from pursuing revenge.[21] Not only is the theme of vengeance a stock-in-trade of westerns, it goes back in the drama past *Hamlet* at least as far as the *Oresteia* of Aeschylus—works the director no doubt knew.[22] What is special is that *The Deadly Companions* deemphasizes retribution. At first, as in *Hamlet,* it is deferred (Yellowleg saves his enemy's life in order to kill him later); then, another possible resemblance to *Hamlet,* it is neglected for another endeavor (in the film, to protect the heroine); and finally, it is abandoned (love makes Yellowleg recognize its futility).

Before continuing to list characteristically Peckinpah themes that *The Deadly Companions* adumbrates, let us examine some subjects that it does not. According to Kitses, its dramatic movement, "clearly looking forward to *Major Dundee*," has two major characters increasingly assume the appearance of Indians as they march through Apache country until they reach their destination.[23] If one overlooks the adverb "clearly," one might grant his assertion, but this dramatic movement does not occur in other Peckinpah films. Philip French, who studies *The Deadly Companions* in terms of its cinematic genre, the western, finds a "complex" exploration of the motif of the ghost town, which he, using T. S. Eliot's phrase, calls "the objective correlative of the impermanence of American life, a pessimistic feeling about the fragility of American civilization and its problems in putting down roots." For hero and heroine, the trip to the ghost town is "the journey of self-discovery."[24] French's observation is convincing, but no other feature film by Peckinpah contains the motif of a ghost town. Neither does the "moral judgment proposed by the code of poker," also cited by French,[25] a game whose only other appearance is in *Pat Garrett and Billy the Kid*.

What specific aspects of *The Deadly Companions* does Peckinpah denigrate? Apart from Fleischman's dialogue, Peckinpah faults plot gimmicks: the scar on Yellowleg's brow derived from Turk's attempt to scalp him (for this reason he does not remove his hat), the bullet lodged in his shoulder (consequently, he cannot control his aim), and the need to carry a corpse across a hot desert for five days.[26] A scar, a debilitating wound[27] (in part, the former visually suggests the latter), the transportation of a corpse in hot weather: all of these contrivances in *The Deadly Companions* reappear in various combinations in Peckinpah's later movies, where he tries to shear them of gimmickry.

In addition, he castigates FitzSimons for having taken over the editing, scrapped his original cut, and so changed the conclusion that "I defy anyone to make sense of the ending." As Peckinpah conceived and shot the film, Yellowleg is going to kill Turk when Billy "steps up in front of him, with his particular kind of little-boy bravado," whereupon Yellowleg "pulls his gun and kills him, a brutal, realistic act." But FitzSimons recut the sequence in such a way that Turk appears to kill Billy.[28] A brutal, realistic action—that is, vividly depicted violence—of which *The Deadly Companions* was shorn by its producer, becomes a trademark of most of Peckinpah's motion pictures, a feature that I analyzed in the last chapter.

To the list of features in *The Deadly Companions* that recur in his later movies, one may add others, all of which, like almost all of those cited earlier, are in Fleischman's writing: former enemies (Yankee and Confederate soldiers) unite (to rob a bank); they become the titular cohorts (whose superficial collegiality masks antagonism); characters disguise themselves (in the film's only famous scene, Indians chase a stagecoach, which is populated not, as first appears, by whites, but by Indians wearing head-gear and other apparel of the whites they killed, in a drunken reenactment of their battle); and people survive long enough to become anachronisms (the former Reb soldier, a deserter to boot, retains his animosity against a Yankee after the war has ended).

* * *

Because this chapter, as its title indicates, focuses on Peckinpah's recur-rent themes—which become his continuing companions, as it were—some of his superior films, notably *Ride the High Country* and *Junior Bonner*, re-ceive shorter shrift than their merits warrant. Let us now turn to the thir-teen feature films Peckinpah made after *The Deadly Companions*.

* * *

Ride the High Country, Peckinpah's second feature film and the first to gain him widespread acclaim as a director by European as well as American critics, subtly picks up several motifs of *The Deadly Companions*. Its two chief characters, Steve Judd and Gil Westrum, become deadly companions on their return trip from the goldmining camp, after Gil tries but fails to persuade Steve to help steal the gold. Their wound is not physical. Rath-er, it is economic: poverty has forced Steve to accept a small-scale job for penny-ante wages, Gil to become a carnival con man. Steve shows scars of this wound, a frayed sleeve, which he unsuccessfully tries to hide from the bankers, and a hole in one of his boots, which he quips derives from the craftsmanship of the bootmaker, who understood the need for prop-er ventilation.

Steve and Gil are living anachronisms not because they harbor old ideo-logical enmities but simply because—the first of Peckinpah's characters to embody this distinctive theme—they have grown old. When Steve first appears in town, one policeman moves him out of the way of a race be-tween a horse and a camel; and another, urging the "old-timer" to take care, ushers him out of an automobile's path. Gil ekes out a living at a sideshow, disguised (less transparently than the Indians of *The Deadly Companions*) in a red wig and beard as one of the last extant gunfighters. Each berates the other for showing his age by failing to understand the needs of young people. More crucially, Steve reveals his years during the first battle with the Hammond brothers, when he remembers that before leaving camp he did not check whether the rifles were loaded—which,

Gil reminds him, he would not have forgotten to do in the old days. Both men have survived into an era with values different from those current in their youth. In these different times, dreams diminish as high expectations give way to modest realities. The mother lode of gold, which the bankers led Steve to expect would be $250,000, will be, they tell him after he arrives, $20,000. In reality, it turns out to be $11,486. At the end of the movie, through sheer force of will, the two old-timers persuade their antagonists to settle their differences in a man-to-man shootout in the open.

As in Peckinpah's first film, respectability links to business values, which contrast with manliness and pioneer adventurousness. In *The Deadly Companions,* the citizens of Gila City ride through Apache territory not to protect a defenseless woman but to retrieve their money, stolen from a bank. In *Ride the High Country,* the elder banker who, like his son, looks physically weak and is ironically surnamed Samson, tells the aging Steve, a gunslinging former lawman, that the days of the steady businessman have supplanted the days of the forty-niners.

Whoredom does not contrast with respectable business in *Ride the High Country,* as it does in *The Deadly Companions. Ride the High Country* romanticizes neither, but each parallels the other. The owner of Kate's Place, the brothel in the mining town of Coarse Gold, is like the city itself vulgar and greedy. Her breasts are grotesquely padded, her lips overly rouged, her hair obviously dyed, her laugh raucous, and her behavior vulgar. Perhaps more significant, her first two appearances are in front of her brothel, where she greets newcomers with a strident laugh and welcome, and at the makeshift bank branch where she deposits her wealth, which associate her business not with glamor but with moneymaking. Kate's whores—what Kit would really be—are functionaries who instantly turn from zombie-like flower girls (disguises, like Gil's red hair and the Indians' clothing) at the wedding ceremony in the town whorehouse (a parallel to the church service at the local saloon in *The Deadly Companions*) to their traditional function when Kate commands them to change their clothes. Perhaps the vilest characters in *Ride the High Country,* the Hammond brothers are at their worst when they go through a ceremony of respectability: Billy's wedding to Elsa. Riding to the whorehouse for the event, they drunkenly sing, "When the Roll Is Called Up Yonder." Afterward, the brothers aim, singly and together, to function as groom with the bride, and their drunken conduct, Billy's included, suits the brothel where the ceremony takes place. With shrewd irony, the film satirizes Elsa's Bible-quoting father for his intransigence, his failure to understand his daughter's needs, and his harshness toward her; yet it also demonstrates the paradox that his view of the young man she wants to marry is accurate.

* * *

The Deadly Companions might well be the title of *Major Dundee,* in which Amos Dundee, in charge of a garrison of Confederate prisoners in the territory of New Mexico toward the end of the Civil War, agrees to accept under his command twenty Confederate prisoners led by a former friend turned personal and national enemy, Captain Ben Tyreen, as they traverse hostile territory (without the burden of a corpse, as in *The Deadly Companions*) to retrieve boys abducted by Apaches led by Sierra Charriba in a savage raid on a ranch, and to remain together until the Apaches are captured or killed. Not only are these enemies deadly companions, so are the Yankee and Rebel troops serving under them. Emphasizing internal strife within the command, mirroring that within the country, both reflecting the protagonist's internal strife, the troupe moves to another country, Mexico, which as Paul Seydor points out is itself "civil-war-torn."[29] Within Dundee's command, also potentially deadly, are the "coloreds," black soldiers in the Union army, and those Rebs who are, in Tyreen's words, "rednecked peckerwoods," a phrase also used, aptly, in *Ride the High Country, The Wild Bunch, The Ballad of Cable Hogue,* and *Pat Garrett and Billy the Kid,* but in no other film of Peckinpah. As if these potentially lethal comrades were insufficient, the company seeking Sierra Charriba includes an Apache scout, Riago, who Dundee suspects is a spy for Charriba. Dundee consents to keep Riago because the white scout, Sam Potts, who believes Riago's assertion that he is a Christian Indian, not an Apache, threatens to leave if Riago goes.[30]

Signifying the potential ominousness of Dundee's soldiers, the group's members assert their disunity at the very start of their mission: the Confederate troops sing "Dixie," the Union soldiers "The Battle Hymn of the Republic," and the western scouts, independent despite their affiliation with the Union Army, "My Darling Clementine." Discord surfaces when one of the Confederate rednecks tries to provoke a fight with Aesop, the African-American Union soldier in charge of the coloreds, and when Dundee decrees that he will shoot a Reb soldier for desertion rather than grant Tyreen's request that the Confederates discipline their own (partly to maintain order, Tyreen prevents Dundee from enforcing the punishment by shooting the man himself). Like America in that period, those who serve Dundee are, as one of them states, "a command divided against itself." Foreshadowing union, Aesop mocks the black African soldiers in the French army to one of the Rebs as being softer than the American colored, since they had not lived in the American South, a statement that bonds the Rebs and the colored. At the end of the film's final battle, between the Americans and the French, whom the former defeat after they have defeated the Apaches, Dundee's soldiers firmly unite as Americans. In this battle, the Confederate Tyreen hoists the Union flag.

Amos Dundee's wound is psychological, not physical. As disciplinary action for disregarding orders at the Battle of Gettysburg, he was transferred to the Far West. Now more of a jailer than a soldier, he aims to mend his wound by proving his value, both to his superiors and himself, when he retrieves the boys stolen by the Apaches and takes or kills their Indian abductors. His internal incapacity is physically manifested when he is shot in the thigh by an Indian arrow after he foolishly goes with Teresa beyond the secure perimeter of the camp. This is one of many bad judgments that demonstrate his failures.[31] While "more than half convinced" that Sierra Charriba has returned the children in order to lead his pursuers into an ambush, which Tyreen warns is probable, Dundee disregards his and Tyreen's better judgment to conduct a raid that Charriba ambushes, resulting in fatalities and loss of supplies. Physically and psychologically, his wound festers. Regardless of when the Civil War ends, Teresa predicts, the war within him will "last forever." Only after the physical wound heals does Dundee prove himself militarily, thereby vindicating himself, first when he ambushes the Apaches who ambushed him, then when he defeats the French army, whose provisions his troops had stolen, in a formal military battle. However, his self-vindication is deeply ambiguous, for he wins it at the expense of many lives, civilian as well as military.

Dundee is not the only wounded or scarred character. Although Sam Potts's left forearm had been amputated, his mutilation, in striking contrast to the major's mutilated pride, does not prevent him from functioning successfully. Emphasizing his victory over his wound, he wrestles Riago in "a friendly contest."

As in *The Deadly Companions* and *Ride the High Country*, disguise figures in *Major Dundee*. Charriba's ambush revolves around Apaches dressed as Union soldiers (as Kitses points out, Tyreen recognizes the trick when they do not react to his whistling "Dixie").[32] In Durango, Dundee's disguise as a Mexican apparently deceives no one.

Like Steve Judd's wound in *Ride the High Country*, Tyreen's wound is poverty, which he tried to overcome in the New World by becoming a part of its ancient régime, the southern aristocracy. Because the northern and southern states are still at war, regional enmities are not anachronistic;

yet because Tyreen places his allegiance with a moribund social class, he is a living anachronism. His personal grievance against Dundee, once his friend, is less because they are on different sides in the war between the states than because Dundee voted against him at a court martial in which he was tried for an archaic method of settling disputes, dueling with a fellow officer, whom he killed. In the dramatic present, in a poverty-ridden Mexican village, he looks "quite the gentleman," as Dundee says; he affectedly kisses Teresa's hand as a courtier might; he addresses her with similar elegance, "with beauty such as yours, this village is rich beyond comparison"; and in her words, he asks her to dance as if they were in a Viennese ballroom. As Dundee charges, he is "a would-be cavalier, an Irish potato farmer with a plumed hat [Tyreen sports a feather in it], fighting for a white-columned plantation house [he] never had and never will." Tyreen admits that he has killed men "in a hopeless war." His death is a romantic *beau geste* that befits his life: when the French commander hoists, as a token of victory, the Union banner he seized from a falling soldier, Tyreen stabs him with his sword, retrieves it, and is shot by the dying commander; but he then rides into the midst of the French soldiers, trying to kill as many as he can, to his certain death.

Revenge deferred and denied is also a theme of *Major Dundee*. Despite Tyreen's announced intention to kill Dundee for having sentenced a deserter to death, he puts his personal vendetta aside "until the Apache is taken or destroyed." As Yellowleg rescues Turk, Tyreen rescues Dundee in Durango. His reason, echoing Yellowleg's, is "So I can kill you myself." When the drunken Major pleads to be left in Durango, Tyreen, prepared to renounce vengeance, mocks him: "You're not worth killing anyway." After Dundee recovers his wits and leaves with Tyreen, they wait until the Apache is destroyed, at which point they prepare to settle their feud—only to be interrupted by the French army, which kills Tyreen before he can try to exact retribution.

Children constitute a minor theme in *Major Dundee*. As Peckinpah maintains, they are innocent, their tastes acquired. When the Apaches return the kidnapped boys to Dundee's camp, the children, who are dressed like Indians, play with bows and arrows.

* * *

As mentioned earlier, *The Wild Bunch*, Peckinpah's best-known movie, has dramatically changed the cinematic treatment of the American western. What was deglamorization in *Ride the High Country* becomes delaundering in this film, which is also rooted in such historical realities as automobiles and airplanes (the time is 1913), references to General Pershing (soon to command American forces in what would be World War I), and the presence of German military advisers in Mexico (German plans to give Mexico the United States Southwest, exposed in 1917, were a factor in drawing Americans into World War I). *The Wild Bunch* also transcends the motifs and gimmicks of *The Deadly Companions*.

An incident in the later film might, at least in part, satirize a gimmick in the earlier, the transportation of a corpse through hostile Apache country in order to bury it in a distant town. In *The Wild Bunch,* after the bank robbery in a south Texas town that Sykes calls Starbuck but that signs in the town variously call Starbuck and San Rafael,[33] the gang flees, pursued by hostile railroad deputies. At the request of a member of the Bunch who was blinded by gunshot, Pike Bishop shoots him so that he will not impede their escape. As if in mockery of *The Deadly Companions,* Tector and Lyle Gorch propose taking time to bury their companion, whereupon Dutch satirically suggests, "I'd like to say a few words for the dear, dead departed. And maybe a few hymns'd be in order, followed by a church supper, with a choir." When Dutch jolts the brothers, and the audience, back to reality, which consists of a life-and-death pursuit of the outlaws, the Bunch rides off.

Whereas disguise is an interruption in *The Deadly Companions,* it is integral to the opening action of *The Wild Bunch.* The gang enters Starbuck costumed as soldiers. In town, they encounter other members of the Bunch, some also in military uniform, others in long dusters that conceal rifles.

What in *The Deadly Companions* are two gimmicks, in *The Wild Bunch* is one small but important characterizing element: the chief character's scar, the result of a wound. Having been shot in his left thigh by a jealous husband after fatally shooting his wife, Pike is scarred. Despite temporary respite in a steam bath, the wound still hurts and sometimes makes physical activities, such as mounting a horse, difficult—but unlike Yellowleg's wounded arm, it is not incapacitating. More important, Pike's wound reminds him of the only woman he wanted to marry and of the family she had no opportunity to give him. The woman with whom Pike spends the night before the final shoot-out seems to be more than a casual whore. Establishing rapport between them, thereby implying an ongoing relationship, she and Pike catch each other's eyes when he first visits Agua Verde. Suggesting family (she has an infant) and religion (a crucifix adorns a wall of her house), she also suggests responsibility, which parallels Pike's as leader of the Bunch. Unlike the woman with whom the Gorch brothers spend the night, she carefully washes herself. While her sexual barter does not differ from that of the prostitute in the next room, her calm smile of acceptance when Pike gives her money, contrasting with the other woman's raucous complaint that she was underpaid, hints that she retains her dignity.

While *The Wild Bunch* does not dramatize men who are or were antagonists in America's Civil War, its main characters go to Mexico, which is in the midst of a civil war, wherein Pancho Villa's forces are in revolt against the federal soldiers. The American groups, one of which contains a Mexican, are not deadly companions but deadly adversaries. Only when there are fallings-out within each group—the Gorch brothers and Angel, Thornton and the "gutter trash"[34]—do comrades threaten to become deadly to each other, but such events are temporary. As the film's title suggests, the adversaries have identity chiefly as groups.

The companions who are potentially deadly to each other do not remain in physical proximity for long and are not intimates. Harrigan, a railroad official, and Deke Thornton, who to save himself from further whippings in Yuma Prison becomes Harrigan's "Judas goat," do not conceal their mutual abhorrence. Although they are banded, they are not bonded. Through Harrigan, Peckinpah derides the respectable world. With the law behind him, Harrigan's pursuit of Pike and his gang—a vendetta that is partly personal (for years, Pike had repeatedly shown him up) and partly professional (the railroad wants to apprehend robbers), which the movie does not dwell on—causes the slaughter of many innocent bystanders in Starbuck. When Thornton asks how it feels to kill with the force of the law behind him, Harrigan replies succinctly, "Good!"

Like Thornton, Peckinpah sympathizes not with respectable society but with the outcasts, the loners, the fugitive Wild Bunch, who have a sort of code of honor, however their profession (theft) and way of life (violence) distort it. "I go for the loners," the director admits. "I'm nothing if not a romantic and I've got this weakness for losers on the grand scale, as well as a kind of sneaky affection for all the misfits and drifters in the world." He also admires the values to which such losers and misfits conform: "Outdated codes like courage, loyalty, friendship, grace under pressure, all the simple virtues that have become clichés, sure. They're cats who ran out of territory and they know it, but they're not going to bend, either; they refuse to be diminished by it." Echoing Dutch's praise of Angel after being seized by Mapache, he adds, "They play their string out to the end."[35] "I gave you my word!" Thornton tells Harrigan, and like Tyreen's parole to Dundee, it is his bond. The same is true of the Bunch, although some members must be reminded of this fact. When Tector angrily prepares to shoot Sykes for failure to pack the horses properly, Pike stops him: "We're gonna stick together, just like it used to be. When you side with a man you stay with him, and if you can't do that you're like some animal. You're finished. We're finished. All of us."

Peckinpah is not sentimental about these outcasts. The violence that inheres in this film reflects the violence "built into the fabric of their lives," as he puts it. "They were people who lived not only by violence but *for* it." He tried to make *The Wild Bunch* depict what violence actually is, not what Hollywood usually shows it to be. He also "tried to make a film about heavies—break up the myth of the western gunfighter. They were bad," and if their only grace is, in Dutch's words, "We don't hang anybody," such grace is ironic. "They don't hang anybody, but they shoot people down, they're terrible, they're awful."[36] As the first page of the screenplay explicitly says of the gang's leader, "Make no mistake, Pike Bishop is not a hero—his values are not ours—he is a gunfighter, a criminal, a bank robber, a killer of men."

Deglamorizing these gunslingers, Peckinpah stresses that the mayhem they create affects the innocent. In *The Wild Bunch,* a boy is not caught in crossfire, but as the gang escapes from Starbuck, numerous adult bystanders are killed, Pike's horse tramples a young woman, and the slaughter terrifies children who are little older than toddlers. One reason that *The Wild Bunch* "is not a pretty picture," the director says, is that "it's the story of violent people in violent times. Violence to the people in the movie is not just a means to an end, it's the end itself. I make that point very clear." Nevertheless, he deleted violent scenes "because I thought they were excessive to the points I wanted to make. . . . I have a story to tell, too, and I don't want the violence, *per se,* to dominate what is happening to the people." To support his views, he invokes Homer's *Iliad:* "The facts about the siege of Troy, of the duel between Hector and Achilles and all the rest of it, are a hell of a lot less interesting to me than what Homer makes of it all."[37]

The movie avoids sentimentality for its characters. "Being sure is my business!" declares Pike, moments before (in a flashback) the law breaks into the brothel where he and Thornton enjoy themselves after a robbery, and the words literally echo in his and Thornton's memory. After Pike's moral lecture on standing by a comrade, Sykes inadvertently reminds him that he had forgotten, not stuck with, the man who at his order remained at the bank and was killed after the Bunch escaped. At this point, one might recall that the self-styled proponent of siding with comrades killed the blinded robber so that the others might more easily escape. Nevertheless, Pike remains loyal to his comrades, insofar as he is capable of it. He insists to Mapache, for instance, that Angel be released to rejoin the gang.

Resonating a quintessential motif of Peckinpah's films, Pike, the other members of the Bunch, and Thornton are anachronistic characters, similar in this respect to Amanda Wingfield in Tennessee Williams's *The Glass Menagerie,* which Peckinpah had directed four times on stage.[38] These figures in the West of 1913 are "unchanged men in a changing land," according to a narrative voice-over at the start of the original script, which Peckinpah discarded, probably because it is unnecessarily explicit. A visual embodiment of their status is the automobile, vividly colored red, which carries Mapache into a town and world in which the audience has so far seen only horses carry human beings (a railroad train appears later). "Now what in the hell is that?" asks Dutch, who has not seen a horseless carriage before. Boasting that he has seen one in Waco, Pike explains that it runs on gasoline. Although Tector is skeptical of Sykes's claim that machines can fly, Pike confirms the old man.

The Wild Bunch articulates as well as visualizes the view that these characters are anachronisms. After the fiasco in Starbuck, the gang members survey their lot. When Sykes reminds them, "you boys ain't getting any younger," Pike concurs: "We gotta start thinking beyond our guns. Those days are closing fast."

Merely to utter such statements, however, does not suffice to make them real. Pike, Dutch, and the Gorch brothers dream of one last robbery that would enable them to retire. "Ain't gettin' around any better," says Pike. "I'd like to make one good score and then back off." "Back off to what?" asks Dutch. Pike's failure to reply suggests that he recognizes the hollowness of his dreams.

Subtly but vividly, this film dramatizes the view of the child as tabula rasa. As the old man in Angel's village observes, "We all dream of being a child again"—that is, of returning to a state of innocence—"even the worst of us, perhaps the worst most of all." In the film's opening credits, as the gang enters Starbuck, children with innocent faces watch a scorpion and ants in ferocious combat. When the members of the South Texas Temperance Union march, other children stride behind them, guilelessly laughing. During the massacre that attends the getaway, a little boy and girl cling to each other in fear as they watch and hear the gunfight surrounding them. When the gang leaves town after the slaughter, the innocent-looking children set fire to the scorpion and ants—an extension and expressionistic reflection of the carnage in town, as well as a foreshadowing of the film's finale. When the Starbuck citizens survey the corpses in front of the bank, children play cops and robbers, pointing their fingers and crying "Bang!" During the falling-out between the Gorch brothers and Angel, which threatens to erupt into shooting, children watch; they hear the gang talk about whores; and they listen in rapt attention when Angel sings a sweet song. In Angel's village, children absorb the innocent dance. The most striking image of the child as tabula rasa may be the first view of General Mapache's camp at Agua Verde, a baby nursing at its mother's breast, around which is a bandolier. The bullet that kills Pike is fired not by an adult soldier but by a uniformed little boy who seems the same age as and who looks like the boy who had idolized the Mexican general[39]— an ironic contrast to *The Deadly Companions*, wherein the chief character accidentally kills a little boy.

Unlike *The Deadly Companions*, deferred revenge is not a major subject but a delicately treated motif in *The Wild Bunch*. As Pike recognizes, his former friend and colleague Deke Thornton pursues him not in retaliation for his having lacked foresight to prevent Thornton's apprehension by the law, but as a way to avoid further punishment, which we see differs little from what Mapache dispenses to Angel when his army captures him. Like the prison authorities at Yuma, Mapache is the law. Like Harrigan, he is vindictive.

Both Pike and the old man in Angel's village try to dissuade Angel from personal retribution. "What difference does it make?" asks Pike when Angel demands to know the name of the soldier who shot his father. "Names in these matters do not have any importance," declares the old man. When Angel screams, "Where is Mapache?" it is unclear whether he seeks revenge for his father or his fiancée, Teresa, who left him for Mapache. Although Angel promises to side with Pike, his attitude toward a personal vendetta is ambivalent. Crying "Puta!" (Whore!), he kills Teresa. Yet he defers personal revenge against Mapache, deflecting it, and in the process changing it to something impersonal, by supplying rifles and ammunition to the peasants who fight the general. In retaliation for Teresa's death, however, her mother informs Mapache that Angel diverted rifles and ammunition to his enemies.[40] Mapache avenges himself by torturing and eventually slitting the throat of Angel. Furthermore, as Seydor notes, revenge is "the reason the woman [whose lover Pike kills behind the mirror] shoots Pike in the back."[41]

Snakelike, the theme of vengeance slithers through the film, deferring its fullest manifestation until the climax. Pike, the object of Harrigan's revenge, had cautioned Angel against personal vindictiveness and maintained that a large sum of money cuts many family ties, but he leads the

Bunch in exacting payment from the object of Angel's vendetta. When Mapache cuts Angel's throat, Pike shoots him—an act of vengeance similar to Angel's vendetta. For a dramatically elongated split second (that echoes the less-elongated split second after Angel kills Teresa), and to the gang's surprise, Mapache's army does nothing. Then, revenge breeds revenge. In a massacre that dwarfs the slaughter at Starbuck and that evokes the scorpion and the ants destroying each other, Mapache's army kills the Bunch, while the Bunch kills them.

* * *

Perhaps to parody the violence in *The Wild Bunch,* a shotgun blows up a gila monster at the start of *The Ballad of Cable Hogue.* The animal also suggests that the latter film may be, in part, a spoof of *The Deadly Companions,* wherein Gila City is prominent. As Hogue learns, the water hole he finds lies midway between Dead Dog and a town sometimes called Lizard, more often Gila City. While the action moves only to Dead Dog, performers at its saloon, according to a prominently displayed placard, are "Arizona Hogan and His Four Gilas." The very name Gila City, foreshadowed by the violence perpetrated upon the deadly lizard and underscored by the show biz sequence, signals parallels between *The Ballad of Cable Hogue* and *The Deadly Companions.* Such themes as vengeance deferred, then denied, and the prostitute as heroine appear in both. Suggesting that these correspondences are deliberate is Peckinpah's revelation that, at least until 1972, *The Ballad of Cable Hogue* was not a directorial assignment but "the only movie I ever picked to do."[42]

After the gila monster explodes, Hogue's companions, Taggart and Bowen, turn deadly. Robbing him of his weapons, horse, and, especially consequential, his water canteen, they leave him to die in the desert. When he miraculously finds water there, he vows vengeance: "I'll whip them bastards. And all I've gotta do is wait."[43]

Forced to become a loner and an outcast, Hogue unlike similar figures in Peckinpah's pictures becomes an entrepreneur whom luck makes prosperous. However, he evokes sympathy as a loner, not as a capitalist. In the role of loner, he fights nature to survive; in that of businessman, he ruthlessly exacts profit from nature's bounty. "Tomorrow ragmen can be kings" is a line sung during the opening credits. As a ragman, he is an attractive character. As a business king (his establishment is called "a one-man kingdom"), his initial action is to shoot his "first customer," who refuses to pay him ten cents for drinking water; but he kills him only after the man pulls a gun on him. Because business precedes pleasure (he worries that someone may put boundary stakes on his claim before he has a chance to do so), he interrupts his first sexual encounter with the prostitute Hildy, which infuriates her. Peckinpah emphasizes what is God's, or nature's, and what is Hogue's. When Reverend Sloane announces that Hogue has "builded an oasis out of this wilderness," Hogue corrects him: "Oh, no, I just stumbled on that mud hole over there and I dug it out a little."

Throughout his prosperous career and love affair with Hildy, revenge is never far from his mind. When Sloane tries to shame him from "that vengeance that gnaws in the very walls of your soul," he dismisses the platitude: "Taggart and Bowen left me out there to die. If my feet don't get cold and my back don't turn yellow and my legs'll stay under me, I aim to kill 'em for it." To Sloane's reminder, "'Vengeance is mine,' saith the Lord," Hogue replies, "Well, that's fair enough, just as long as he don't take too long and I can watch." Like Sloane, Hildy cannot persuade Hogue that instead of retaliating for past injuries, he should leave with her for San Francisco. "Revenge always turns sour," she argues, and asks, "Why don't you just forget it?" He is adamant: "There are some things a man can't forget. . . . I've been waiting a long time, Hildy." In a subplot, Hogue saves Sloane from a jealous husband who seeks revenge on the minister for having seduced his wife, which foreshadows his decision not to kill one of the men from whom he plans to exact retribution.

Three and a half years after Taggart and Bowen leave Hogue to die in the desert, they inadvertently return on the stagecoach that makes its routine stop at Hogue's water hole between Dead Dog and Gila City. Upon discovering his prosperity, they decide to rob him again. After tricking them into digging a huge hole where they think he buried his money, Hogue shoots at them when they stick up their heads, then lobs rattlesnakes into the hole, forcing them to scurry up without their rifle. At gunpoint, he orders them to remove all their footwear and clothing except underwear, to walk into the waterless hills, and to stay off the road, where, he threatens, he will kill them if he finds them. Bowen strips to his longjohns. When Taggart draws a pistol, Hogue shoots him. Interrupting Bowen's pleas for his life, an automobile drives by, its passengers laughing at the man in his longjohns. Hogue perceives that instead of stopping, the horseless carriage drove past his watering place—indicative that the days of stagecoach stops will soon end. He decides not to remain, since he would then become, like his business, an anachronism. After he orders Bowen to bury Taggart, a stagecoach arrives with mail but no passengers—confirmation that times are changing. Partly for this reason, he forgoes the remainder of his anachronistic retribution and gives his business to Bowen.

Another automobile arrives, carrying Hildy, who is en route from San Francisco to New Orleans. Interrupting her reunion with Hogue, who agrees to join her, her chauffeur cries that the car, overheated by the desert sun, needs a tankful of water. Bowen orders him to drive the car onto a rise and to help him get water for it. As Hogue deposits his gear in the horseless carriage, he accidentally disengages the brake. The auto slides downhill in Bowen's direction. To save the life of the erstwhile object of his revenge, further emphasizing his abjuration of the action that Sloane had reminded him was exclusively God's, Hogue pushes Bowen out of the way and is run over. Hogue's abandonment of vengeance occurs too late. Having remained in the desert long enough to become an anachronism, he is killed by an emblem of what has replaced his world.

Another wave of the future enters, this time a motorcycle, carrying Reverend Sloane, clad in his usual black suit,[44] who offhandedly calls the vehicle "just a means of transportation," in contrast to Bowen, who in a remark that recalls *The Wild Bunch* boasts that the car bringing Hildy is the third such machine he has seen. As Sloane preaches a eulogy for Hogue, an exquisitely photographed and edited montage accelerates time to show Hogue dying, dead, and buried. As Philip French perceives, the montage signifies "not just the death of a man but of a way of life."[45]

The second major theme of *The Ballad of Cable Hogue* to derive from *The Deadly Companions* is the whore as heroine. As Paul Seydor notes in connection with *The Wild Bunch,* Peckinpah's frequent employment of prostitutes in his westerns constitutes fidelity to his material, "and part of that truth requires that he deal with the kind of woman . . . men like [his characters] would probably be associated with."[46] Hildy may represent one way Peckinpah might have treated Kit had the producer of *The Deadly Companions* permitted him to rewrite the screenplay. As in the earlier film, respectable townswomen sneer at the whore. The one upright woman the movie dramatizes is a hypocrite, a housewife who commits adultery with Sloane. In marked contrast, Hildy rejects Sloane's advances when she has an exclusive relationship with Hogue. Her visit to Hogue's home is occasioned by the demands of "the good people of the town," as she puts it, that she leave. His response—that Hildy is the only good person he met at Dead Dog—constitutes his recognition of her dignity and value as a human being, which makes him worthy to receive her gift, not sale, of love. Peckinpah emphasizes these qualities in Hildy more than he does her profession. Before she permits Hogue to purchase what she sells, she bathes him, which suggests that she will not accept a client for money alone. Beneath a pink heart snapped on the crotch of her underwear, a symbol of her profession, is her name, which like Hogue's distinctive name (as several characters acknowledge when they have difficulty spelling it) signals individuality. Linking the uniqueness of each via their names is the alliterativeness of what they call each other, Hildy and Hogue. Solidifying that connection, she answers his question, "Do ya remember my name?" with another, "Do you remember mine?" Affirming her independence, Hogue tells Sloane, "Hildy ain't mine. Nobody owns Hildy."

Partly because of her profession and partly because he too sells nature's goods, he is ambivalent about her. "You can't convince Hildy with anything but hard cash," he says, the words reverberating on himself. Their idyllic tryst before she leaves for San Francisco is a honeymoon in which buying and selling have no place. "You've been awful nice to me, Hogue," she says. "Never bothered you none what I am?" "Hell, no, it never bothered me," he replies. He calls what she is "a human being. . . . We all got our own ways of livin'." "And lovin'?" she asks. "It gets mighty lonesome without it," he answers. Perhaps exaggerating the number, Peckinpah claims to have developed "some kind of warm personal relationship" with some 90 percent of the whores he has known. "We've been human beings together," he states, echoing Hogue. "I never thought of these women as objects to be used." Much of his association with them, he claims, he has put into Hogue's and Hildy's love story. "They had a relationship that was truer and more tender than between most husbands and wives. The fact that she was a whore and went to bed with men for money didn't change anything."[47] Her immediate decision to leave Hogue derives from Hogue's inability to maintain an uncommercial view of human associations. When he demands that Sloane, his guest, pay for his dinner—Hogue seems to be upset because he declined the reward offered by the man Sloane cuckolded—Hildy points out that Hogue charged her nothing. "That's because you haven't charged me nothing," he snorts. Since he puts their alliance on a barter basis, she decides to depart for San Francisco in the morning. Because she loves him, however, she relents in her demand that he sleep outside. Also for love, she returns to give him another chance to leave his business and join her on a trip to New Orleans. This time, Hogue has changed, and he shares her values: a view of human beings based on love, not money, and his abandonment of vengeance. When she tells him that the man she married in San Francisco died of a stroke in bed, "but he died happy," he laughs—affirming sex, love, and life.

* * *

Although *Straw Dogs* is set and was filmed in England, and although Englishmen wrote the novel on which it is based and coauthored the screenplay, elements of the western inhere in this movie. Peckinpah not only emphasizes the rustic setting—when Amy Sumner drives her husband, David, home from town, a horse is in the background—he stresses, more important, their house's remoteness: a farm isolated in an open space. Yet he explicitly relates the film not to westerns but to a literary tradition that includes Bernard Shaw's *The Devil's Disciple,* in which, says Peckinpah, a man of peace discovers in time of trial that he is really "a man of action, a man of violence."[48]

Although *Straw Dogs* may have fewer features of *The Deadly Companions* than any other Peckinpah film discussed so far, the reasons are the nature of the source and of the job he agreed to do. Based on *The Siege of Trencher's Farm* by Gordon M. Williams, *Straw Dogs* draws its basic situation from it: a battle between an American academic, who is on leave in a remote English hamlet, and some of the local inhabitants. In the director's comments on *Straw Dogs,* unlike those on *The Deadly Companions* or *Major Dundee,* he does not castigate a producer or studio for having prevented him from making a good film or for ruining one he made. Instead, he justifies the behavior and feelings of the characters from their viewpoints, and he stresses the film's source and his job as director. "Look," he argues, "what if they'd given me *War and Peace* to do instead of *Trencher's Farm?* I'm reasonably sure I'd have made a different picture." Calling the novel "a lousy book with one good action-adventure sequence in it—the siege itself," he explains a movie director's usual job: "You get hired to take this bad book and make a picture out of it . . . the best way you know how, that's all." You "take the material and try . . . to tell a story, above all, in terms of the material." With David Zelag Goodman, his collaborator on the screenplay, he "tried to make something of validity out of this rotten book. We did. The only thing we kept was the siege itself."[49]

The climactic sequence of *Straw Dogs,* the battle at Trencher's Farm between the besieged David Sumner and the locals intent on destruction and murder, may be one of the longest, most sustained, and most artistically graphic depictions of violence in cinema. In part, it rebukes the deletion of the single brutal act in the final sequence of Peckinpah's *The Deadly Companions.* Essentially, the siege revolves around one of the basic themes of *The Deadly Companions:* revenge deferred, then denied. In *Straw Dogs,* however, the delayed retribution is not of the protagonist David but of his antagonists, Tom Hedden and his cronies, for what Henry Niles may have done to Tom's daughter Janice. In contrast to *The Deadly Companions,* they do not abjure vengeance; rather, David thwarts them.

Not only is David an American, he is also, like Reverend Hood, an outsider. In the film, not the novel, both are intellectuals. The vicar recognizes in David's friendly jibe (that there has never been a kingdom so fully given to bloodshed as that of Christ) a paraphrase of Montesquieu, which his wife does not (a hint that she, like Amy, is not an intellectual). Before David battles Tom Hedden physically, he spars with Reverend Hood verbally; and his success in this battle anticipates his success in the other.

Although David bears no wound or scar, the people associated with him—in the film, not the novel—do. The magistrate, representing the law to which David appeals, lacks an arm. Henry Niles, whom David protects, limps.[50] Amy bears a psychic wound, her rape by Charlie Venner and Norman Scutt, which occurs while they and two cronies victimize David; her inability to cleanse her mind of what she has endured (in quick cuts, her memory flashes back to it) makes her so distraught that David drives her home from the church social. As in the novel, his car accidentally hits Henry, whom he takes to Trencher's Farm. When the magistrate arrives to prevent the violence Tom Hedden is bent on perpetrating, Peckinpah links all scars and wounds to David's besiegement at the farm.

In *Straw Dogs,* no innocent boy is killed, but an innocent cat is, and it is hanged in the closet to demonstrate that the locals can enter the Sumner home at will.[51] Nevertheless, *Straw Dogs* retains the motif of children as tabula rasa. While *The Deadly Companions* ends in a cemetery, *Straw Dogs* begins in one, where children play, indifferent to the dead and to death. Some, holding hands, dance a circle around tombstones, while others, also holding hands, encircle a dog. Furthermore, grown men in *Straw Dogs* behave as children—perhaps the worst more than others, as the old Mexican in *The Wild Bunch* says. During the violent siege, Scutt and the rat catcher cavort on children's tricycles. More important are the children who observe, thereby learning to emulate, what adults do. Outside the farmhouse, fourteen-year-old Janice and her thirteen-year-old brother spy on David and Amy as they prepare for bed, and immediately prior to their lovemaking the camera cuts to the girl and boy, watching. Sex is among the primary interests of this adolescent girl, who is eager to learn and to enact what her budding instincts make her desire. At the church social, the miniskirted Janice tries sexually to interest David in her. When he ignores her, she acts provocatively toward Henry Niles, whom she treats as David's surrogate. More so than Amy, she flaunts her sexuality (when she and her brother spy on the Sumners, she appears eager to experiment with her sibling).

Amy is not one of Peckinpah's prostitutes. She is a respectable married woman whose relationship with her husband is less harmonious and tender than that of the whore Hildy's is with Hogue during the period when they play at being married. More circumspect than Amy, Hildy becomes upset that people in the stagecoach might see her naked. When Peckinpah makes a heroine of a whore, she is a bona fide prostitute, not simply a woman who defies orthodox dress codes or who may enjoy sexual intercourse with a man who used to be her lover.

* * *

The credit sequence that opens *Junior Bonner* dramatizes the wound inflicted on J.R. ("Junior") Bonner: during a rodeo, a brahma bull named Sunshine throws him from its back; as he walks he feels the pain; and he bandages his aching body. Throughout much of the film, his very bones seem to ache. Not a gimmick, as it is in *The Deadly Companions,* the protagonist's wound in *Junior Bonner* is a consequence of his profession and inheres in his being. Like Pike's wound, it is a frequent reminder of what he did, what he does, what he has been, and what he cannot repudiate without repudiating his very self.

A rodeo cowboy may be, as I have heard rodeo announcers call him, the last of the individualists. Like J.R.'s father, Ace Bonner, the title character of *Junior Bonner* is a loner, a maverick, a nonconformist—dissimilar to respectable moneymakers and salaried employees. J.R.'s brother Curly, the film's most prominent moneymaker, is a real estate developer who sells tract houses and mobile homes, urges J.R. (whom he calls "as genuine as a sunrise") to join his firm, and condescendingly brags, "Hey, boy, I'm just making money hand over fist here." When J.R. insists, individualistically, "I got to go down my own road," Curly sardonically draws a businessman's conclusion, which opposes his own road ("my first million") to his brother's ("eight seconds"). J.R. also contrasts with Charmagne's wealthy boyfriend, who takes her to the Frontier Days rodeo in Prescott, Arizona. An independent person, J.R. rejects a friendly offer by Buck, a rancher who supplies animals to rodeos, to serve as his assistant. By having J.R.'s mother, Elvira, agree to run a curio shop connected with one of Curly's tracts, Peckinpah stresses the moral and ideological ties between them. The director emphasizes ties between J.R. and his father, a prospector who continually falls short of the mother lode and who aims to pan for gold in Australia, the final frontier. Both men are former rodeo champions (Ace boasts of his kinship to heavyweight boxing title holder Jack Dempsey, and the announcer at the rodeo parade informs onlookers that Junior was "twice Frontier Days champion bull rider"), they ride on one horse in the rodeo parade, they enter a wild cow milking competition together, and since the wealthy Curly refuses to grubstake Ace to a trip to Australia, Junior buys him a ticket there—not in the economy coach section, but in first-class.

As members of a dying breed of individualists, rodeo riders are virtual anachronisms. The West is no longer what it used to be. Developers are subdividing the prairie, caged animals are part of the hoopla surrounding real estate sales, and as a bulldozer demolishes the Bonner home, it buries a photograph of young Ace in his glory. Once J.R. and Ace leave the regular path of the parade on J.R.'s horse, they find not wide open spaces but a backyard clothesline, which knocks them off the animal, prompting a woman to yell, "Get that damn horse out of my yard!" Pointedly, Curly calls rodeos "part of history." Though nicknamed "Junior," J.R. was, as Buck reminds him, "a champion in his day" but he is "not the rider [he] was a few years back." Still independent, J.R. determines to prove Buck wrong by winning the main event at Prescott's Frontier Days rodeo, which as the rodeo announcer tells the audience is "the oldest professional rodeo in America," having begun on the Fourth of July 1888.

Although J.R.'s aim—to win that event by riding Sunshine, the bull that defeats him in the film's opening credit sequence—resembles deferred revenge, he is not retributive. In *Junior Bonner,* Peckinpah transcends the theme of a delayed vendetta, which he transforms into a test of the protagonist's skill in bettering a worthy opponent who has proved his mettle by having defeated him. Partly for this reason, and partly for its superb characterization, *Junior Bonner* is one of Peckinpah's best movies.

While the bulls are being penned in preparation for the rodeo, J.R. enters Sunshine's pen. Each stares at the other, taking his measure as, in a quick cut, Peckinpah shows J.R.'s memory of Sunshine throwing him; and when Sunshine begins to charge, J.R. is forced to jump over the fence. "I want to ride that Sunshine bull of yours again," he tells Buck after the incident. Whereas most cowboys would pay Buck to fix the draw so that they will not ride Sunshine, says J.R., he offers half of the prize money so that he will. "Just one of him and one of me" is what he wants, that is, the opportunity to defeat a formidable adversary. Acknowledging that his prime years are behind him and ambiguously referring both to a chance at winning and to his dignity, J.R. confesses, "I need it, Buck. It's my home town." The eponymous rodeo rider's victory does not consist of killing his antagonist but of staying on his back for eight seconds with grace and poise. Thus, it is an act of skill, and for all the brutalities a rodeo inflicts on its participants, it is not primarily or mainly a brutal event; rather, it is a festival that demonstrates and celebrates the expertise of those engaged in it. Whereas Junior Bonner achieves his goal of staying on Sunshine for eight seconds, Curly has not yet gained his first million. Whereas the rodeo rider wins the main event with ninety-two points, a high score, the real estate developer's float wins only second prize in the commercial division. "Well," J.R. ironically comments to his brother, "second's better'n third." Vindicating Junior Bonner and the way of life he represents, the rodeo announcer confirms J.R.'s triumph: "after eighty-four years they still make cowboys as tough as they ever was."

* * *

In *The Deadly Companions,* a blonde boy is accidentally shot by the protagonist. In *The Getaway,* a black boy intentionally shoots the protagonist—with his water pistol—and later "triggers" him, so to speak, when he and his brother identify his photograph for the police. Instead of a sentimental desire to bury a dead son, a man demands that his underlings dump his brother's corpse down a dry well, and when one of them suggests that he be properly buried, he is ordered to do as he is told. None of these actions is in the novel from which *The Getaway* derives.[52]

Both *The Deadly Companions* and *The Getaway* dramatize a falling-out among partners, companions who as professional thieves and killers are indeed deadly; but the later film, which inverts the first movie's motifs and themes, is more complex and better motivated than the earlier. Initially, Doc McCoy does not aim to doublecross Rudy. When, as prearranged, he meets Rudy, he rightly infers that the absence of Rudy's accomplice Jackson means that Rudy killed him and plans to kill McCoy, who shoots Rudy first; but Doc's bullets are not fatal. Doc does not intend to doublecross Beynon, who contracted him for their robbery. Only after Doc's wife, Carol, shoots Beynon, because he tells of her marital infidelity with him, does Doc take all the money. Although the desire to get the money stolen from the bank is Rudy's chief motivation, he also pursues Doc in revenge for having shot him. "Kill him, kill that mother," he mutters upon recovery. Of necessity, this attempt at vengeance is deferred until Rudy catches up with Doc, who frustrates it by killing him instead.

Whereas Peckinpah intended Yellowleg to shoot Billy as a brutal act but was thwarted by the producer, who made the sequence appear as if Turk shoots him, Peckinpah forcefully demonstrates the brutality of his modern outlaws in *The Getaway,* where they employ more effective disguises (ski masks) than their counterparts in *The Wild Bunch* or the Indians in *The Deadly Companions.* Yet he contrasts Doc, who like Yellowleg is brutal when he feels he must be, with Rudy, who like Billy and Turk is brutal because it is his nature to be. "Careful he doesn't panic and go and shoot somebody," Doc instructs Rudy and Jackson about the bank guard. These cohorts are unnecessarily savage. They pistol-whip the guard on the head and roughly hurl a bystander to the ground. Failing to exercise care about his own actions, much less the guard's, Jackson shoots him. As he and Rudy drive away, Rudy in the driver's seat tells him to take the wheel. When he does so, watching the road as he drives, Rudy calmly pulls out his gun, shoots him twice in the groin and once in the heart, and kicks his screaming accomplice from the car, driving away as Jackson falls dead onto the ground. Stressing Rudy's savagery, Peckinpah intercuts his actions with the timed, diversionary dynamite explosion of a truck filled with hay. As indicated, Doc is brutal when he must be: he shoots Rudy before Rudy can kill him, and he fires at Rudy's inert body to make certain he is dead; when Doc finds the con man who switched keys with Carol to steal the briefcase (filled with the loot), he elbow-punches him unconscious. Upon the arrival of policemen at the radio store, where he has been recognized, Doc shoots not them but their car; but when the police chase him and Carol at the drive-in restaurant, where he has also been recognized, he prudently shoots to kill, which he and Carol also do during the final, violent battle in a seedy El Paso hotel.

Perhaps the chief inversion of *The Deadly Companions* is the theme of the heroine-whore in contrast to respectable women. Carol McCoy is a loving, respectably married woman who, at her husband's request to win his release from prison, prostitutes herself with an influential member of the parole board. "Get to Beynon," Doc orders her. "Tell him I'm for sale. His price." Until Beynon's revelation, which Carol confirms by shooting him, Doc imagines that the price consists solely of his committing a robbery for Beynon. Despite the fact that both McCoys are killers, Peckinpah presents them as a loving and sensitive married couple. After Doc's release, as they prepare to go to bed but are fearful of embracing, they try to articulate their anxieties. "It does something to you, you know," he says, trying to explain his self-doubts after having been incarcerated for so long. "It does something to you. It does something to you in there." "We've got time, Doc. We've got lots of time," she sympathizes, confessing, "I'm just as nervous as you are." "Really?" he asks. "Really," she responds. Only then do they kiss and make love. The next morning, he thanks her for getting him out of jail. "It was a pleasure," she quips. These words may reverberate in his mind when he learns the price Beynon exacted for arranging his parole. After they leave Beynon's home, Doc slaps his tearful wife, demanding that she explain why she did not tell him. "There wasn't any way to explain it," she says. "You sent me to him, you know."

Doc's discovery of Carol's action is analogous to Yellowleg's wound. As in *The Deadly Companions,* a man and woman travel through hostile territory, pursued by the police as well as by Rudy and Beynon's minions. Instead of journeying to a ghost town for an emotional reason, they flee to safety in Mexico. As they travel, in both films, they perceive that they still love each other. In *The Getaway* their acknowledgment is not a cliché but is earned, the result of an effort to achieve mutual understanding. "Maybe we should split up," says Doc at one point. "I'll cut up the money with you." Carol refuses. Although he tries not to press the issue, his wound festers. "I think you liked it with him," he jeers later. She reminds him why she had sex with Beynon. Continuing to bicker, he points to money as all he can trust. "Just keep that up, Doc, and it won't matter how far we get away," she snaps, "'cause there won't be anything left between us." After they spend a night in a garbage truck to hide from the police, their shared danger seems to heal his wound. Their positions reverse. "It's not going to mean anything if we don't make it together," he says. "I don't think we can make it," she argues. "I think if we ever get out of this dump I'll just split." He persists: "We made it together so far." She contradicts him, "We've come a lot of miles but we're not close to anything," but she also reminds him, "I chose you, not [Beynon], you know that?" He insists, "We pick it up, or we leave it. And we leave it here or there's no other way." "No more about him!" she stipulates. He agrees. They make these renewed vows in a garbage dump, which represents a past they decisively reject. Agreeing to remain together, Doc and Carol McCoy achieve the most emotionally mature male-female relationship in any Peckinpah movie. When they escape to Mexico, fulfilling the promise of the film's title, the trucker who drives them there approves the fact that they are married, thereby underscoring their union as a couple. Reversing their physical separation at the start of the movie, *The Getaway* ends on a note of their union.[53]

Carol McCoy is a criminal who, to help her criminal husband, commits adultery with an apparently respectable businessman. Fran Clinton, who is married to a veterinarian, is unfaithful with a criminal because he sexually appeals to her. Fran takes the initiative with the wounded Rudy, stroking his pistol as if it were a penis and seductively telling him he does not need it to make her do anything he wants. Unlike Carol, who hopes to conceal her action from Doc, Fran flaunts her infidelity while her husband watches, until it drives him to suicide.[54]

* * *

The second title character of *Pat Garrett and Billy the Kid* is also suicidal, in that he returns to the territory where he knows the first title character will gun him down. A statement Peckinpah made the year before he was invited to direct *Pat Garrett and Billy the Kid* reveals a key bond between this movie and *The Deadly Companions*: "Billy the Kid was no hero. He was a gunfighter, a real killer."[55] Apart from reminding us that in each film the gunman who is killed is named Billy, the remark recalls Peckinpah's comment that Yellowleg's killing his erstwhile companion was "a brutal, realistic act."

Pat Garrett and Billy the Kid portrays a brutal world wherein people kill without mercy or warning. Whereas *The Deadly Companions* presents a Hollywood view of the West, *Pat Garrett and Billy the Kid* dramatizes a realistic view that on one level is a gloss on the director's first feature film. As soon as one of Billy's gang, upon awakening in the morning, steps outside the door of the bunkhouse, for instance, Garrett's posse, without a word of warning or call to surrender, opens fire on him. In Peckinpah's film, not in the original screenplay, Garrett's deputy Ollinger is a religious zealot who is as vicious as any outlaw. To force Billy to repent, Ollinger hits him with the butt of his rifle, which he has loaded with dimes, so that if he shoots Billy, the shot will be more painful than it would otherwise be. When Billy eventually shoots him with that rifle, Peckinpah shows the dimes spread as they move toward the camera. In Rudolph Wurlitzer's script, when Billy is about to escape from jail, Billy draws his pistol on Bell, another deputy, and fires. "*The shot misses Bell and ricochets against the wall. Bell turns to run out the building, and Billy shoots him in the back, sending him flying out the door.*"[56] Going further than Wurlitzer, Peckinpah has Bell state that Billy would not shoot him in the back, turn, and begin to run, whereupon Billy unhesitatingly shoots him in the back, without missing—"a brutal, realistic act." The outlaw Black Harris tells Garrett, "If it's straight up one to one you want, then I'm your man," while he crawls along a rooftop to shoot Garrett from behind, which Garrett knows he is doing and therefore positions himself to do the same to Harris. Characters on both sides of the law ambush their enemies, whom they kill before the latter can defend themselves. In this respect, the film stresses their similarity, not their dissimilarity. As the Kid recalls, "It wasn't long ago when

I was the law, riding for Chisum [one of the wealthy landowners who has hired Garrett to gun down Billy], and old Pat was an outlaw. The law is a funny thing, ain't it."

Witnesses to this savage world are children, a familiar motif in Peckinpah's films. In his prologue, which is not in Wurlitzer's script and which Wurlitzer repudiates, kids watch Billy and his gang amuse themselves killing chickens, planted in the earth, for target practice—flies that exist for the sport of the outlaws and Garrett, who themselves are flies for wealthy landowners. Poe and two confederates kill Garrett, whose dying moments are intercut with shots of the chickens being shot thirty years earlier. The wealthy landowners who speak to Garrett at Governor Wallace's mansion treat him as a hired hand, and Chisum is so disdainful of him that he takes no pains either to conceal or to reveal his contempt. Children play on the gallows, swinging on the rope from which Billy is to hang, and they watch the murder of Ollinger, even stand close to his corpse—touches that are not in Wurlitzer's script. In that script, however, children point up attitudes toward Garrett: early in the film, a young boy respectfully obeys his orders; at the end, another young boy throws a rock at him as he rides away after killing the Kid.

Exemplifying the brutal realism of these professional killers, including Billy the Kid, whom Peckinpah takes pains to deromanticize, is a scene wherein, on neutral territory, at a friend's family meal table, he accidentally meets the cognominally similar Alamosa Bill, Garrett's deputy, who has been searching for him. Not knowing how to avoid a confrontation, they step outside, prepared to duel. As Wurlitzer writes the sequence, Billy tells Bill to start counting. "*Standing back-to-back, they begin walking away from each other, stepping and counting simultaneously. At nine, Alamosa whirls and fires. His shot is hurried, and he misses. Billy, smiling slightly, shoots him through the stomach as he counts ten*" (p. 70). More strongly than Wurlitzer does, Peckinpah satirizes the Hollywood convention of a fair gunfight at high noon (which, this movie reminds us, is customarily an undramatic lunchtime). Bill and Billy turn their backs to each other. Billy makes Bill count to ten, but while Bill marches as he counts, Billy simply turns and draws. When Bill turns at the count of eight (not nine), Billy shoots him. Although both Bill and Billy, who in Peckinpah's film share more than a name, are brutal and realistic, Billy is more devious. In both screenplay and film, Garrett's murder of Billy, whom he takes by surprise, occurs not at noon but in the dead of night.

Peckinpah reverses the theme of enemies whom time and circumstances turn into companions. Time and circumstances turn Garrett and the Kid, who are friends, into enemies. Despite the Kid's explanation in the film's prologue, that he did not kill Garrett because Garrett is his friend, their friendship formally though not emotionally ends, as Garrett warns him it will, when he officially becomes sheriff. Thus, the title's conjunction *and* is more apt than *versus*. Contrasting the reversed theme in regard to the title characters, Garrett and John Poe, deputized by the governor, and answerable to him and the large landowners, to spy on Garrett and ensure that he kills his former friend, are truly the film's deadly companions, who ride together to track down Billy.

Unlike such films as *Ride the High Country* and *The Wild Bunch*, *Pat Garrett and Billy the Kid* does not treat the theme of gunslingers who have lived long enough to become anachronisms, but it treats a related theme: bandits who know that since the country is changing, they will, unless they too alter, become either anachronisms or corpses. The bulk of *Pat Garrett and Billy the Kid* is set in the territory of New Mexico in 1881—thirty-one years before it became a state. At that time, former Union general and president Ulysses S. Grant was alive and the Apache chief Geronimo had not surrendered. While the frontier had not closed, the more prescient westerners recognized that the old era would soon end. Because of their consciousness, thus their greater explicitness on the subject, the world of *Pat Garrett and Billy the Kid* makes the chief characters seem more anachronistic than those of Peckinpah's earlier films. To Garrett's assertion (in the prologue) that times have changed, Billy replies, "Times, maybe. Not me." In part, perhaps, to reassure himself, Garrett frequently enunciates his position. "I aim to live to be rich, old, 'n' grey," he asserts in Peckinpah's film. In an exchange only slightly altered from Wurlitzer's screenplay, Poe declares, "The time's over for drifters and outlaws and them as got no backbone." Despite Garrett's antagonism toward Poe and his aversion to gunning down a former friend, Garrett confirms Poe's view: "This country's getting old, and I aim to get old with it. Now the Kid don't want it that way."

* * *

An aura of brutality, corruption, and evil permeates *Bring Me the Head of Alfredo Garcia* more than it does any other film by Peckinpah. In its pitiless, malignant, and savage world, anyone can become a victim of violence: not only a person who commits an infraction or opposes a gunman, but a bar girl who strokes the inside of a man's thigh (in response, he knocks her unconscious) or a man and woman who picnic a few yards from a road (motorcycle thugs draw guns so that one of them may rape her). In such a world, love exists only as an interlude, destroyed before it can flourish, and both a discovery of pregnancy and a baptismal ceremony occasion a command for murder.

In *Bring Me the Head of Alfredo Garcia*, Peckinpah takes the theme of anachronistic conflicts (*The Deadly Companions*), which he had developed into people who become anachronisms (*The Wild Bunch*) or might do so (*Pat Garrett and Billy the Kid*), and dramatizes that, far from being anachronistic, the code of revenge, the values embraced by such people, and the violent and brutal way of life they represent are as much a part of contemporary civilization as they are of El Jefe's fiefdom. In a dazzlingly edited sequence in the prologue to *Bring Me the Head of Alfredo Garcia*, such sights as horses, men with boots and spurs, a formal baronial room in a hacienda, and women wearing stately black dresses and mantillas give the impression that the film is set in the old West—or rather, an old somewhere south of the border. Although, in this prologue, El Jefe's chief henchman, Max, wears a contemporary shirt and tie, his costume only momentarily jars. Once El Jefe gives the order for Alfredo Garcia's head, the movie enters a disorienting time warp as it cuts to a moving motorcycle and automobiles in the same frame as horses, then to shots of a jet plane taking off and landing in Mexico City. In the twentieth century, as in earlier times, the baronial El Jefe can command murder to satisfy his sense of honor. The vendetta remains a way of life. In this respect, Elita's reminiscence of a place she would like to revisit is apposite: "It's a beautiful, old Spanish town. It's a sixteenth- or a seventeenth-century—I don't know. I get mixed up with the centuries."[57] The centuries she cites are unlikely to be accidental on Peckinpah's part: they are the period when revenge tragedies flourished in English drama.

Unlike *The Deadly Companions*, the protagonist of *Bring Me the Head of Alfredo Garcia* does not instigate the quest for vengeance, which in the later film is treated in a complex manner. Unlike the vindictive character in *The Deadly Companions*, El Jefe, who offers a million dollars for the head of the man who impregnated his daughter, which is a traditional Mexican method of taking revenge,[58] does not renounce his vendetta. Ironically, retribution is denied nonetheless, since Garcia is already dead as a result of drunken driving.[59] More ironically, El Jefe does not discover this fact, for not only does no one tell him, he also expresses no interest in learning the circumstances of Garcia's death. It is for the audience to recognize the futility of vengeance, which breeds further vengeance until each revenger is avenged and, with greater irony, the woman who tried to avoid the vendetta takes revenge. El Jefe's order sets in motion a chain

of events—Max contracts Quill and Sappensly,[60] who employ two underlings and who subcontract Bennie for the head—that turn against him and
the man who kills him.

When Bennie claws his way up from where the underlings buried him
alive after knocking him out with a shovel and decapitating Garcia, his
discovery of Elita's death spurs him to retributive action. Driving after her
murderers, he mutters to himself, "Come out of the dark, I'll meet you
bastards. I'm going to nail you. Somewhere I'm going to nail you." He
does, and after he puts Garcia's head in his car, he shoots one of the dead
bodies. "Why? Because it feels so goddamned good," he says, before shooting it again.

As Garcia's relatives prepare to kill Bennie in revenge for having dese-
crated the grave and mutilated the corpse, Quill and Sappensly arrive and
save him by shooting most of them. However, one of the relatives shoots
Quill. To avenge himself on the death of his friend (and perhaps, the actors but not the words imply, his homosexual lover), Sappensly draws a
pistol on Bennie for having got them into this situation; but Bennie kills
him first. Bennie wonders why the head is so valuable that Elita and others were killed for it. Upon delivering it to Max, he asks, "What do you want
it for? Not you guys. You don't want it." Max's refusal to answer precipitates another gunfight, of which Bennie is the sole survivor. He takes a card
with El Jefe's address and flies to the hacienda, where a baptismal party for
El Jefe's grandson, Garcia's son, takes place. After El Jefe pays Bennie, he
orders the head to be thrown to the pigs. His daughter, whom he had tortured to reveal the name of the man responsible for her pregnancy, commands Bennie to kill her father, which he does. Although she helps Bennie to flee the hacienda, El Jefe's guards slaughter him with a barrage of
bullets before he can get more than a few yards from the compound.

In what may be the movie's most ironic aspect—"I regard everything with
irony," Peckinpah has said, "including the face I see in the mirror when I
wake up in the morning"[61]—almost every person who instigates vengeance
becomes the victim of vendetta. The mother of Garcia's newly baptized son
proves to be her father's daughter by avenging herself for her lover's death.
If audiences perceive a rough justice in her causing her father's murder, they
thereby ignore the facts that it results in Bennie's death and that she goes
scot free. If she personifies the righteous avenger, why is she more virtuous than Bennie, who follows her directive after, moving upward through
the chain of command, he kills those responsible for Elita's death? The
movie ends not with his murder but with a machine gun spitting bullets
directly at the camera—that is, at the spectators.

Bring Me the Head of Alfredo Garcia elaborates the themes, motifs, and gimmicks of *The Deadly Companions*. While the later film is not a simplistic retelling of the earlier as the director would have told it thirteen years before if the producer had given him leeway, their parallels and reversals are too prominent to be coincidental. In the earlier movie, a boy's coffin is carried to a cemetery; in the later, children carry a coffin to one. Instead of a boy accidentally killed, one is accidentally engendered. Instead of transporting a corpse by wagon or pallet to bury it, the protagonist unearths a grave in order to cut off a corpse's head, which he drives by automobile—but in both movies he is a Caucasian American traversing territory rendered hostile by the area's natives. Whereas the corpse in *The Deadly Companions* seems immune to decay or stench inflicted by time, road conditions, and the hot sun, Alfredo Garcia's head, although it is wrapped, is not similarly protected. When the car hits bumps in the road, the head is knocked about. Since flies swarm around it, the protagonist packs it in ice. Bennie does not suffer from an arbitrarily inflicted wound. Rather, his life is his wound. At a glance, one of the gangsters appraises him in an aside that he does not care is overheard: "A loser." "Nobody loses all the time," Bennie responds. To him, the prospect to earn an apparently easy ten thousand dollars is a last chance to improve his life. Contrivances notwithstanding, Peckinpah manages to a surprising extent to transcend gimmickry in *Bring Me the Head of Alfredo Garcia,* whereas the most he was able to accomplish in *The Deadly Companions,* as he recognizes, was to keep the audience's mind off the gimmicks.[62]

Both films treat the prostitute as heroine, but only the later one does so unconventionally. When the whore is about to be raped at gunpoint, she warns the protagonist not to interfere, since "I've been here before, and you don't know the way." He admits to himself, "She can handle it a lot better than I can." The loser falls in love with the whore and to the surprise of both he proposes marriage, which in an extremely touching moment makes them so happy that she cries and he all but does the same. Particularly important, the whore of *Bring Me the Head of Alfredo Garcia* acquires dignity when she falls in love and becomes engaged to marry her man, loser though he may be.

Their admission of love and engagement to marry betoken mutual respect, which they demand from others. When Elita's rapist rips off her sweater with a knife, she slaps his face, an assertion of pride, and she neither flinches nor cries when he hits her in return. Only after he denies her plea—"Please don't. Please"—does she submit, for in her phrases she has been there before and knows the way. After Bennie prevents the rape by shooting the man and his accomplice, he and Elita go to a rural hotel, where the clerk refuses them a room. "This hotel does not allow—," he says, and he completes the sentence by glancing at her. Bennie breaks down the door to his cubicle, grabs his collar, insists that he and Elita are married, and demands accommodations. Gratified that her lover-fiancé has retrieved her honor, she orders the best room in the hotel. In contrast to El Jefe's requirement for the satisfaction of his honor, which involves the torture of his daughter and the decapitation of her lover, Bennie's centers upon the recognition of a woman's dignity. In contrast to the patriarchal society dominated by El Jefe, which renders his daughter a virtual slave, the society formed by the union of Bennie and Elita consists of mutual respect, not domination. Only when Bennie invades El Jefe's society is El Jefe's daughter capable of overthrowing its ruler.

* * *

Instead of antagonists who, as Billy says at the end of *The Deadly Companions,* keep shooting at each other without hitting anything, those of *The Killer Elite,* as the title indicates, are among the aristocracy of murderers, whose expertise the movie amply demonstrates. Although *The Killer Elite* has no innocent child killed in crossfire, the explosion set off by Mike Locken and George Hansen during Peckinpah's opening credit sequence kills a mother bird feeding its young—an image not in the novel from which the film derives.[63]

Locken's debilitating wound and his scar are not gimmicks but are integral parts of character and plot. ComTeg (Communications Integrity), a private American company with paid mercenaries, contracts jobs, some for the CIA, which provides 10 percent of its operating funds. The tasks this movie dramatizes are the protection of an Eastern European defector and of the head of an Asian democratic movement. In a company hideout, Hansen, who for higher pay has sold his services to a rival organization (perhaps another country's), kills the defector while his best friend and partner, Locken, is showering. When Locken emerges, Hansen shoots him in the left elbow and knee, stating, "You've just retired, Mike. Enjoy it." Not malicious, the act is as affectionate as Hansen's profession permits. Unknown to Locken, the two elite killers are deadly companions at the film's start.[64] After Hansen's action, they become enemies, although Hansen later offers Locken the opportunity to join his side. When the stitches come off Locken's joints, scars remain; but a doctor says they will disappear in time. Through will, training, and exercise, Locken overcomes his disabilities.

Yet his desire for revenge remains. "I'll get even," he promises after Hansen plays a practical joke on him early in the movie—foreshadowing what happens. When Cap Collis offers him an office job, Locken makes his goal clear: "I just want to get closer to George." "So you find him and you zap him," says Cap. "Will that give you back your knee and your elbow?" "Oh, no," Locken replies, "but wherever they are I know they'll be a lot happier." When the CIA offers ComTeg the job to protect the democratic Asian leader Chung while he is in the United States with his daughter, ComTeg's head, Lawrence Weyburn, accepts because Chung's opposition has hired Hansen to kill him. Weyburn too wants vengeance. He orders Cap to give Locken the job and tell him "to tag" Hansen. Although Locken's primary goal is to protect Chung, his secondary aim, more prominent to him, is "a chance to get Hansen." After a shootout in San Francisco's Chinatown, Locken spirits Chung and his daughter to a hideout more suited to his subordinate goal than to his primary mission. "Hey, this is a mousetrap, Mike," says his cohort Mac when they arrive, "We're using them as bait." As if to confirm Mac's observation, Locken declares, after those he has been assigned to protect have gone upstairs, his certainty that Hansen will arrive. "Is that why you made 'em put the lights on upstairs?" asks Mac. "He really blew you apart, didn't he? Whatever he does dictates the way you go. You're getting to be his prisoner, Mike," pointing to his forehead, "up here." In contrast to *The Deadly Companions,* the protagonist of *The Killer Elite* is not in a position to revenge himself on the person who debilitated him. Using the daughter as hostage, Hansen orders Locken and Mike to throw down their guns, which they do. It is Miller, another cohort, who, instead of surrendering as ordered, kills Hansen. Actually, the three companions—alliteratively called Mike (Locken), Mac, and Miller—represent three facets of Yellowleg: the revenger, the voice of conscience, and the killer. Demonstrating the ambivalence of seeking revenge against a former friend, a person who deliberately let him live, Locken punches Miller for having shot Hansen.

The question of retaliation is more complex than the settlement of personal scores just described. Learning that Hansen's superior in the rival company is Cap, who works for both organizations, Locken shoots him, repeating Hansen's words, "You've just retired." However, when it becomes clear that Weyburn masterminded the entire scheme of retribution in order to eliminate Cap, whom he suspected of treason, Locken does not kill him as well, but turns his back on the entire affair.

Going beyond the perception of the futility of revenge, he accepts the validity of Mac's views, reflecting those uttered by Peckinpah in 1972,[65]

that all power systems manipulate people into killing each other for supposedly noble aims, that "you're so busy doing their dirty work, you can't
tell who the bad guys really are," and that "all the goddamn power systems, all the wheelers and dealers at the top with their gin and fizzes . . .
need guys like you to do their bloodletting while they're busy making
speeches about freedom and progress. They're all full of bullshit. There's
not one power system that really cares about a civilian."[66] One civilian,
Mac's wife, Josephine, becomes almost hysterical whenever he accepts a
ComTeg assignment, and she implores him to renounce that part of his
life—revealing the brutal reality about women whom the supposedly romantic and heroic gunfighters leave behind. The film's attack on power
systems includes that represented by Chung, who is called not a freedom
fighter but "an Asian politician." Against Locken's advice, Chung agrees,
in the best tradition of an honorable shootout at high noon, to personal
combat with his chief enemy. "If I don't survive, I'm not the man who's
needed," he asserts. Repudiating the ethos of movie westerns, Locken says,
"I never heard so much bullshit in my life." When he would interfere in
Chung's behalf, Mac stops him: "Don't. Who cares?" The final ritual sword
combat mocks the western gunfight, for while the supposedly good guy
wins, his victory is essentially meaningless. Apart from the fallacy that the
better fighter is therefore the better person to lead his country's government, Chung represents a power system that, in the film's terms, is no
better than others.

In *The Killer Elite*, Peckinpah metamorphoses the theme of the American Civil War in *The Deadly Companions*. The battle between Hansen and
ComTeg suggests that of rebel and country. Instead of a national north
and south, the film presents a global north and south, America and
Chung's unnamed Asian country. While the countries are not in conflict,
the CIA supports Chung only minimally, requiring merely that he not be
assassinated on American soil. Furthermore, a civil war rages in Chung's
country and his opponents want him dead. Reflecting this strife is that
of the titular killers, one trying to protect Chung, the other trying to ex-
terminate him in behalf of his domestic opponents.

* * *

A prime example of Peckinpah's motif of children, the credit montage in
Cross of Iron begins with three Hitler Youth boys climbing a mountain as
they carry a Nazi flag that, later in the montage, they plant on the top.
This montage alternates shots of artillery explosions, huge rallies, soldiers
being decorated, troops in battle, Nazi flags, parades, Hitler, tanks, soldiers

shooting civilians, and battlefield corpses with shots of a little boy blowing a horn, an innocent-looking lad amidst a group of children gazing heavenward, Hitler patting a youngster's cheek, boys playing soldier as they march with stick guns, and Hitler shaking hands with a little girl. Near the end of this montage, a return to the Hitler Youth boys and the innocent-looking lad, following photographs of war horrors, suggests the betrayal of youth and innocence—a hint that the film's closing credits buttress, for they include stills of children who are victims of the Nazis.

Evoking *The Deadly Companions* is a short subplot that starts with a battle following the credits. After overcoming a Russian artillery position, Steiner and his reconnaissance company find one survivor, a blonde boy who looks thirteen years old. Upon being captured, the frightened youth, recalling the boy of *The Deadly Companions*, plays a harmonica. Not only does Steiner bring him with them, in defiance of the German army policy to take no prisoners, his response to Captain Stransky's order to shoot him is, "You shoot him, sir." "I will," says the Captain, "on the spot. And then I'll deal with you." "No need," interrupts Corporal Schnurrbart, saving the situation, "I'll see that it's taken care of, sir." Removing the boy, he hides him in the company's bunker. Conforming to Peckinpah's view that children are innocent, with good and evil an acquired taste, the boy responds in kind to Steiner's and Schnurrbart's acts of goodness. When Steiner returns to the bunker, he tosses his cap, fatigue jacket, and shoulder holster on his bed. The holster falls behind the bed, where the Russian boy is hiding. Perceiving that he might kill one or more of his German captors, he removes the pistol; but he then decides against this course of action and replaces it in the holster, which he returns to Steiner. Before dawn, when a major enemy offensive is to start, Steiner—who has children of his own, though he does not know where they are—frees the Russian youth, whom he leads to a place where he can rejoin his own people. The boy turns back, calls Steiner, and as a token of gratitude throws him his harmonica. Each smiles. Directly after the lad leaves, advancing troops of his own side, beginning their attack, inadvertently kill him—an analogue to being caught in crossfire. The harmonica becomes an emblem of goodness and childlike purity. Later in the film, after Steiner plays a note on it, one of his men takes it to play a sweet, nonmartial tune that the others sing, thereby relieving their tensions and fatigue in a peaceful moment between fighting. In the movie's final battle, a dark-haired Russian soldier, who is about the same age as the blonde boy, fires a machine gun at Stransky—resonating the two boys in *The Wild Bunch*. What is noteworthy about Peckinpah's employment of these themes and actions is not only their thematic integration into this film, in marked contrast to their use in *The Deadly Companions,* but also the fact that none of them, including Steiner's children and the prohibition against taking prisoners, is in the novel from which *Cross of Iron* is adapted, Willi Heinrich's *The Willing Flesh,* or in an early draft of the screenplay that served as the basis of Peckinpah's film.[67]

Corresponding to the motif of living anachronisms in *The Wild Bunch* and *Junior Bonner,* as well as *The Deadly Companions,* the German soldiers in *Cross of Iron* are fighting a war they know is already lost. Before the end of the opening credits, a subtitle informs us of the state of this war, plus time and place: "Russia / The Taman Peninsula—1943 / The Retreat." When, upon arriving at the front, Stransky states his belief in the German soldier's ideals, Colonel Brandt interrupts: "The German soldier no longer has any ideals. He is not fighting for the culture of the West, not for one form of government that he wants, not for the stinking Party, he's fighting for his life, God bless him." Before the massive Russian attack at the end of the movie, Stransky learns from "reliable sources that headquarters have already written off the Taman bridgehead and soon the whole Crimea will be a cul-de-sac." The film's battles constitute not glorious victory but inglorious defeat. Corresponding to Caucasian Americans traversing hostile Indian or Mexican territory, the Germans are foreigners traveling across hostile Russian land. Their Moselle wine, says Brandt, is as out of place as they themselves are.

Unsentimentally, Peckinpah depicts doomed losers fighting for a monstrous cause. The only saving graces of those among them with saving graces are hatred of the war and those who caused it, pride in professionalism, humane instincts exercised under pressure of combat, and loyalty for individual human beings. In addition to saving the life of the Russian boy and refusing to obey Stransky's command to kill him, thereby placing his own life in jeopardy, Steiner does not order the execution of the Russian female soldiers his men capture; and he leaves behind, for the women to deal with, the Nazi Party soldier who brutalized one of them. He understands, as his counterpart in the novel does not comprehend, that the cause which will conquer his forces is no better than the cause which he serves: "One extreme to another, and neither works, or will ever." In the movie's climax, Peckinpah dramatically integrates the motif of disguise—the Germans don Russian uniforms to pass through enemy lines into their own (an action early in the novel, late in the film).

Ideologically as well as personally, the individualist Steiner opposes the elitist Stransky who, exemplifying the aristocratic and military side of the class conflict, reminds the enlisted man that everything Steiner is and may become after the war depends on himself (Stransky). In a sequence not in the novel, Lieutenant Meyer reminds Steiner that Stransky is not merely a Nazi but "is pure Prussian military aristocracy, and rich. You know the ruling classes." "Come now, lieutenant, what's left for them to rule?" asks Steiner. "Don't be naive," Meyer replies. "Stransky will survive this war one way or another, and he'll still have his land, his wealth, and his status. But he can be very dangerous in defeat." Stransky reminds Steiner that distinctions between them are matters "of ethical and intellectual superiority, which is caused, whether you like it or not, by class differences." Steiner insists that a man is often what he feels himself to be and points out that Kant was the son of a shoemaker and Schubert of a schoolmaster. "Talent, sensitivity, and character," he adds, "are no longer privileges of the so-called upper class." Stransky admits that his own statement was a general concept to which there may be individual exceptions.[68] To Steiner's mocking remark, "Didn't your Führer say that all class distinctions were to be abolished?" Stransky draws himself up proudly: "I am an officer of the Wehrmacht. I have never been a Party member. I am a Prussian aristocrat and I don't want to be put into that same category."[69]

Later, Captain Kiesel asks Steiner why he displays such ingratitude toward Colonel Brandt, who early in the film says that Steiner is "a first-rate soldier, so we look the other way."[70] "What do I have to be grateful for, Captain?" demands Steiner bitterly, "Your tolerance? You think that just because you and Colonel Brandt are more enlightened than most officers that I hate you any less? I hate all officers—all the Stransky's, all the Triebigs, all the Iron Cross scavengers, the whole German army. . . . Do you know how much I hate this war and everything it stands for?" Correctly, Steiner perceives that the difference between officers like Brandt and Kiesel and those like Stransky is merely cosmetic.

During the general retreat at the film's finale, Brandt explains his decision to evacuate Kiesel before anyone else: "You're a brave man, braver than you think you are. One of these days there will be a need for brave civilians. . . . In the new Germany, if such a thing is allowed to exist, there will be a need for builders, for thinkers, for poets. . . . You will search out and contact all of these—'better people,' you call them?—and together you will take on the responsibility that goes with survival."[71] As if such a speech were insufficient to demonstrate that Peckinpah does not idealize the Third Reich, whose soldiers are the subjects of *Cross of Iron*, or portray a person like Brandt sympathetically rather than ironically, he quotes a poem by Bertolt Brecht after the closing credits: "Don't rejoice in his defeat, you men. / For though the world stood up and stopped the bastard, / The bitch that bore him is in heat again." This theme does not exist in the novel.[72]

War may constitute the essence of realistically brutal violence, but in *Cross of Iron*—a great film that is perhaps one of the greatest war movies ever made (Orson Welles called it the finest antiwar picture he had ever seen)[73]—Peckinpah attaches neither glory nor idealism to war or violence. Compared to war, the realistic, brutal act Peckinpah wanted at the end of *The Deadly Companions* is mild. In *Cross of Iron,* the sounds of battle rarely let up, and bunkers shake when bombs fall nearby. Rifle, pistol, and machine gun bullets, mortar and cannon shells, aerial bombs and tanks maim and kill, as do bayonets. Shells explode in faces and they toss soldiers onto barbed wire. Screams of pain rend the air. A troop truck travels along a muddy road over tracks made by other trucks, which cover a body imprinted in these tracks. A headless corpse incarnadines the water in which it lies. Like menacing prehistoric reptiles, giant tanks attack men. The wounded are armless, legless, scarred. Graphically, the director depicts Steiner's shell shock, a result of brain concussion, partly from Steiner's viewpoint. When his nurse, Eva, states, "Violence should stop. It must stop," Steiner recollects what he has undergone and laughs. Stransky demonstrates his personal brutality not only when he unhesitatingly prepares to shoot the Russian boy but when, after entrapping the young lover of his aide Lieutenant Triebig into stating that Triebig admitted his homosexuality, he threatens: "If you get caught, you will be hanged, slowly, both of you, together."[74]

As in *The Deadly Companions,* a delayed, then denied vendetta is a theme of *Cross of Iron,* in which the deadly companions are officers and enlisted men. Steiner refuses to certify, as Triebig has, that Stransky led the counterattack that repelled the Russians, which would earn Stransky the Iron Cross he covets. "Lieutenant Meyer led the attack," Steiner tells Brandt. "Captain Stransky was nowhere in sight." Since Brandt will begin disciplinary proceedings against Stransky unless Steiner confirms Triebig, he asks if Steiner stands by his statement. Steiner hedges, for he considers his feud with Stransky "a personal matter." Whereas the independent Steiner refuses to permit an organization to settle his vendetta for him, Stransky has no such compunction. When Kiesel directs Stransky to pull out all rear guard soldiers, including those under Steiner's command, and orders him to make everyone join the evacuation immediately, Stransky conveys the command to Triebig, who asks whether it includes Steiner. Although Stransky says "Yes," he silently disconnects the phone wires when Triebig begins to ring Steiner, thereby trapping Steiner's platoon behind enemy lines. Wearing captured Russian uniforms, Steiner's men make their way past the Russian front lines to the German rear lines, where Stransky and Triebig arrange to have Steiner's troops machine-gunned as they advance. Because some of the German gunners recognize the soldiers as their own, they stop firing, giving a few members of the group enough time to cross the lines safely. When Triebig pleads that he acted under Stransky's orders, Steiner machine-guns him, then goes in search of Stransky, "To pay my debts."

Stransky's effort to brazen out his dilemma with the excuse that Triebig acted on his own does not deceive Steiner, who fires at Stransky to prevent him from leaving, contemptuously taunting the "aristocratic pile of Prussian pig shit" about his Iron Cross. Reclaiming his dignity, as Mapache in *The Wild Bunch* does before an admiring little boy in the midst of Villa's attack, Stransky asserts the pride of his social class and military caste to demand the whereabouts of the remainder of the sergeant's company. Sensing mettle, Steiner forgoes vengeance to accept the gauntlet and issue his own challenge, that Stransky is the rest of his troops. Deliberately, he throws Stransky a rifle and turns his back on him. Instead of shooting Steiner, the potentially deadly companion smiles: "I accept. I'll show you how a Prussian officer can fight." Acknowledging his acceptance and abnegation of revenge, Steiner replies, "And I will show you where the Iron Crosses grow." In contrast to *The Deadly Companions,* the decision of both commoner and aristocrat to abjure vengeance derives from their individualistic characters, which possess dignity and pride.[75]

* * *

Unlike Peckinpah's earlier films, including *The Deadly Companions, Convoy* lacks any "brutal, realistic act." For all the fighting and wrecking of automobiles, furniture, and buildings, these actions are photographed to appear comic. In *Convoy,* his use of slow motion is almost entirely balletic, and except for his depiction of the aftermath of violence in the face and body of Spider Mike, the violence of this film is nullified. Symptomatic of its avoidance of brutality is the motif of children caught in the middle of violence. Whereas Yellowleg accidentally shoots a boy, Pig Pen swerves his truck to avoid hitting children as they cross the street; but the truck accidentally hits an ice cream wagon, knocking down the vendor, who though uninjured angrily throws ice cream at Pig Pen's side window. Instead of bullets, *Convoy* has sweets.

While Rubber Duck is not a western outlaw or a cowboy, Spider Mike links him to that tradition: "I heard more stories about you than Jesse James." When the truckers sound their horns as they pass a cowboy herding steers, he raises his hat in fraternal salute. Pig Pen ruminates, "These lonely lost highways sure grind the soul out of us cowboys." As Governor Haskins says, notwithstanding his political hyperbole, the truckers who form the titular convoy are "the living embodiment of the American cowboy tradition."

For this reason, and because they are individualists, not conformists, they are anachronisms in the contemporary world. Although the Teamsters union has tried to organize truckers, the Duck is among those who have refused to join. "I'm independent," he insists. "At least we got one thing in common," concedes Sheriff Lyle Wallace. Those in the convoy, young and old, are anti-Establishment individualists who protest a variety of sociopolitical and personal grievances, from the treatment of black Vietnam War veterans to the recently lowered speed limit ("the whole fifty-five double-nickle was a jive-ass turkey rap and I don't like people giving me bullshit"). Since the governor recognizes that the convoy has more public support than he does, he aims by negotiating with its apparent leader, Rubber Duck, to use the truckers to spur his election to the United States Senate.

The truckers' code of honor resembles that enunciated by Pike in *The Wild Bunch:* stand by a friend, come what may. When Spider Mike, an African American, leaves the convoy to return to his pregnant wife, the Alvarez, Texas, sheriff detains and beats him (offscreen). To save Mike, Governor Haskins does not want to postpone his meeting and photo opportunity with the Duck, much less to forfeit his image as a forceful leader. "Sometimes you have to sacrifice the individual," he insists. "Bullshit," says a trucker. "I'll do all I can to help you," the governor tells the Duck, "but I'm afraid he's just going to have to fend for himself for a while." Without considering whether or not anyone will join him, the Duck leaves to help his friend.

In the background of *Convoy* is Peckinpah's familiar theme of revenge deferred and denied. Lyle has not seen the Duck, on whom he has therefore delayed vengeance, for six years. While the movie is unclear as to the reason for their animosity, it hints that Violet, who gives herself to the Duck as a birthday present, is Lyle's wife. After the fight in the diner, during which Mike hits Lyle and the Duck handcuffs him to a counter stool, Lyle pursues them. When the truckers destroy the jail and other property in Alvarez, Lyle is caustic: "I knew you'd come, but I never figured you'd need help too. . . . This is between you and me. . . . And now look what you've done. You're nothing but a two-bit, lyin', cheatin', law-breakin' trucker." Calling Lyle "a broke down old bribe-takin' piece of meanness," the Duck asks, "What good are you?" Lyle's response recalls Harrigan in *The Wild Bunch:* "I am the law. . . . I represent the law." "Well, piss on you," says the Duck, "and piss on your law." Although the Duck would forget their feud and abandon further vengeance, Lyle refuses to do either and self-righteously insists the Duck should be shot. At a bridge on the Rio Grande, over which the vehicles in the convoy hope to pass into Mexico (as the Wild Bunch and the McCoys in *The Getaway* do), where they would be safe from American law, Lyle leads police and National Guardsmen with pistols, rifles, a machine gun, and a tank; and he fires the machine gun at the Duck's truck when the Duck ignores the warning to stop. A pistol shot hits the truck's load of inflammable chemicals, which explode, plunging truck and driver into the river. Lyle looks sad, as if surprised at this consequence of his actions.

When the truckers see that the governor has turned the Duck's funeral into a media event to bolster his senatorial campaign, they leave, one by one, with such comments as "He's using the truckers for a red carpet to the White House" and "Somebody ought to de-horn that rotten son-of-a-bitch." Lyle notices that Rubber Duck is alive, disguised (another recurrent image) as a "Jesus freak" in a van that has joined the convoy. Instead of informing, he laughs—partly because he is humane enough to favor the triumph of life over death, partly because he tacitly accepts the Duck's willingness to abandon revenge, and partly because he applauds the triumph of the Duck's defiant individualism over the conformist political Establishment repudiated by the truckers.

*   *   *

Whereas *Cross of Iron* dramatizes the heat of combat, *The Osterman Weekend* portrays the cold war. Unlike the stylized photography and editing of *Convoy,* and like those of Peckinpah's usual work, those of *The Osterman Weekend* do not soften or nullify violence. Such set pieces as the kidnapping and rescue of John Tanner's wife and son, and the battle at Tanner's home, which is vastly different from and more vivid than their counterparts in the Robert Ludlum novel from which the film derives, contain "brutal, realistic" actions that Peckinpah with customary skill arranges to generate considerable impact.[76] In addition, individual deeds, none of which is in the novel, are redolent of Yellowleg's shooting Billy, for instance: Joseph Cardone tries to drown Tanner while they are playing pool-basketball; when Virginia Tremayne urges the men to beat Tanner, his wife, Ali, punches her; Bernard Osterman karate-chops the CIA agent who accosts him in the dark; and when Tanner tries to beat Osterman with a baseball bat, Osterman throws him onto a table and prepares to choke him with the bat.

In *The Osterman Weekend,* the central character does not shoot a boy in crossfire but, analogously, Lawrence Fassett, the plot's prime mover though not the central character, thrusts Tanner's young son into danger by seizing him and holding a gun to his head in order to stop his mother from shooting Fassett's underling, who is trying to kill the boy's father. At the movie's start, Fassett's wife is murdered as a result of what one might consider crossfire: she is a victim of manipulations by both KGB and CIA. Neither incident is in Ludlum's novel.

Nor is the film's basic foundation, Fassett's revenge on his employer, Maxwell Danforth, head of the CIA, who is not in the book. The movie revolves around Fassett's deferral of retribution until he has manipulated Tanner—an investigative television reporter ("the king of the exposé," one of his friends calls him) at whose home the titular weekend, a reunion of friends, takes place—into exposing Danforth during a live television interview in which Danforth has agreed to participate. Unknown to Danforth, Fassett is his deadly companion in the CIA. The novel's major situation, which may have attracted Peckinpah to it or activated his imagination once he agreed to direct the film version, is that the relationship between Tanner and his guests who visit him for the weekend becomes—when Fassett makes Tanner believe they are KGB agents, which results in his acting in such a way that they think he is trying to expose their illegal deposit of money in Swiss banks to avoid taxation—an association of deadly companions.

Different from *The Deadly Companions* and from the novel that is this film's source, *The Osterman Weekend* dramatizes the incident that provokes vengeance, the murder of Fassett's wife, which the CIA recorded on film. Fassett's scar is psychological, not physical. Ironically, neither Danforth nor his aide Stennings recalls why she was terminated, save that the action cleared up "a potentially messy situation." Both mistakenly believe Fassett does not know that Danforth sanctioned her murder by the KGB. While investigating his wife's killing, Fassett found a videotape of the assassination. Far more elaborately than any disguise in *The Deadly Companions* or Peckinpah's other films, all of Fassett's actions mask his plans—from the CIA as well as from the CIA's pawns. He explains why he sets up Tanner and his friends: "I want revenge for my wife. Maxwell Danforth murdered her, and I will have him exposed." To this end, after fabricating KGB dossiers on a Soviet contact and concocting evidence against Tanner's friends, he persuades Danforth to let him turn Tanner against them and convinces both that the friends are Soviet agents. Shrewdly, Fassett perceives that Tanner's price for helping the CIA will be Danforth's agreement to appear on his television interview program. Sardonically, he calls the killing of his wife, "while my employers watched on closed-circuit TV," merely "another episode in this whole snuff soap opera we're all in." But so is Fassett's murder of Tanner's four friends, whom he callously dispatches by blowing up a camper they are driving. In an ironic touch, Peckinpah shows that Fassett regards the murder of innocent people to achieve his ends as lightly as Danforth does. He likens Tanner's dead friends to fleas on a dog that is "hit by a stolen car, driven by a drunk teenager, whose girl friend's just given him the clap."

In their interview early in the film, Tanner dubs Danforth "big brother Max." On the air, he refers to him as "arguably the most powerful man in the nation, if by powerful you mean whoever has the greatest effect on your privacy, your personal well-being, and your possible prospects of survival," and he quotes Danforth's statement, "counterintelligence and public accountability make uneasy bedfellows." Partly through Tanner, partly through Fassett's testimony, and partly through Danforth's own words, the head of the CIA exposes himself as a cold warrior with presidential ambitions,[77] which he first denies but immediately admits: "If it is my destiny to be called on by the American people to assume that exalted office, I should feel compelled to accept. I have always sought out my country's enemies and foiled their designs against us. And as president of these United States I would continue to do so." Tanner airs Fassett's videotape of his wife's death. Admitting his culpability as a killer of innocent people, Fassett insists on the guilt of Danforth, who "is prepared to use the power of his office and all its techniques in order to further his own personal ambition."

In contrast to *The Deadly Companions*, the avenger of *The Osterman Weekend* does not abjure vengeance as foolish and futile. As in *Bring Me the Head of Alfredo Garcia*, he is the victim of the forces he sets in motion. Tanner, whom Fassett manipulates, maneuvers Fassett into a false sense of security by making him think that he (Tanner) is at the studio interviewing Danforth (Tanner and Osterman prerecord Tanner's questions, which Osterman intercuts with Danforth's live response) and arrives at the hideout (whose whereabouts he may know because of the television hookup), where he kills him. These aspects are not in the novel.

Unlike the novel, which is a simple spy yarn, the film revolves around broader implications of Fassett's actions. As if to call attention to these connotations, the movie's Fassett approvingly quotes the observation of Osterman, which is not in the novel, "The truth is a lie that hasn't been found out." Upon learning what Fassett did, Osterman says, "I was just kind of wondering how we got in this mess." "It's called being programmed," says Tanner. Fassett's manipulation of relatively few people, largely by means of television, is a microcosm of the television medium's manipulation of many people who watch it and who, in doing so, as Fassett puts it, are "worshiping graven images." As Peckinpah said as early as 1972, "We're all television oriented now. We'd better all wake up to the fact that Big Brother is here. And now, with TV and video cassettes coming in, . . . it's awful." Anticipating *The Osterman Weekend* by eleven years, he adds what Tanner's statement in the movie virtually paraphrases, "We're all being programmed, and I bitterly resent it."[78] Not only is Tanner's phrase not in the original novel, it is not in the final draft of Alan Sharp's screenplay. In it, Tanner responds to Osterman's query by berating his own self-righteousness and hypocrisy, whereupon Osterman says, not "It's called being programmed," but rather, "It's called being human, John."[79] As coproducer William N. Panzer states, Peckinpah wanted the audience "to feel the same confusion everyone in the movie felt as they were being manipulated to know nothing about it."[80] In my judgment, he succeeded. At the end of the film, after the confrontation between Fassett and Danforth, Tanner tells the viewing public: "You saw a liar talk to a killer and you couldn't tell them apart. Who cares? It's only television." Since television programs merely fill gaps between efforts to steal the public's money, if the viewers want to save their money, they could easily switch off by using their hands "and what is left of your free will. This is the moment. My bet is you can't do it. Go ahead and try."

Apart from changing Fassett's motivation and altering the theme, Peckinpah's film makes him more prominent than he is in the novel. Moreover, it makes him a variant of the key figures who populate Peckinpah's other movies. As Stennings, the CIA man who thereby occupies the same position as the respectable bankers and railroad men of the westerns, says of him, "He's too much of an individual." This quality appeals to Danforth, who sees it as a characteristic they share, although he expresses the matter differently: "He's something you're not and never will be. He's a field operator." By linking Fassett and Danforth in this manner, Peckinpah conveys their similarity in another way, as mentioned earlier, and thus he reveals what the westerns—because their aura may, in the view of some spectators, transcend his demythologizing themes and techniques—do not always make convincing, the dark side of the individualist, the loner, the outcast.

In addition to Stennings, Tanner's guests, who are all tax evaders, are figures of respectability. Cardone is a corporate lawyer who specializes in tax shelters for the wealthy; Richard Tremayne is a fashionable, feel-good doctor who panders to rich patients; and Osterman is a screenwriter who quips, "I'm not a revolutionary. What I am is a nihilistic anarchist who lives on residuals," and who admits that money has always informed his decisions.

Although prostitutes as such do not people *The Osterman Weekend,* two wives who arrive for the weekend, Betty Cardone and Virginia Tremayne, are—unlike the disreputable Kit in *The Deadly Companions,* the scandalous Hildy in *The Ballad of Cable Hogue,* and the unrespectable Elita in *Bring Me the Head of Alfredo Garcia*—respectable women who differ little from prostitutes. In bed, Betty behaves as if her husband were a client. When he reminds her not to chew gum when she is about to perform fellatio, she dispassionately sticks it on the bedpost, and after sexual intercourse she replaces the wad in her mouth, patting him on the back in approval—suggestive that only he had an orgasm. A cocaine addict whose habit her physician-husband supports, Virginia manipulates him sexually, enhancing her attractiveness verbally, by wearing provocative underwear, by lying to him during telephone conversations as to what she is or is not wearing, and in general, by "playing the bitch in heat." The phrase is Ali Tanner's, whose mature relationship with her husband, which differs from that of the other women and their husbands, includes candor, comprehension of his work (when Danforth telephones, she understands the implications of the call), and open discussion of mutual problems (when he tries to make her leave for the weekend without disclosing what Fassett told him, she straightforwardly asks if he intends to dissolve their marriage). Also unlike the other couples, they have a child, which makes their marriage a family, not simply (or complexly) a man and woman cohabiting.

* * *

The Deadly Companions adumbrates themes, motifs, and gimmicks that in varying combinations and with different emphases inform all of Peckinpah's feature films. To say that his employment of them following his first feature becomes increasingly sophisticated would be to damn with faint praise, since his first movie is unsophisticated; yet the statement is true. Symptomatic of his growing skill is the treatment of the central gimmicks of *The Deadly Companions:* the scar and wound, which increasingly become more emblematic of the psychological (*The Wild Bunch*) and as psychological only (*Bring Me the Head of Alfredo Garcia, The Osterman Weekend*). Increasingly too, he motivates and integrates motifs and gimmicks of *The Deadly Companions* into the fabric of character and situation: for instance, children and the accidental shooting of a boy (*Cross of Iron*), traversal across hostile terrain (*Bring Me the Head of Alfredo Garcia, Cross of Iron*), companions deadly to each other (*The Getaway, The Osterman Weekend*), and disguises (*Major Dundee, Cross of Iron*). After *The Deadly Companions,* he treats whores with fewer of the constraints imposed by Hollywood conventions, and he does so with understanding, humanity, and variety, as he also contrasts them with respectable women (*The Ballad of Cable Hogue, Bring Me the Head of Alfredo Garcia*). The outcast, loner, or individualist reappears continually, also in thematic opposition to respectable society, and also handled with great variety and skill (*The Wild Bunch, Junior Bonner, Pat Garrett and Billy the Kid, Cross of Iron*). The theme of revenge deferred and perhaps denied recurs in a variety of combinations (*The Ballad of Cable Hogue, Straw Dogs, The Getaway, The Killer Elite, Convoy, The Osterman Weekend*), as does the theme of people who have become anachronisms (*Ride the High Country, The Wild Bunch, Junior Bonner, Pat Garrett and Billy the Kid*). The single act of brutal realism mushrooms into what are perhaps the most personal, artistic, and graphic, yet extremely varied, depictions of violence in cinematic history (*The Wild Bunch, Straw Dogs, Cross of Iron*).

Incipient in Peckinpah's first feature film are trademarks of his canon. They have become his artistic rather than deadly companions, continuing to appear in his entire body of cinematic work. Is their reappearance deliberate? Does it reveal a psychological preoccupation with problems he worked out while making motion pictures? Since I cannot read his mind or communicate with his spirit, I do not know. Even if I did, the answer would not matter. Of consequence is the result, that is, to use the title of my first chapter, "what he did," which was to produce a unified body of work that is the fruit of a consistent intellectual vision and, as often observed, a consistent style. In and of itself, the thematic unity of his films does not create greatness, goodness, or even adequacy. What it does is to help one perceive some of the artistry in works that have clarity of vision, psychological and social understanding, and organic coherence. The themes, motifs, and transformed gimmicks that are continuing companions in Peckinpah's career as a director of feature films demonstrate a unifying characteristic of his greatness.

* * *

Ongoing themes and motifs, consistent philosophical underpinnings, solid directorial technique: these aspects of Sam Peckinpah's extraordinary corpus of feature films are stable; yet as we have seen, their dramatically cinematic execution has enormous variety. One source of the fascination and the very artistry of Peckinpah's feature films is his passionate realization of a set of themes and motifs established by stimulating groups of characters who diversely reveal or embody them in relationship to each other and to their environment. These characters and their situations exhibit the director's view of life, which is also consistent and has a sound philosophical basis. It is with extraordinary skill and variety that he stages, shoots, and edits the violent actions which derive from his characters, themes, and ideas. These features inform the art of this great American director.

Notes

Chapter 1: What He Did

1. Kauffmann, *Figures of Light,* p. 181.

2. Heston, *The Actor's Life,* p. 216.

3. That the restored version is, unlike the MGM version initially released, an excellent film, does not mean that it is entirely the director's cut. For one thing, it omits a short scene between Garrett and his wife, whom the restored film's credits cite. (See Seydor, *Peckinpah: The Western Films: A Reconsideration,* p. 299. To distinguish this book from Seydor's earlier book, cited below, I will hereafter cite it as *Reconsideration.*) For another, it substitutes Poe hurting old Rowland to make him tell where Billy is for Garrett hitting Ruthie Lee for the same reason. Possibly, Peckinpah's print would have kept both, partly because dialogue (in both prints) indicates that Garrett and Poe learn of Billy's whereabouts at about the same time, and partly because the inclusion of both, suggesting similarities between the men, would have greater dramatic impact than either one by itself.

4. Simmons, *Peckinpah,* pp. 185–86. Fielding's name does not appear in the credits of the restored version either. For credits of Peckinpah's feature films, see the filmography. Since Fielding's contribution to the score of the restored film is problematic, I have not added his name. Apropos cinematic credits, Peckinpah sometimes makes self-referential jokes in those that appear at the end of his movies. In *Convoy,* for instance, one figure is dubbed Deke Thornton, which is the name of the Robert Ryan character in *The Wild Bunch,* and the minister who leads the "Jesus Freaks" is called Reverend Sloane, the name of the David Warner character, also a minister, in *The Ballad of Cable Hogue.*

5. Bayer, *The Great Movies,* p. 27.

6. Kauffmann, *Field of View,* pp. 44–45.

7. Seydor, *Peckinpah: The Western Films* (hereafter, *Peckinpah*), p. 255; Seydor, *Reconsideration,* p. 340.

8. Quoted in Simmons, p. 39.

9. Quoted in Joel Reisner and Bruce Kane, "Sam Peckinpah," in Thomas, *Directors in Action,* p. 126.

10. Quoted in Fine, *Bloody Sam,* p. 290.

11. Seydor, *Reconsideration,* p. 351.

12. "Playboy Interview," p. 74.

13. Quoted in Simmons, p. 86.

14. Fine, p. 284.

15. Ernest Callenbach, "A Conversation with Sam Peckinpah," *Film Quarterly* 17 (Winter 1963–64), in Sarris, *Interviews with Film Directors,* p. 376.

16. Seydor, *Peckinpah,* p. 24; Weddle, *"If They Move . . . Kill 'Em!"* p. 200.

17. Simmons, p. 47.

18. Reisner and Kane, p. 128; Seydor, *Peckinpah,* p. 145n; Fine, p. 164.

19. Simmons, p. 140.

20. Ibid., pp. 158, 166–67.

21. Hill, *The Getaway,* pp. 25–26.

22. Wurlitzer, *Pat Garrett and Billy the Kid,* p. viii; Seydor, *Peckinpah,* p. 190.

23. In his introduction (p. viii), Rudolph (Rudy in the screen credits) Wurlitzer emphasizes that unlike Peckinpah's film his screenplay begins with Billy's escape from the jail in Lincoln, and that Billy and Garrett do not meet until the final scene. Wurlitzer adds, "The director wanted their relationship in front, so that everyone would know they were old buddies. . . . The beginning was changed completely." Because of Peckinpah's cuts, additions, and changes, I consider it proper to label those parts of Wurlitzer's screenplay that Peckinpah retained in the movie as Wurlitzer's, the rest as Peckinpah's. Unless otherwise indicated, quotations are from the film, not the published screenplay. Where relevant, I cite distinctions between Peckinpah and Wurlitzer.

24. Simmons, pp. 213–14, 216–17, 220.

25. Fine, p. 164.

26. Weddle, p. 505; Simmons, p. 228.

27. Whitehall, "Talking with Peckinpah," p. 175; "Shoot!" p. 6.

28. Simmons, p. 171.

29. Weddle, p. 537.

30. "Sam Peckinpah Lets It All Hang Out," p. 18.

31. Seydor, *Reconsideration,* p. xxii.

32. Seydor, *Peckinpah,* p. 80, and *Reconsideration,* pp. 139–40, give two hours and fifteen minutes for the cut version. Fine, p. 288, gives two hours and fourteen minutes.

33. Weddle, p. 9.

Chapter 2: Their Own Laws, Their Own Trails, Their Own Ways

1. Shaw, *Everybody's Political What's What?* p. 191.

2. McKinney, *Sam Peckinpah,* p. 242.

3. Sartre, *No Exit and Three Other Plays*, pp. 122–23. Further references to *The Flies* will be given in the text by act and scene. References to the one-act play *No Exit* will be given by title, as will a reference to Steve Martin's play *Picasso at the Lapin Agile*.

4. Selland quoted in Seydor, *Peckinpah*, p. 256.

5. Seydor, *Reconsideration*, p. 345.

6. Weddle, *"If They Move . . . Kill 'Em!"* pp. 73–74.

7. Seydor, *Reconsideration*, pp. 347–48.

8. Having taught in its Department of Drama from 1960 to 1962, and having known one of Peckinpah's mentors, James Butler, and other teachers with whom he studied, I can certify that Aristotle was still alive and influential at USC years after Peckinpah left.

9. Seydor, *Peckinpah*, p. 256.

10. Ibid., p. 256; Weddle, pp. 73–74.

11. Interview with Tom Milne, *Sight and Sound*, Winter 1971–72, quoted in Parrill, *Heroes' Twilight*, p. 46, and in Seydor, *Reconsideration*, p. 219.

12. Camus, *The Myth of Sisyphus*, p. 88.

13. Burke, *A Grammar of Motives*, p. 219.

14. Sartre, *Being and Nothingness*, p. 496.

15. Camus, p. 64.

16. This should, but today unfortunately does not, go without saying. I reject "or she" instead of one pronoun because it is wordy, and the faddish "s/he" because it is stilted.

Sartre, *Being and Nothingness*, p. 554.

The first interview is in *Film Quarterly*, Fall 1969, the second in *Adam Film* March 1970, both quoted in Fine, *Bloody Sam*, p. 123.

"Cowboy Interview," 70, 72.

pp. 74–75.

Although some critics give the name as one word, a sign in the film itself reads. See Bliss, *Justified Lives*, p. 313.

p. 203.

The Words, p. 149.

Being and Nothingness, pp. 48–49, 68, 56.

The ramifications of this incident, which was inspired by David Lean's film, written by Robert Bolt, were clearer before Columbia Pictures *Dundee*. As the dismembered film now exists, the scene is a condensation than its source, where T. E. Lawrence executes a man (his man's life) who committed a crime in order that he may between rival tribes, one of which would take offense if the man murder of the other tribe, who plans to slay him, the other of avenged if the man were pardoned. Lawrence, who belongs to man and thereby preserves the unity of his command. In Confederate prisoner-soldiers are the equivalent of the former necessarily all the Union troops) of the latter. The view that one dramatic point of the scene is to show Tyreen doing the Union's work (another point is that Dundee's stubbornness fractures the fragile unity within his command) is an inference that Peckinpah's full film might or might not support, and the complete film might make the sequence comparable in quality to that in *Lawrence of Arabia.*

26. Quoted in Simmons, *Peckinpah,* p. 60. Silke's last phrase is odd. Perhaps his memory conflates Tyreen and Dundee, who as his costume in Durango displays, turns into an animal. Nevertheless, Silke's point is valid: Tyreen's clothing, which reflects the man inside, becomes increasingly that of a Union officer.

27. Slotkin, *Gunfighter Nation,* p. 565.

28. Quoted in Simmons, p. 67.

29. This statement may have misled some critics, such as the usually astute Slotkin, who errs somewhat when he says, "the original objective of the mission (rescuing the captives) is achieved, but Dundee continues the mission, with the desire to avenge his recent defeat as an additional motive" (p. 751). While Slotkin is correct about the additional motive, the original mission, as I have quoted Dundee's statement of it, includes capturing or killing the Apache.

30. Barnes, *Humanistic Existentialism,* p. 87.

31. Ansen, "The Return of a Bloody Great Classic," p. 71.

32. Ibid.

33. Weddle, p. 2.

34. Ibid., p. 315.

35. Camus, pp. 89–91; Sartre, *Being and Nothingness,* pp. 538–39.

36. Camus, pp. 3–4.

37. Bishop's decision not to abandon his tortured comrade Angel echoes the decision of another Holden character not to abandon a wounded comrade, Major Warden, in David Lean's *The Bridge on the River Kwai.* In both films, too, the Holden character helps to blow up a bridge.

38. Seydor, *Peckinpah,* pp. 98, 100.

39. Simmons, p. 96; Seydor, *Peckinpah,* p. 137.

40. Casty, *Development of the Film,* p. 380.

41. Seydor, *Peckinpah,* p. 165.

42. Butler, *Crucified Heroes,* pp. 32, 73.

43. Haskell, *From Reverence to Rape,* pp. 363, 353. Although Amy gropes at husband twice, he does the same at her, which Haskell does not say makes sexually obsessive.

44. Scutt's sodomy is much clearer in the U.K. print than in the U.S. print, which more explicit moments were excised. All but a few shots in the U.K. which is 5 minutes longer than the original U.S. print, were restored when t was released on videocassette in the U.S. These few shots, which total less minute, emphasize Amy's humiliation and victimization. In 1998, they were stored in a widescreen videocassette released in the U.S.

45. Kael, *Deeper into Movies,* pp. 495, 500–501.

46. Interview by F. Anthony Macklin, 1975, quoted in Weddle, p. 399.

47. Weddle, p. 395.

48. Kael, p. 498.

49. Simon, *Reverse Angle*, p. 66.

50. Casty, p. 385.

51. Camus, pp. 10–11.

52. Quoted in Seydor, *Peckinpah*, p. 193.

53. Barrett, *Irrational Man*, p. 253.

54. In the film's credits he is Rudy, in the published screenplay Rudolph. The quotations are from a 1973 interview quoted in Weddle, p. 457, and the author's introduction to *Pat Garrett and Billy the Kid*, p. vi.

55. Wurlitzer, *Pat Garrett and Billy the Kid*, p. 63.

56. Sartre, *Being and Nothingness*, pp. 538–39.

57. Camus, p. 11. One also recalls that in *The Deadly Companions,* a character named Billy jokingly shoots the image of himself in a mirror, and he does so twice. For the relationship of *The Deadly Companions* to Peckinpah's other films, see chapter 4.

58. While Butler (p. 124) cites the names of these characters, the film's credits and dialogue do not. Quill identifies himself to Bennie as Fred C. Dobbs (the name of the Humphrey Bogart character in *The Treasure of the Sierra Madre,* a film Peckinpah greatly admired [Whitehall, "Talking with Peckinpah," p. 175]); and Sappensly calls him Johnny.

59. The names of the other chief ComTeg characters are also significant. Weyburn indicates that he has not followed the way dictated by his birth: his father was a minister and wanted him to be one. "Did you ever consider, my dear Cap," the CIA man asks, using Collis's given name, "how much energy you've wasted over your forty-seven years, mustering up that good-fellow smile and that insincere handshake?"—a clue that Cap's name covers something, which is a meaning of "cap." At another point, Hansen tells him Cap's style is "setting people against each other," suggesting that Collis may relate to collision.

60. Bernhardi made the statement in *Germany and the Next War* (1912). Karl von Clausewitz's dictum, whose first key phrase is more often translated as "a continuation of politics," is from *On War* (1833).

61. For example, McKinney says that "hope is allowed by letting Kiesel, an officer of conscience, escape" (p. 243).

Chapter 3: I Would Give You Some Violence

1. "Playboy Interview," p. 66.

2. Bond, *Lear*, p. v.

3. "Playboy Interview," p. 68.

4. Simmons, *Peckinpah*, p. 2.

5. Quoted in Joel Reisner and Bruce Kane, "Sam Peckinpah," in Thomas, *Directors in Action*, p. 126.

6. By, respectively, Evans, Fine, and Weddle.

7. Ansen, "The Return of a Bloody Great Classic," 70–71.

8. Kauffmann, *Living Images*, p. 207.

9. McKinney, *Sam Peckinpah*, p. 238.

10. Judith Crist, "The Great Dozen: A Critique," in Thomas, p. 124.

11. I must reiterate that I enjoyed the movie too, since I want no one to take this account as disparagement of the woman or as Schwarzenegger-bashing. Although I saw little merit in his previous films, this one turned me into a Schwarzenegger fan, a position that, eccentric or not, was reinforced by both the imaginatively witty *The Last Action Hero* and the clever parody of James Bond films, *True Lies*.

12. "Playboy Interview," p. 68.

13. Seydor, *Peckinpah*, p. 118.

14. Shaw, *Misalliance*, in *Bodley Head Shaw*, vol. 4, p. 168.

15. "Playboy Interview," p. 68.

16. Kauffmann, *Living Images*, pp. 168–69.

17. David Denby, "Violence, Once Again," in Denby, *Film 72/73*, pp. 117, 120.

18. Kael, *Deeper into Movies*, pp. 169–70.

19. Kauffmann, *Living Images*, pp. 241, 95, 167.

20. Simmons, p. 51.

21. Slotkin, *Gunfighter Nation*, p. 593.

22. Simmons, pp. 84–85; Weddle, pp. 333–34.

23. Fine, p. 145.

24. Weddle, p. 356.

25. According to Weddle, p. 356, Lombardo said that he fine-cut the opening gunfight to just five minutes. After so many years, Lombardo apparently mixed up the duration of it and the closing gunfight, which lasts slightly over five minutes.

26. "Sam Peckinpah Lets It All Hang Out," p. 20.

27. John L. Simon makes much more of this "distorted echo." See "The Tragedy of Love in *The Wild Bunch*," in Bliss, *Doing It Right*, p. 104.

28. "Playboy Interview," p. 70.

29. Quoted in Reisner and Kane, p. 127.

30. Bliss, *Justified Lives*, p. 79.

31. Robert Culp, "Sam Peckinpah, the Storyteller and *The Wild Bunch*: An Appreciation," in Bliss, *Doing It Right*, pp. 6–7.

32. Else, *Aristotle's* Poetics: *The Argument*, chapter 13 and his gloss on the chapter, especially pp. 423–24.

33. Peckinpah's superb use of camera and editing, not to mention actors, who are as much at the heart of his films as their technical devices, is so varied, he gives the lie to the notion that the arts of stage and screen drama are inimical to each other. Restricted space is a challenge that a great director surmounts, not one from which he exempts himself.

34. According to Roger Spottiswoode, one of the film's editors, he and Peckinpah compressed the siege from one hundred to thirty to eighteen minutes (Fine,

p. 207), which is shorter than my count even without the aftermath. One main reason for the disparity may be Spottiswoode's memory. Another may be that he is considering only the most violent sequences, phases 3–5 and 8–15, which come to about nineteen minutes, of which eighteen is a good approximate figure.

35. The U.K. print of *Straw Dogs*, which, as mentioned in the last chapter, is slightly longer than the U.S. print, makes the sodomy and Amy's revulsion clearer, as it does her different responses toward Scutt and the man who was once her lover.

36. Cleverly and subtly, Michael Bliss elaborates the sexual symbolism of the man trap. See *Justified Lives*, p. 153.

37. As far as I know, no other critic has noticed that this is the third shell in a double-barreled shotgun. The first shoots Tom Hedden's foot; the second kills Scutt. To my mind, this is a subject for trivia pursuit rather than critical chastisement. In fact, it is a compliment to Peckinpah that his artistry enables him to have got away with the error for so long before someone detected it.

38. Bliss, *Justified Lives*, p. 168. From a different viewpoint, Bliss gives a detailed analysis of this sequence (pp. 168–74) that helped my understanding of it.

39. Although the cowboy stunt man doubling for Steve McQueen in the flashback is made up to look like the actor, the intercutting between past and present in this climactic sequence reveals a minor error not noticeable in the opening credits sequence. Whereas Junior Bonner in the flashback is left-handed, since he holds the rope with his left hand, McQueen and his double in the Prescott rodeo are right-handed and hold the rope with their right hands. According to Casey Tibbs, a former rodeo rider who was technical adviser and stunt coordinator for *Junior Bonner*, McQueen "did do some of his own stunts. He wanted to do a bunch of 'em. . . . He even got on this one bull and insisted on coming out of the chute on him. You know, many things can happen right in the chute, and even just jumpin' off a bull can get you hurt." With a star actor, however, "there is a big insurance problem in things like that" (quoted in Simmons, p. 144). According to Marshall Fine, McQueen "got close enough to horses and bucking bulls to sprain a finger, gash his nose and nearly break his wrist" (p. 218).

40. Bliss, *Justified Lives*, p. 219. My analysis of the killing of Garrett resembles Bliss's, but our viewpoints differ, as do some of our conclusions. For example, I am unconvinced that one effect of the "temporal reversal" is that "Billy has avenged Garrett's shooting of him" (p. 221).

41. Hoberman, "Once upon a Time in America," p. 63.

42. Bliss, *Justified Lives*, p. 248. Bliss observes that Garrett does not wear his badge when he stalks and kills Billy, "perhaps to indicate that he is acting on his own and not as a lawman in the employ of the Santa Fe Ring." I disagree, partly because Garrett is acting in his capacity as lawman. The explanation, it seems to me, is simply that Garrett's covert operation is on Billy's turf, and he does not want his badge to attract the attention of anyone sympathetic to the Kid.

43. Ibid., p. 249.

44. Ibid., pp. 249–50.

Chapter 4: Continuing Companions

1. "Sam Peckinpah Lets It All Hang Out," p. 18.

2. Ernest Callenbach, "A Conversation with Sam Peckinpah," in Sarris, *Interviews with Film Directors*, p. 378; "Shoot!" p. 5.

3. "Playboy Interview," p. 73.

4. Quoted by Simmons, *Peckinpah*, p. 37.

5. "Shoot!" pp. 3, 5; "Playboy Interview," p. 73; Callenbach, p. 380.

6. Callenbach, pp. 377, 380.

7. Simmons, pp. 39–40.

8. Among the exceptions is Doug McKinney, to whom *The Deadly Companions* "is of interest in retrospect. . . . Ignoring its place in Peckinpah's work, the film does not stand up too well" (*Sam Peckinpah*, p. 40). Left-handedly, William Parrill calls it "not without merits" (*Heroes' Twilight*, p. 8).

9. Kitses, *Horizons West*, pp. 151–53.

10. Butler, *Crucified Heroes*, pp. 35, 37.

11. Seydor, *Peckinpah*, p. 18.

12. French, *Westerns*, pp. 74–75.

13. Whitehall, "Talking with Peckinpah," p. 175.

14. Despite the statement in the film credits that the screenplay is from the novel of the same title, Fleischman wrote the screenplay first, then adapted it into a novel, which was published in 1960 under the title *Yellowleg*, before the movie was made. In the novel's second printing (1961), after the movie was released, the title changed to that of the film, *The Deadly Companions*. I thank A. S. (Sid) Fleischman for generously sending me a copy of the novel, which has long been out of print and which I was unable to locate.

15. French, pp. 64–66.

16. Butler, pp. 35–36.

17. Seydor, *Peckinpah*, p. 20.

18. Callenbach, p. 379.

19. At the University of Southern California, his master's thesis analyzed the production of a one-act play for stage and television, Williams's *Portrait of a Madonna*, whose protagonist is an early sketch for Blanche DuBois in *A Streetcar Named Desire*. Simmons, pp. 22–23; "Sam Peckinpah Lets It All Hang Out," p. 18.

20. Butler, p. 37.

21. Seydor, *Peckinpah*, p. 147.

22. In "Playboy Interview," p. 68, Peckinpah, a former drama major and theater director, refers to Shakespeare, Sophocles, Euripides, "and those other Greek cats." See also Seydor, *Peckinpah*, pp. 255–56.

23. Kitses, p. 154.

24. French, pp. 109–10. Eliot's phrase is in his 1920 essay "Hamlet and His Problems."

25. Ibid., p. 133.

26. Callenbach, p. 378; Simmons, p. 37. Unlike the film, the novel attempts to account for how Kit might carry the body in the heat of the desert without being overcome by the stench of decaying flesh. According to the blacksmith, "'They fixed the body to travel in the heat'" before they nailed the coffin shut (Fleischman, *The Deadly Companions*, p. 45).

27. Parrill, p. 8, briefly mentions that "the wounded hero" of *The Deadly Companions* anticipates later use of this figure.

28. "Shoot!" p. 5; Callenbach, p. 380. In fairness to Charles FitzSimons, his explanation has merit: "I was trying to show a moral man who somebody had done something dastardly to . . . and despite his morality, he was going to find the son of a bitch and kill him. But he wasn't going to kill other people. . . . How can you have a man shoot another against whom he bears no grudge and then turn around and be unable to kill the man he's hated for years?" (quoted in Simmons, pp. 38–39). Fleischman displays no ill will toward Peckinpah: "I don't have any unhappy memories of Sam; he certainly did less violence to my work than other directors of less ability." As to the shootout at the end, he writes, "It was Charles' idea to have Yellowleg walk dead ahead in the shootout, virtually ignoring Billy (finishing him off with hardly a glance) as he guns for the real object of his fury, Turk. During the shooting, Sam turned things around, regarding Billy as the real threat. In this, Sam was dead wrong. And that produced the cutting room battle" (letter, Sid Fleischman to Dukore, 26 April 1988). Actually, Peckinpah's treatment is closer to the final shootout in the novel than the author remembers. In the novel, as Yellowleg strides toward Turk, Billy challenges him: "'I'm ready any time you turn around.'" "'I told you before, Billy. My fight's not with you,'" is the reply. Turk and Yellowleg exchange fire again. Billy mocks Yellowleg for having missed Turk and challenges him once more. Accepting the challenge "meant turning his back on Turk, but he supposed he would have to risk it. . . . Yellowleg drew only one gun, his left, and nailed Billy's hide to an awning post. Billy curled around it, still on his feet, and then slid into the weed-grown street." Yellowleg then goes after Turk (Fleischman, pp. 138–39).

29. Seydor, *Peckinpah*, p. 56.

30. In no print of *Major Dundee* that I have seen is the issue of whether Riago is a spy resolved. According to Kitses (p. 140), one of the many cuts made by the studio (Columbia) is "the discovery of Riago's mutilated corpse strapped to a tree by the Apache, Potts insisting that Dundee himself cut down the scout whose loyalty he doubted throughout." Other cuts include a massacre of settlers by Apaches soon after the movie begins.

31. Although, as this paragraph demonstrates, the released film reveals his failures, they are apparently clearer in the uncut version. "I shot a series of progressive incidents in which Dundee kept failing in what he was doing," says Peckinpah, and adds, "All of which was cut and junked" ("Shoot!" p. 6).

32. Kitses, p. 149.

33. The most prominently displayed sign, above a large building, says San Rafa-

el, but signs on the hotel and beside the bank office have Starbuck. The screen-play (dated 9 February 1968, not the final shooting script) consistently calls the town San Rafael (Green and Peckinpah, *The Wild Bunch*, pp. 2, 105). According to David Weddle, Peckinpah deliberately had signs with different names "to reflect the confused identity" of this Texas border town, which the United States had seized in the Mexican-American War (*"If They Move . . . Kill 'Em!"* p. 326). Before reading Weddle, I thought the San Rafael signs in the film were an oversight, built before Peckinpah, not the American settlers, changed the name. Audiences who have not read the explanation may have the same reaction.

34. As numerous critics have noted, several themes of *The Wild Bunch* derive from John Huston's *The Treasure of the Sierra Madre*, particularly laughter. Other resemblances are the idyllic Mexican village and, perhaps not yet noted, the dispute over the boots of people killed by the human vultures of both films, the bandits of Huston's film and the "gutter trash" of Peckinpah's.

35. "Playboy Interview," p. 72.

36. Ibid., p. 70; "Sam Peckinpah Lets It All Hang Out," p. 20.

37. "Shoot!" p. 8; Whitehall, p. 175; "Playboy Interview," p. 72.

38. "Sam Peckinpah Lets It All Hang Out," p. 18. This theme is also prominent in a movie Peckinpah admired, George Stevens's *Shane,* whose title character tells the villains that he and they have become anachronisms in a changed West, but that unlike them he is aware of the fact. Another theme Peckinpah's films share with *Shane* is the ubiquitousness in the West of children, who (as discussed below) are tabula rasa, imitating adults who dance or who shoot guns.

39. Seydor documents that "Peckinpah had always intended that he be played by the *same* child actor; but the production manager had by mistake already returned the boy to Mexico City, and it was impossible to get him back in time for the Agua Verde sequence" (Seydor, *Reconsideration,* p. 154).

40. So says Mapache. Later, Lyle Gorch says it was Angel's parent. No wonder some reviewers and critics confused this point.

41. Seydor, *Reconsideration,* p. 159.

42. "Playboy Interview," p. 66.

43. Seydor mentions that after Peckinpah establishes a revenge theme, he drops it for much of the film (*Peckinpah,* p. 163). As Seydor does not state, such dramaturgy has antecedents—notably *Hamlet* and, in the movies, another Peckinpah favorite, John Ford's *My Darling Clementine,* in which a Shakespearean actor recites a few lines of Hamlet's "To be or not to be" soliloquy and Doc Holliday picks up where he leaves off.

44. As Seydor says, "his black attire now makes him seem a minister of death arrived just in time to preside over Cable's funeral" (*Peckinpah,* p. 155). Death and the motorcycle also suggest Jean Cocteau's *Orphée.*

45. French, p. 125. In French's view, however, the sequence is "elaborately" but "laboriously" made.

46. Seydor, *Peckinpah,* p. 90.

47. "Playboy Interview," p. 70.

48. Ibid. Although Peckinpah's interpretation of Shaw's play is accurate, I suspect he is chiefly thinking of the 1959 movie version, which builds up the role of Anderson (acted by Burt Lancaster, who coproduced it) and shows him commiting acts of violence.

49. Ibid., pp. 66, 68. Whatever the merits of Peckinpah's evaluation, the novel from which *Straw Dogs* derives is, compared to that from which *The Getaway* derives (see below), on the artistic road to *War and Peace*. It is true that he retained little besides the siege. In Williams's novel, the protagonist is an English professor who is on a sabbatical leave to write about an eighteenth-century diarist, not (as in the film) a mathematical expert on a grant; his English wife, who is not a native of the village but decided to rent the farm on the basis of an advertisement in *The Times,* is not raped; they have an eight-year-old daughter; Henry Niles is explicitly a convicted child-murderer who escaped from an institution for the criminally insane; Janice Hedden is a mentally defective eight-year-old, not a sexually provocative adolescent; and so forth. Peckinpah or Goodman changed the protagonist's name from George Magruder to David Sumner—perhaps, as Pauline Kael says, to allow David to suggest the biblical character who fights Goliath (*Deeper into Movies*, p. 498); also, the authors may have thought the name Magruder would seem more Scottish than American. The third draft of the screenplay, dated 24 November 1970, which retains the novel's title, changes the protagonist's surname to Matlock (the script precedes the TV series *Matlock* by quite a few years). Not until 30 December 1970, the date on pages inserted into this screenplay, does Matlock become Sumner (see Goodman and Peckinpah, *The Siege of Trencher's Farm*, pp. 3–4). The screenwriters may have changed the name Louise to Amy to suggest *aimée.*

50. Although he limps because David Warner, who acts the role (without screen credit), limped as a result of a motor accident, it was Peckinpah's decision to cast Warner, limp and all.

51. Near the start of the novel, a cat is gratuitously strangled and buried in a snowdrift. Goodman and Peckinpah make the killing of the cat more organic to the film than Williams does to the novel.

52. In Jim Thompson's novel *The Getaway,* a seven-year-old boy does not encounter Doc McCoy (or his wife, Carol, who is with him in the train) but aims his gun at the train conductor, who identifies the McCoys (pp. 105, 112); Beynon has no brother and Doc buries his corpse in a coal bin (p. 68). In the second draft of Walter Hill's screenplay of *The Getaway,* a seven-year-old boy shoots Doc with a water pistol, but as in the novel the conductor identifies Doc for the police; in this draft, as in the novel but not the film, Carol is with Doc on the train (pp. 97, 99–100). The differences between the film and the novel, which (notwithstanding Thompson's high reputation in some quarters) is merely pulp fiction, are extensive. Rather than bloat these endnotes unnecessarily, I will restrict my comparisons.

53. The growing maturity of their relationship is not in the novel, which has a farfetched crime-does-not-pay ending (the McCoys get away to where they become

worse off than before). Critics who oppose what they consider Peckinpah's misogyny tend to ignore or explain away the relationship of Carol and Doc as much as they ignore Hildy in *The Ballad of Cable Hogue.*

54. Disregarding Carol's marriage and focusing on Fran's, John Simon infers, with more certainty than the evidence warrants, that Peckinpah's sympathies, "very clearly, are not with the victim" of marital infidelity; and he generalizes, without apparently considering the McCoys and Beynon in *The Getaway* or Clete, Claudia, and Sloane in *The Ballad of Cable Hogue,* that "it is no longer possible to avoid the notion that Peckinpah thinks of women as generally inferior beings who always attach themselves to the stronger or more powerful man" (*Reverse Angle,* p. 100). Carol McCoy, hardly an inferior being, does not attach herself to the more powerful person, and Clete is stronger than Sloane. While Peckinpah is unable to "inject life" into Carol McCoy, Molly Haskell states, using her own subjective inferences rather than evidence in *The Getaway,* "he obviously gets—and gives—his kicks in the relationship between the sluttish wife . . . and the sadistic villain" (*From Reverence to Rape,* p. 364). Whereas the character of Carol differs greatly from that of her counterpart in the novel, Haskell fails to consider, the character of Fran Clinton does not. The second draft of Walter Hill's screenplay develops the relationship between Carol and Doc further than the novel does, but with less depth and complexity than Peckinpah's film.

55. "Playboy Interview," p. 73.

56. Wurlitzer, *Pat Garrett and Billy the Kid,* p. 7.

57. The last two sentences of this quotation have been cut from the videocassette version of *Bring Me the Head of Alfredo Garcia.* My quotation is from the film itself.

58. Butler, p. 92.

59. Peckinpah says that a longtime friend, Frank Kowalski, presented him with the original idea: "'I got a great title: *Bring Me the Head of . . . ,*' and he had some other name—'and the hook is that the guy is already dead'" (Simmons, p. 189). However, the revenge motif is Peckinpah's.

60. As mentioned earlier (p. 203, n. 58), Butler cites these characters' names, but neither the film's credits nor its dialogue does so.

61. Quoted in Seydor, *Peckinpah,* p. 228.

62. Callenbach, p. 378.

63. Rostand, *The Killer Elite.* Rostand is the pseudonym of Robert S. Hopkins (for this information, I thank Charles A. Carpenter). Most of what the following paragraphs analyze is not in the novel, which is set in London, not San Francisco.

64. In the novel, Locken and Hansen do not meet until Hansen shoots him. In it, however, Locken and Miller are deadly companions, Miller joining Locken at the order of Cap Collis, whose lover as well as double agent he is.

65. "Playboy Interview," p. 192. Through the writer of credit, Stirling Silliphant, and through improvisatory work with the actors, Peckinpah contributed a great deal to the script (Simmons, chapter 15, especially pp. 210–11, 216–17).

66. This speech has a counterpart in the novel, where Locken states that "'while the gentlemen sip away at their gin and tonics, a Collis or Miller down at the bottom of the pyramid makes it [killing someone] happen. Business as usual. Killing called a lot of things, so the good men at the top can go home clean at the end of the day'" (Rostand, p. 216). In the novel, Locken became a hired assassin as a result of disillusionment with the Cuban revolution and Fidel Castro, with whom he fought. "'I . . . decided that the things we'd done in the name of revolution were no different than the things Batista [the dictator Castro overthrew] did to stay in power. The killing, the torture, they were all the same no matter what people said they believed in. No good guys or bad guys. . . . One cause just as rotten as the next'" (Rostand, p. 48).

67. In the novel, when Steiner brings back a Russian captain for interrogation, Stransky says nothing; Lieutenant Meyer later orders Steiner "to take as many prisoners as possible" (Heinrich, *The Willing Flesh,* pp. 120, 160). The draft of the screenplay available for inspection, dated 7 April 1975, which bears the name Julius J. Epstein (the film credits have two more writers, Walter Kelley and James Hamilton), is titled *Sergeant Steiner.* The sequence about shooting prisoners echoes the movie version of Irwin Shaw's *The Young Lions,* in which Maximilian Schell and Marlon Brando play German officers. After a battle, the Schell character commands, "Shoot all wounded. Leave no one alive here. We cannot take prisoners. Our movements must not be reported. These wounded can give information, and their planes would be on us before we got back." Except for the Brando character, German soldiers obey him. When an unarmed, dazed, wounded straggler stumbles forward, Schell orders Brando, "Shoot him." Brando lowers his gun. He and Schell stare at each other. "That's an order," says Schell. They continue to stare at each other until Schell removes his revolver and shoots the wounded man. Perhaps Peckinpah created the comparable sequence in *Cross of Iron* after Schell was cast.

68. After Steiner comments on what a man feels himself to be, the novel's Stransky replies, less complexly, "'you can feel as you like, but as long as you talk with me do not forget that you are wearing a uniform'" (Heinrich, p. 123).

69. Their conversation about Hitler is not in the novel. There the less complex but more representative Stransky agrees to converse on the basis of equality, not of military subordinate and superior, but the moment Steiner does so, Stransky repudiates his agreement: "'Your impertinence can only arise from stupidity. . . . I have encountered more than one person of your type,' he went on, 'and I have always crushed them like repulsive vermin.'" In civilian life, "'I would have had dogs chase you over the countryside until your feet were bloodless straps.'" As punishment, he orders the battle-weary Steiner to dig a bunker ten feet deep that evening (Heinrich, pp. 203–4).

70. The novel makes more of Brandt's and Kiesel's attitude toward Steiner. Both actively intercede in his behalf when Stransky punishes him (see n. 69). Brandt's affection toward Steiner derives partly from Steiner's resemblance to his son, killed in combat, whose photograph he shows Kiesel as proof; and Steiner not only saved

Brandt's life, which the film mentions, he also saved the life of Kiesel's brother-in-law (Heinrich, pp. 27, 184, 218, 244, 228).

71. In the novel, Brandt has a different motive to save Kiesel: "'Noah built the ark and saved himself and his family from the Flood. He became the bridge between the old and the new humanity, and he took elements of both into the new world: the good and the evil. I am trying to do the same. I have given evil a chance, in the special case of Stransky [whom he permitted to transfer to France, as arranged by one of Stransky's influential relatives], and I shall give the good a chance also'" (Heinrich, p. 279).

72. The poem is from the epilogue to Brecht's *The Resistible Rise of Arturo Ui.* Its most easily accessible translation, which is somewhat different, is by Ralph Manheim, in Brecht, *Collected Plays,* vol. 6.

73. Simmons, p. 236.

74. By contrast, the film's Steiner is compassionate when a member of his platoon kisses another to stop the latter's hysteria, a scene not in the novel, which treats homosexuality differently. In it, after Stransky traps Triebig, he reminds Triebig of his obligation to be courageous while a soldier; and Steiner uses his discovery of Triebig in bed with his lover as justification to beat Triebig for having verbally humiliated him before Stransky and Meyer (Heinrich, pp. 89–90, 169–70).

75. The novel ends differently. When Steiner aims his machine gun at Stransky, the stunned officer flees to safety. Instad of firing, Steiner lowers his weapon and murmurs, "'It's pointless' without any awareness of what his words meant" (Heinrich, p. 275). In the final paragraph, Steiner dies of a wound inflicted by a Russian shell. The early draft of the screenplay ends with Steiner blowing up himself and Stransky with a hand grenade (Epstein, pp. 160–61).

76. Apparently, neither Peckinpah, a former university drama major, nor Robert Ludlum, a former professional actor, was familiar with Shaw's *Man and Superman,* whose protagonist is also named John Tanner. Since the apparent Shavian allusion makes no sense, the choice of name is probably accidental. However, the novel, but not the movie, makes much fuss over the village where Tanner lives, Saddle Valley, and its supposed Soviet code name, translated by the CIA as "Chasm of Leather," which connect to the name Tanner (Ludlum, *The Osterman Weekend,* pp. 7–8, 66–67).

77. Burt Lancaster (Danforth) played a similar character in John Frankenheimer's *Seven Days in May.*

78. "Playboy Interview," p. 192.

79. Sharp, *The Osterman Weekend: A Screenplay,* p. 115. This so-called final draft, which may have been superseded by other final drafts, is dated 7 October 1982, revised 9 October 1982.

80. Fine, *Bloody Sam,* p. 353.

Filmography:
Feature Films Directed by Sam Peckinpah

The Deadly Companions
(1961, released in Great Britain 1962)

Running Time: 93 minutes (subsequently cut to 79 minutes)
Producer: Charles B. FitzSimons
Production Company: Carousel, released through Pathé-America
Screenplay: A. S. Fleischman
Cinematographer: William H. Clothier (filmed in Panavision; Color Process, Pathé Color)
Editor: Stanley E. Rabjohn
Assistant Editor: Leonard Kwit
Special Effects: Dave Kohler
Music: Marlin Skiles
Conductor: Raoul Kraushaar
Song: "A Dream of Love," by Marlin Skiles and Charles B. FitzSimons, sung by Maureen O'Hara
Production Manager and Assistant Director: Lee Lukather
Script Supervisor: Dikie McCoy
Sound Recording: Robert J. Callen, Gordon Sawyer
Costumes: Frank Beetson Sr., Sheila O'Brien
Makeup: James Barker
Hairstyles: Fae Smyth

Cast:

Kit Tilden	Maureen O'Hara
Yellowleg	Brian Keith
Billy	Steve Cochran
Turkey	Chill Wills
Parson	Strother Martin
Doctor	Will Wright
Cal	Jim O'Hara
Mayor	Peter O'Crotty
Mead Tilden	Billy Vaughan
Gambler	Robert Sheldon
Gambler	John Hamilton
Bartender	Hank Gobble
Indian	Buck Sharpe

Ride the High Country

(1962, released in Great Britain as **Guns in the Afternoon**)

Running Time: 94 minutes
Producer: Richard E. Lyons
Production Company: Metro-Goldwyn-Mayer
Writer: N. B. Stone Jr.
Director of Photography: Lucien Ballard (filmed in Cinemascope; Color Process, Metrocolor)
Film Editor: Frank Santillo
Music Composer and Conductor: George Bassman
Art Direction: George W. Davis, Leroy Coleman
Set Decoration: Henry Grace, Otto Siegel
Color Consultant: Charles K. Hagedon
Assistant Director: Hal Polaire
Sound: Franklin Milton
Makeup: William Tuttle
Hairstyles: May Keats
Recording Supervisor: Franklin Milton
Cast:

Steve Judd	Joel McCrea
Gil Westrum	Randolph Scott
Elsa Knudsen	Mariette Hartley
Heck Longtree	Ron Starr
Joshua Knudsen	R. G. Armstrong
Judge Tolliver	Edgar Buchanan
Kate	Jenie Jackson
Billy Hammond	James Drury

Sylvus Hammond	L. Q. Jones
Elder Hammond	John Anderson
Henry Hammond	Warren Oates
Jimmy Hammond	John Davis Chandler
Saloon Girl	Carmen Phillips

Major Dundee

(1965)

Running Time: 122 minutes (initially released at 134 minutes)
Producer: Jerry Bresler
Production Company: Jerry Bresler Productions for Columbia Pictures Corp.
Screenplay: Harry Julian Fink, Oscar Saul, Sam Peckinpah
Story: Harry Julian Fink
Director of Photography: Sam Leavitt (filmed in Panavision; Color Process, East-
  man Color by Pathé)
Film Editors: William A. Lyon, Don Starling, Howard Kunin
Second Unit Director: Cliff Lyons
Assistant Directors: John Veitch, Floyd Joyer
Assistant Director, Mexico: Emilio Fernandez
Art Director: Al Ybarra
Assistant to the Producer: Rick Rosenberg
Production Manager: Francisco Day
Music: Daniele Amfitheatrof
Songs: "Major Dundee March," by Daniele Amfitheatrof and Ned Washington,
  sung by Mitch Miller's Sing Along Gang; "Laura Lee," by Liam Sullivan and
  Forrest Wood, sung by Brock Peters
Special Effects: August Lohman
Costumes: Tom Dawson
Property Master: Joe La Bella
Makeup: Ben Lane, Larry Butterworth
Sound Supervisor: Charles J. Rice
Sound: James Z. Flaster
Cast:

Major Amos Dundee	Charlton Heston
Captain Benjamin Tyreen	Richard Harris
Lieutenant Graham	Jim Hutton
Samuel Potts	James Coburn
Tim Ryan	Michael Anderson Jr.
Teresa Santiago	Senta Berger
Sergeant Gomez	Mario Adorf
Aesop	Brock Peters
O. W. Hadley	Warren Oates

Sergeant Chillum	Ben Johnson
Reverend Dahlstrom	R. G. Armstrong
Arthur Hadley	L. Q. Jones
Wiley	Slim Pickens
Linda	Begonia Palacios
Captain Frank Waller	Karl Swenson
Sierra Charriba	Michael Pate
Jimmy Lee Benteen	John Davis Chandler
Priam	Dub Taylor
Captain Jacques Tremaine	Albert Carrier
Riago	Jose Carlos Ruiz
Melinche	Aurora Clavell
Doctor Aguilar	Enrique Lucero
Old Apache	Francisco Reyguera

The Wild Bunch

(1969)

Running Time: 144 minutes (Great Britain; in the United States, 143 minutes, subsequently cut to between 135 and 121 minutes, then restored to 144 minutes)

Producer: Phil Feldman

Production Company: Warner Brothers–Seven Arts

Screenplay: Walon Green, Sam Peckinpah

Story: Walon Green, Roy N. Sickner

Director of Photography: Lucien Ballard (filmed in Panavision; Color Process, Technicolor)

Film Editor: Louis Lombardo

Music: Jerry Fielding

Art Director: Edward Carrere

Associate Producer: Roy N. Sickner

Wardrobe Supervisor: Gordon Dawson

Assistant Directors: Cliff Coleman, Fred Gammon

Second Unit Director: Buzz Henry

Special Effects: Bud Hulburd

Associate Film Editor: Robert L. Wolfe

Makeup: Al Greenway

Sound: Robert J. Miller

Production Manager: William Faralla

Script Supervisor: Crayton Smith

Music Supervisor: Sonny Burke

Cast:

Pike Bishop	William Holden
Dutch Engstrom	Ernest Borgnine
Deke Thornton	Robert Ryan
Freddy Sykes	Edmond O'Brien
Lyle Gorch	Warren Oates
Angel	Jaime Sanchez
Tector Gorch	Ben Johnson
Mapache	Emilio Fernandez
Coffer	Strother Martin
T.C.	L. Q. Jones
Harrigan	Albert Dekker
Crazy Lee	Bo Hopkins
Wainscott (Temperance Preacher)	Dub Taylor
Zamorra	Jorge Russek
Herrera	Alfonso Arau
Teresa	Sonia Amelio
Aurora	Aurora Clavell
Don Jose	Chano Urueta
Colonel Mohr (German Officer)	Fernando Wagner
Captain Ernst (German Officer)	Jorge Rado
Ross	Paul Harper
Elsa	Elsa Cardenas
Jess	Bill Hart
Buck	Rayford Barnes
Sergeant McHale	Steve Ferry
Ignacio	Enrique Lucero
Rocio	Elizabeth Dupeyron
Yolis	Yolanda Ponce
Juan Jose	Jose Chavez
Juan	Rene Dupeyron
Benson	Pedro Galvan
Emma	Graciela Doring
Perez	Major Perez
Paymaster	Ivan Scott
Margaret	Sra. Madero
Luna	Margarita Luna
Gonzalez	Chalo Gonzalez
Lilia	Lilia Castillo
Carmen	Elizabeth Unda
Julio	Julio Corona
Boy in Starbuck	Matthew Peckinpah

The Ballad of Cable Hogue

(1970, released in Great Britain 1971)

Running Time: 121 minutes
Producer: Sam Peckinpah
Executive Producer: Phil Feldman
Production Company: A Phil Feldman Production for Warner Brothers
Writers: John Crawford, Edmund Penney
Director of Photography: Lucien Ballard (Color Process, Technicolor)
Editors: Frank Santillo, Lou Lombardo
Music: Jerry Goldsmith
Songs: "Tomorrow Is the Song I Sing," music by Goldsmith, lyrics by Richard
    Gillis, sung by Gillis; "Wait for Me, Sunrise," by Gillis, sung by Gillis; "But-
    terfly Mornings," by Gillis, sung by Stella Stevens and Jason Robards
Orchestrations: Arthur Morton
Art Director: Leroy Coleman
Set Decorator: Jack Mills
Property Master: Robert Visciglia
Music Supervision: Sonny Burke
Special Effects: Bud Hulburd
Sound: Don Rush
Associate Producer: Gordon Dawson
Co-Producer: William Faralla
Unit Production Manager: Dink Templeton
Assistant Director: John Guadioso
Dialogue Supervisor: Frank Kowalski
Costumes for Stella Stevens: Robert Fletcher
Titles: Latigo Productions
Makeup: Gary Liddiard, Al Fleming
Hair Stylist: Kathy Blondell
Wardrobe: Robert Fletcher
Cast:

Cable Hogue	Jason Robards
Hildy	Stella Stevens
Reverend Joshua Duncan Sloane	David Warner
Bowen	Strother Martin
Taggart	L. Q. Jones
Ben Fairchild (Stagecoach Driver)	Slim Pickens
Cushing	Peter Whitney
Quittner	R. G. Armstrong
Clete	Gene Evans
Claudia	Susan O'Connell
Jensen	William Mims

Mrs. Jensen	Kathleen Freeman
Powell	Vaughn Taylor
Webb Seely (Stagecoach Shotgun)	Max Evans
William	Felix Nelson
The Stranger (First Customer)	Darwin W. Lamb
Preacher	James Anderson
Dot	Mary Munday
Lucius	William D. Faralla
Matthew	Matthew Peckinpah
Stage Office Clerk	Victor Izay
Easy	Easy Pickens

Straw Dogs

(1971)

Running Time: 118 minutes (cut to 113 minutes for initial United States release)
Producer: Daniel Melnick
Production Company: Talent Associates Films Ltd. and Amerbroco Films Ltd. for ABC Pictures Corp.
Screenplay: David Zelag Goodman, Sam Peckinpah; based on the novel *The Siege of Trencher's Farm,* by Gordon M. Williams
Director of Photography: John Coquillon (Color Process, Eastman Color)
Music: Jerry Fielding
Film Editors: Roger Spottiswoode, Paul Davies, Tony Lawson
Editorial Consultant: Robert Wolfe
Production Designer: Ray Simm
Production Design Consultant: Julia Trevelyan Oman
Art Director: Ken Bridgeman
Set Decorator: Peter James
Property Master: Alf Pegley
Titles Designer: Anthony Goldschmidt
Assistant Director: Terry Marcel
Dialogue Director: Katy Haber
Camera Operator: Herbert Smith
Makeup: Harry Frampton
Wardrobe: Tiny Nicholls
Hairdresser: Bobbie Smith
Special Effects: John Richardson
Stunt Coordinator: Bill Cornelius
Sound Editor: Garth Craven
Sound Recordist: John Bramall
Associate Producer: James Swann
Production Supervisor: Derek Kavanagh

Continuity: Pamela Davies
Casting: Miriam Brickman
Cast:

David Sumner	Dustin Hoffman
Amy Sumner	Susan George
Tom Hedden	Peter Vaughan
Major Scott	T. P. McKenna
Charlie Venner	Del Henney
Chris Cawsey	Jim Norton
Norman Scutt	Ken Hutchison
Phil Riddaway	Donald Webster
Henry Niles	David Warner (uncredited)
Reverend Barnard Hood	Colin Welland
Janice Hedden	Sally Thomsett
Bobby Hedden	Len Jones
Harry Ware	Robert Keegan
John Niles	Peter Arne
Mrs. Hood	Cherina Schaer

Junior Bonner

(1972)

Running Time: 103 minutes
Producer: Joe Wizan
Production Company: Joe Wizan–Booth Gardner in association with Solar Productions, Inc., for ABC Pictures Corp.
Screenplay: Jeb Rosebrook
Director of Photography: Lucien Ballard (filmed in Todd AO-35; Color Process, Movielab)
Film Editors: Robert Wolfe, Frank Santillo
Second Unit Director: Frank Kowalski
Music: Jerry Fielding
Songs: "Arizona Morning" and "Rodeo Man," written and sung by Rod Hart; "Bound to Be Back Again," by Dennis Lambert and Brian Potter, sung by Alex Taylor
Production Manager: James C. Pratt
Assistant Directors: Frank Baur, Malcolm R. Harding, Newt Arnold
Art Director: Edward G. Haworth
Set Decorator: Gerald F. Wunderlich
Production Assistants: Raymond Green, Betty J. Gumm, Katy Haber
Production Secretary: Dorothy Whitney
Script Supervisor: John Franco

Dialogue Director: Sharon Peckinpah
Special Effects: Bud Hulburd
Property Master: Robert J. Visciglia
Location Assistant: Chalo Gonzalez
Costumes: Eddie Armand
Men's Wardrobe: James M. George
Women's Wardrobe: Pat L. Barto
Makeup: Donald W. Robertson, William P. Turner
Hair Stylist: Lynn del Kail
Title Design: Latigo Productions; Titles, Pacific Titles
Sound Mixer: Charles K. Wilborn
Rerecording Mixer: Richard Portman
Rodeo Stunt Coordinator: Casey Tibbs
Stunt Coordinator: E. Michael Gilbert
Sound Effects and Music Editing: Edit International Ltd.
Casting: Lynn Stalmaster
Associate Producer: Mickey Borofsky
Cast:

Junior Bonner	Steve McQueen
Ace Bonner	Robert Preston
Elvira (Ellie) Bonner	Ida Lupino
Buck Roan	Ben Johnson
Curly Bonner	Joe Don Baker
Charmagne	Barbara Leigh
Ruth Bonner	Mary Murphy
Red Terwilliger	William McKinney
Nurse Arlis	Sandra Deel
Del (Bartender)	Dub Taylor
Homer Rutledge	Donald "Red" Barry
Burt	Charles Gray
Tim Bonner	Matthew Peckinpah
Nick Bonner	Sundown Spencer
Flashie	Rita Garrison
Merla Twine	Roxanne Knight
Janene Twine	Sandra Pew
Rodeo Official	William E. Pierce
Dudettes	P. K. Strong, Toby Sargent, Bonnie Clausing
Rodeo Secretary	Francesca Jarvis
George	George Weintraub
Barmaid	Irene Simpson

The Getaway

(1972, released in Great Britain 1973)

Running Time: 122 minutes
Producers: David Foster, Mitchell Brower
Production Company: A Solar/Foster-Brower Production for First Artists
Associate Producer and Second Unit Director: Gordon T. Dawson
Screenplay: Walter Hill, based on the novel of the same title by Jim Thompson
Director of Photography: Lucien Ballard (filmed in Todd-AO; Color Process, Technicolor)
Film Editor: Robert Wolfe
Editorial Consultant: Roger Spottiswoode
Assistant Film Editors: Mike Klein, William G. Lindemann
Production Manager: Donald Guest
Assistant Directors: Newt Arnold, Ron Wright
Art Directors: Ted Haworth, Angelo Graham
Set Decorator: George R. Nelson
Music: Quincy Jones
Harmonica Solos: Toots Thielemans
Musical Voices: Don Elliott
Assistant to the Producer: Joe Gould
Dialogue Director: Katy Haber
Production Secretary: Joan Arnold
Property Master: Robert J. Visciglia
Assistant Property Masters: Chalo Gonzalez, Les Hallett
Script Supervisor: Michael Preece
Casting Director: Patricia Mock
Costume Supervisor: Ray Summers
Men's Costumes: Kent James
Women's Costumes: Barbara Siebert
Makeup: Al Fleming, Jack Petty
Hair Stylist: Kathy Blondell
Special Effects: Bud Hulburd
Title Design: Latigo Productions; Titles, Pacific Title
Still Photographer: Mel Traxel
Sound Mixer: Charles M. Wilborn
Sound Consultant: Garth Craven
Rerecording Mixer: Richard Portman
Sound Editors: Joe von Stroheim, Mike Colgan
Music Editor: Dan Carlin
Cast:

Doc McCoy	Steve McQueen
Carol McCoy	Ali MacGraw

Jack Beynon	Ben Johnson
Fran Clinton	Sally Struthers
Rudy Butler	Al Lettieri
Cowboy (Truck Driver)	Slim Pickens
The Thief	Richard Bright
Harold Clinton	Jack Dodson
Laughlin	Dub Taylor
Frank Jackson	Bo Hopkins
Cully	Roy Jenson
The Accountant	John Bryson
Swain	Bill Hart
Hayhoe	Tom Runyon
The Soldier	Whitney Jones
Boys on the Train	Raymond King, Ivan Thomas
Boys' Mothers	C. W. White, Brenda W. King
Parole Board Chairman	W. Dee Kutach
Parole Board Commissioner	Brick Lowry
McCoy's Lawyer	Martin Colley
Field Captain	O. S. Savage
Bank Guard	Dick Crockett
Hardware Store Owner	A. L. Camp
TV Shop Proprietor	Bob Veal
Sporting Goods Salesman	Bruce Bissonette
Carhop	Maggie Gonzalez
Cannon	Jim Kannon
Max	Doug Dudley
Stacy	Stacy Newton
Cowboy's Helper	Tom Bush

Pat Garrett and Billy the Kid

(1973)

Running Time: 106 minutes (initial release), 123 minutes (restored version)
Producer: Gordon Carroll
Production Company: A Gordon Carroll–Sam Peckinpah Production for Metro-Goldwyn-Mayer
Writer: Rudy (Rudolph) Wurlitzer
Director of Photography: John Coquillon (filmed in Panavision; Color Process, Metrocolor)
Film Editors: Roger Spottiswoode, Garth Craven, Robert L. Wolfe, Richard Halsey, David Berlatsky, Tony de Zarraga
Music: Bob Dylan, sung by Bob Dylan

Art Director: Ted Haworth
Assistant Director: Newton Arnold
Second Assistant Director: Lawrence J. Powell
Special Visual Effects: A. J. Lohman
Set Decoration: Ray Moyer
Sound: Charles M. Wilborn, Harry W. Tetrick
Second Unit Director: Gordon Dawson
Second Unit Director of Photography: Gabriel Torres G.
Unit Production Manager: Jim Henderling
Property Master: Robert John Visciglia
Music Editor: Dan Carlin
Camera Operator: Herbert Smith
Makeup: Jack P. Wilson
Wardrobe: Michael Butler
Casting: Patricia Mock
Production Manager, Mexico: Alfonsa Sanchez Tello
Assistant Director, Mexico: Jesus Marin Bello
Cast:

Pat Garrett	James Coburn
Billy the Kid	Kris Kristofferson
Alias	Bob Dylan
Sheriff Kip McKinney	Richard Jaeckel
Sheriff Baker	Slim Pickens
Mrs. Baker	Katy Jurado
Lemuel	Chill Wills
Governor Wallace	Jason Robards
Chisum	Barry Sullivan
Deputy Bob Ollinger	R. G. Armstrong
Eno	Luke Askew
John Poe	John Beck
Holly	Richard Bright
Deputy J. W. Bell	Matt Clark
Maria	Rita Coolidge
Lewellyn Howland	Jack Dodson
Alamosa Bill	Jack Elam
Paco	Emilio Fernandez
Pete Maxwell	Paul Fix
Black Harris	L. Q. Jones
Horrell	Gene Evans
Beaver	Donnie Fritts
Luke	Harry Dean Stanton
Silva	Jorge Russek
Bowdre	Charlie Martin Smith

Cody	Elisha Cook Jr.
Josh	Dub Taylor
Sackett	Don Levy
Mrs. Horrell	Claudia Bryar
Norris	John Chandler
Denver	Mike Mikler
Ida Garrett	Aurora Clavell [credited in restored version but does not appear]
Ruthie Lee	Rutanya Alda
Rupert	Walter Kelley
Will (Coffinmaker)	Sam Peckinpah
Tom O'Folliard	Rudy (Rudolph) Wurlitzer

Bring Me the Head of Alfredo Garcia

(1974)

Running Time: 112 minutes
Producer: Martin Baum
Production Company: A Martin Baum–Sam Peckinpah Film for Optimus Production (Hollywood)–Estudios Churubusco (Mexico City) Co-Production
Screenplay: Gordon Dawson, Sam Peckinpah
Story: Frank Kowalski, Sam Peckinpah
Music: Jerry Fielding
Director of Photography: Alex Phillips Jr. (Color Process, De Luxe)
Supervising Editor: Garth Craven
Editors: Robbe Roberts, Sergio Ortega, Dennis E. Dolan
Associate Producer: Gordon Dawson
Executive Producer: Helmut Dantine
Executive Production Manager and Assistant Director: William C. Davidson
Second Assistant Director: Jesus Marin Bello
Assistant to Director: Katy Haber
Art Director: Agustin Ituarte
Set Dresser: Enrique Estevez
Production Coordinator: Yanquella Wakefield
Dialogue Director: Sharon Peckinpah
Production Assistant to the Director: Katherine Haber
Songs: "Bennie's Song," written and sung by Isela Vega; "A Donde Ir," by Javier Vega, sung by Isela Vega; "Bad Blood Baby," by Sam Peckinpah; "J.P.," by Arturo Castro
Unit Production Manager: Carlos Terron Garcia
Special Effects: Leon Ortega, Raul Falomir, Federico Farfan
Property Master: Alf Pegley

Wardrobe: Adolfo Ramirez
Sound Mixer: Manuel Topete
Makeup: Rosa Guerrero
Sound Editor: Mike Colgan
Rerecording Mixer: Harry W. Tetrick
Music Editor: Dan Carlin
Orchestration: Greg McRitchie, Leonard Niehaus
Music Coordinator, Mexico: Arturo Castro
Script Supervisor: Trudy von Trotta
Production Assistants: Jim Preminger, Dan York
Stunt Coordinators: Gary Combs, Whitey Hughes, Duffy Hambledon
Casting Director: Claudia Becker
Titles: Latigo Productions/Pacific Title
Cast:

Bennie	Warren Oates
Elita	Isela Vega
Sappensly	Robert Webber
Quill	Gig Young
Max	Helmut Dantine
El Jefe	Emilio Fernandez
Paco	Kris Kristofferson
Bartender	Chano Urueta
John	Donny Fritts
Cueto	Jorge Russek
Chalo	Chalo Gonzalez
Frank	Don Levy
Esteban	Enrique Lucero
Teresa	Janine Maldonado
Grandmother Moreno	Tamara Garina
Bernardo	Farnesio De Bernal
El Chavito	Ahui Camacho
Dolores de Escomiglia	Monica Miguel
Carpenter	Paco Pharres
Paulo	Juan Manuel Diaz
Angel	Rene Dupeyron
Yolo	Yolanda Ponce
Juan	Juan Jose Palacios
Tourist Guide	Manolo
Maria	Neri Ruiz
Chavo	Roberto Dumont

The Killer Elite

(1975, released in Great Britain 1976)

Running Time: 123 minutes
Producers: Martin Baum, Arthur Lewis
Production Company: An Arthur Lewis-Baum/Dantine Production, An Exeter/
    Persky-Bright Feature
Music: Jerry Fielding
Director of Photography: Philip Lathrop (filmed in Panavision; Color Process,
    De Luxe)
Screenplay: Marc Norman, Stirling Silliphant; from the novel of the same title
    by Robert Rostand (pseudonym of Robert S. Hopkins)
Executive Producer: Helmut Dantine
Supervising Editor: Garth Craven
Editors: Tony De Zarraga, Monte Hellman
Music Editor: Dan Carlin
Assistant Editors: David Marshall, Robert Pergament, Sergio Ortega, Margo
    Anderson, Gordon Davidson
Production Designer: Ted Haworth
Construction Coordinator: John Lasalandra
Set Decorator: Rick Gentz
Property Master: Robert J. Visciglia
Production Coordinator: Yanquella Wakefield
Production Manager: Bill Davidson
Production Secretary: Joan Arnold
First Assistant Director: Newton Arnold
Second Assistant Directors: Ron Wright, Jim Bloom
Second Unit Director: Frank Kowalski
Second Unit First Assistant Director: Cliff Coleman
Dialogue Director: Walter Kelley
Production Assistant to Director: Katherine Haber
Sound Editor: Fred Brown
Special Effects: Sass Bedig
Stunt Supervisor: Whitey Hughes
Sound Mixer: Charles M. Wilborn
Rerecordist: Richard Portman
Wardrobe Designer: Ray Summers
Costumes: Kent James, Carol Brown
Camera Operators: Bill Johnson, Frank Thackeray, Frank Holgate
Production Assistants: Charles Titone, Charles Milhaupt, Janet Healy
Hair Stylist: Kathy Blondell
Makeup: Jack Wilson, Jack Petty
Assistant Art Director: Ron Hobbs

Script Supervisors: Frank Kowalski, Ray Quiroz
Casting: Mike Fenton, Jane Feinberg
Title Sequence: Burke Mattsson
Cast:

Mike Locken	James Caan
George Hansen	Robert Duvall
Cap Collis	Arthur Hill
Jerome Miller	Bo Hopkins
Yuen Chung	Mako
Mac	Burt Young
Lawrence Weyburn	Gig Young
O'Leary	Tom Clancy
Tommie Chung	Tiana
Walter	Walter Kelley
Amy	Kate Heflin
Josephine	Sondra Blake
Rita	Carole Mallory
Tao Yi	James Wing Woo
Vorodny	Helmut Dantine
Bruce	George Kee Cheung
Hank	Hank Hamilton
Wei Chi	Victor Sen Young
Negato Toku	Tak Kubota
Ben Otake	Rick Alemany
Donnie	Johnnie Burrell
Eddie	Billy J. Scott
Jimmy Fung	Simon Tam
Doctor	Arnold Fortgang
Sam the Mechanic	Tommy Bush
Mat (Kid)	Matthew Peckinpah
Fake Police Officer	Eddie Donno
Association Guard	Kim Kahana
Security Policeman	Edward R. White
Security Policeman	Gary Combs
Wilfie	Wilfred Tsang
Miltie	Milton Shoong
Cop	Alan Keller
Soldier at Party	Charles Titone
Man at ComTeg	Joseph Glenn
Eloise	Eloise Shoong
Waiter	Mel Cenizal
Tai Chi Master	Kuo Lien Ying

Cross of Iron

(1977)

Running Time: 132 minutes

Producer: Wolf C. Hartwig

Production Company: An Arlene Sellers and Alex Winitsky Presentation for Anglo–EMI Productions Ltd. (London) and Rapid-Film GmbH (Munich), Terra Filmkunst GmbH ([West] Berlin), Production Services by Palladium Film (Munich)

Technical Services and Facilities: Jadran Film (Zagreb), supervised by Stipe Gurdulic

Music Composer and Conductor: Ernest Gold

Production Designers: Ted Haworth, Brian Ackland Snow

Director of Photography: John Coquillon (Color Process, Technicolor)

Editors: Tony Lawson, Michael Ellis, Murray Jordan

Screenplay: Julius Epstein, Walter Kelley, James Hamilton; based on the novel *The Willing Flesh*, by Willi Heinrich

Camera Operator: Herbie Smith

Assistant Cameraman: Tony Breeze

Sound Mixer: David Hildyard

Assistant Director: Bert Batt

Second Unit Director: Walter Kelley

Second Assistant Director: Chris Carreras

Second Unit Assistant: Cliff Coleman

Associate Producer: Pat Duggan

Production Supervisor: Dieter Nobbe

Production Assistant to the Director: Katherine Haber

Art Director: Veljko Despotovic

Makeup Supervisor: Colin Arthur

Hair Stylist: Evelyn Döhring

Costumes: Kent James, Carol James

Wardrobe Supervisor: Joseph Satzinger

Special Effects: Sass Bedig, Richard Richtsfeld, Helmut Klee, Zdravko Smojvar

Property Master: Robert Visciglia

Action Arranger: Peter Brayham

Script Supervisor: Trudy von Trotha

Stills Photographer: Lars Looschen

Military Consultants: Major A. D. Schrodek, Claus von Trotha

Assistant Editors: George Akers, Pat Brennan, Ronny Reyer

Orchestration: Gerard Schurmann

Sound Editor: Rodney Holland

Dubbing Mixers: Bill Rowe, Ray Merrin, Jerry Stanford, Rodney Holland

Music Editor: Robin Clarke

Music Rerecorder: John Richards

Cast:

Sergeant Rolf Steiner	James Coburn
Captain Stransky	Maximilian Schell
Colonel Brandt	James Mason
Captain Kiesel	David Warner
Kruger	Klaus Löwitsch
Kern	Vadim Glowna
Lieutenant Triebig	Roger Fritz
Anselm	Dieter Schidor
Maag	Burkhard Driest
Corporal Schnurrbart	Fred Stillkraut
Private Dietz	Michael Nowka
Eva (Nurse)	Senta Berger
Marga	Veronique Vendell
Zoll	(Nazi Soldier) Arthur Brauss
The Russian Boy	Slavco Stimac

Convoy

(1978)

Running Time: 106 minutes

Producer: Robert M. Sherman

Executive Producers: Michael Deeley, Barry Spikings for EMI

Director of Photography: Harry Stradling Jr. (filmed in Panavision; Color Process, De Luxe)

Supervising Film Editor: Graeme Clifford

Screen Story and Screenplay: B. W. L. Norton, based on the song recorded by C. W. McCall

Film Editors: John Wright, Garth Craven

Music (title song): Chip Davis

Supervision and Lyrics (title song): Bill Fries

Songs: "Convoy," by Chip Davis and Bill Fries, sung by C. W. McCall; "Don't It Make My Brown Eyes Blue," by Richard Leigh, sung by Crystal Gayle; "Blanket on the Ground," by Roger Bowling, sung by Billie Jo Spears; "Keep on the Sunny Side," by A. P. Carter and Gary Garett, sung by Doc Watson; "Okie from Muskogee," by Merle Haggard and Eddie Burris, sung by Merle Haggard; "Lucille," by Roger Bowling and Hal Bynum, sung by Kenny Rogers; "Southern Nights," by Allen Toussant, sung by Glen Campbell; "Walk Right Back," by Sonny Curtis, sung by Anne Murray; "Cowboys Don't Get Lucky All the Time," by Dallas Harms, sung by Gene Watson; "I Cheated on a Good Woman's Love," by Del Bryant, sung by Billy "Crash" Craddock

Production Designer: Fernando Carrere

Art Director: J. Dennis Washington

Set Decorator: Francis Lombardo
Property Master: Robert J. Visciglia Sr.
Prop Man: Robert J. Visciglia Jr.
Makeup: Steve Abrums, Jim McCoy
Hair Stylist: Marina Pedraza
Costumes: Kent James, Carol James
Special Effects: Sass Bedig, Marcel Vercoutere, Candy Flanagin
Stunt Coordinator: Gary Combs
Second Unit Directors: Walter Kelley, James Coburn
Second Unit Director of Photography: Richard Kelley
Additional Photography: Robert Hauser
Camera Operators: Tim Vanik, Ralph Gerling, Robert Simson, Steve Lydeker,
    Gary Kibbe, John Kiser, William Gereghty, Joe Valentine
Production Sound Mixer: Bill Randall
Sound Effects: Fred Brown, Ross Taylor, Michele Sharp Brown, Robert Henderson
Assistant Film Editors: Timothy Tobin, Ellen Ring, Ed Fantl, Ken Morrisey
Assistant Sound Editors: Antonio Torres, Sam Crutcher, Scott Hecker
First Assistant Directors: Tom Shaw, Richard Wells, Pepi Lenzi, John Poer, Cliff
    Coleman, Newton Arnold
Second Assistant Director: Ron Wright
Rerecording Mixers: Don Mitchell, Bob Litt, Steve Maslow
Dialogue Editors: Norman Schwartz, Jerelyn Golding
Music Editor: Dan Carlin
Production Managers: Tony Wade, Tom Shaw
Production Coordinators: Ann Shaw, Sheila Warner
Production Executive: Ron Cook
Production Assistant: Elie Cohn
Casting: Lynn Stalmaster
Location Casting: P. K. Strong
Script Supervisors: Barbara Hogan, Harry Harvey, Dolores Rubin
Stunts: Jophery Brown, James Burk, Jade David, Jerry J. Gatlin, Allen Gibbs,
    Robert D. Herron, Tom Lupo, Gary McLarty, Karen McLarty, Alan Oliney, Re-
    gina Parton, Charles A. Tamburro, Glenn A. Wilder, Walter Wyatt
Titles and Opticals: Metro-Goldwyn-Mayer
Post-Production Sound: Samuel Goldwyn Studios
Cast:

Rubber Duck (Martin Penwald)	Kris Kristofferson
Melissa	Ali MacGraw
Sheriff "Dirty" Lyle Wallace	Ernest Borgnine
Pig Pen	Burt Young
Widow Woman	Madge Sinclair
Spider Mike	Franklin Ajaye
Chuck Arnoldi	Brian Davies

Governor Haskins	Seymour Cassel
Violet	Cassie Yates
Federal Agent Hamilton	Walter Kelley
Big Nasty	J. D. Kane
Pack Rat	Billy E. Hughes
White Rat	Whitey Hughes
Old Iguana	Bill Foster
Lizard Tongue	Thomas Huff
Bald Eagle	Larry Spaulding
Sneaky Snake	Randy Brady
Rosewell	Allen R. Keller
Frick	James H. Burk
Bookman	Robert Orrison
Chief Stacey Love	Tom Bush
Fish	William C. Jones Jr.
Tony Alvarez	Jorge Russek
Runyon	Tom Runyon
Thelma	Vera Zenovich
Maria	Patricia Martinez
Reverend Sloane	Donald R. Fritts
Jesus Freaks	Bobbie Barnes, Turner S. Bruton, Sammy Lee Creason, Cleveland Dupin, Gerald McGee, Terry Paul, Michael Utley, Wayne D. Wilkinson
Deke Thornton	Charles Benton
Septic Sam	George Coleman
Silver Streak	Greg Van Dyke
Roger	Ed Blachford
Samantha	Paula Baldwin
Mechanic Bob	Herb Robins
Ice Cream Seller	Robert J. Visciglia Sr.
Senator Myers	Don Levy
18 Wheel Eddie	Spec O'Donnell
Motorcycle Cop	James R. Moore
Doug (Press Man)	Jim Edgecomb
Jack (Garage Attendant)	John R. Gill
Bart	Daniel D. Halleck
Bubba	Stacy Newton
Madge	Sabra Wilson
TV News Crewman	Pepi Lenzi
TV News Sound Man	Sam Peckinpah
Texas Governor	John Bryson

The Osterman Weekend

(1983)

Running Time: 102 minutes

Producers: Peter S. Davis, William N. Panzer

Production Company: A Michael Timothy Murphy and Guy Collins Presentation of a Davis-Panzer Production, released by Twentieth Century Fox Film Corp.

Director of Photography: John Coquillon (filmed in Panavision; Color Process, De Luxe)

Music: Lalo Schifrin

Editors: Edward Abroms, David Rawlins

Associate Producers: Don Guest, E. C. Monell

Executive Producers: Michael Timothy Murphy, Larry Jones, Marc W. Zavat

Screenplay: Alan Sharp

Adaptation: Ian Masters, from the novel by Robert Ludlum

Stunt Coordinator: Thomas J. Huff

Stunt Players: Joanne Anderson, Bobby Bass, Janet Brady, Carl Ciarfalio, Justin DeRosa, Donna Garrett, Steve M. Davison, Steve Hublin, Norman Howell, Rex Pierson, Alan Quiney, George P. Wilbur, Fred Waugh, Scott Wilder, Glenn A. Wilder

Casting: Michael McLean and Associates

Production Manager: Don Guest

First Assistant Director: Win Phelps

Second Assistant Director: Robert Rooy

Art Director: Robb Wilson King

Set Decorator: Keith Hein

Music Supervisor: David Franco

Camera Operator: Michael Benson

Assistant Camera: Don Fauntleroy, Dick McNartis, Eugene Earle, Julio Macat

Still Photographer: Roger Sandler

Second Unit Director: Rod Amateau

Second Unit Assistant Director: Laura Andrus

Second Unit Director of Photography: Jacques Haitkin

Video Coordinator: Todd Grodnick

Sound Supervisor: Jim Troutman

Sound Mixer: Richard Bryce Goodman

Sound Recordist: Bayard Carey for Glen Glenn Sound

Rerecording Mixers: William L. McCaughey, Mel Metcalfe, Terry Porter

First Assistant Film Editor: Randy D. Thornton

Assistant Film Editor: David Lloyd

Music Editor: Dan Carlin Sr.

Music Mixer: Rick Ricco

Electronic Sound Design: Alan Howarth
Makeup: Robert Sidell
Hair Stylists: Shirley Padgett, Paul Abascal
Script Supervisor: Susan Malerstein
Production Coordinators: Judith Pritchard, Karen Altman
Assistant to the Producers: Katie Carlson
Assistants to Mr. Peckinpah: Susan Figueroa, Bonnie Engels
Visual Consultant: C L O U D I A
Key Costumer: George Little
Costumer: Bernadene C. Mann
Property Master: Douglas Madison
Special Effects Coordinator: Peter Chesney for Image Engineering
Titles: Ray Mercer and Co.
Optical Effects: Movie Magic
Cast:

John Tanner	Rutger Hauer
Lawrence Fassett	John Hurt
Bernard Osterman	Craig T. Nelson
Richard Tremayne	Dennis Hopper
Joseph Cardone	Chris Sarandon
Ali Tanner	Meg Foster
Virginia Tremayne	Helen Shaver
Betty Cardone	Cassie Yates
Maxwell Danforth	Burt Lancaster
Stennings	Sandy McPeak
Steve (Chris) Tanner	Christopher Starr
Marcia Heller	Cheryl Carter
Honeymoon Groom	John Bryson
Honeymoon Bride	Anne Haney
Tremayne's Secretary	Kristen Peckinpah
Martial Arts Instructor	Marshall Ho'o
Mikhailovich	Jan Triska
General Keever	Hansford Rowe
Zuna Brickman	Merete Van Kamp
Floor Manager	Bruce Block
Kidnapper	Buddy Joe Hooker
Motorcycle Cop	Tim Thomerson
Nurse	Deborah Chiaramonte
Agent #1 (Kelley)	Walter Kelley
Agent #2 (Burke)	Brick Tilley
Agent #3	Eddie Donno
Assailant #1	Den Surles
Stage Manager #1	Janeen Davis

Stage Manager #2	Robert Kensinger
Technician	Buckley F. Norris
Helicopter Pilot	Gregory Joe Parr
Helicopter Agent	Don Shafer
Executive Assistant	Irene Goodman Wright

Bibliography

Ansen, David. "The Return of a Bloody Great Classic." *Newsweek,* 13 March 1995, pp. 70–71.

Aristotle. *Aristotle's Theory of Poetry and Fine Art.* Translated by S. H. Butcher. New York: Dover, 1951.

———. *The Rhetoric of Aristotle.* Translated by Lane Cooper. New York: Appleton-Century-Crofts, 1960.

Barnes, Hazel E. *Humanistic Existentialism: The Literature of Possibility.* Lincoln: University of Nebraska Press.

Barrett, William. *Irrational Man: A Study in Existentialist Philosophy.* Garden City, N.Y.: Doubleday Anchor, 1962.

Bayer, William. *The Great Movies.* New York: Grosset and Dunlap, 1973.

Bliss, Michael. *Justified Lives: Morality and Narrative in the Films of Sam Peckinpah.* Carbondale: Southern Illinois University Press, 1993.

———, ed. *Doing It Right: The Best Criticism on Sam Peckinpah's* The Wild Bunch. Carbondale: Southern Illinois University Press, 1994.

Bond, Edward. *Lear.* London: Eyre Methuen, 1972.

Brecht, Bertolt. *Collected Plays.* Vol. 6, edited by Ralph Manheim and John Willett. New York: Vintage, 1976.

Burke, Kenneth. *A Grammar of Motives.* New York: Prentice Hall, 1954.

Butler, Terence. *Crucified Heroes: The Films of Sam Peckinpah.* London: Gordon Fraser, 1979.

Camus, Albert. *The Myth of Sisyphus and Other Essays.* Translated by Justin O'Brien. New York: Vintage, 1955.

Casty, Alan. *Development of the Film: An Interpretive History.* New York: Harcourt Brace Jovanovich, 1973.

Denby, David, ed. *Film 72/73: An Anthology by the National Society of Film Critics*. Indianapolis: Bobbs-Merrill, 1973.

Else, Gerald F. *Aristotle's* Poetics: *The Argument*. Cambridge, Mass.: Harvard University Press, 1957.

Epstein, Julius J. *Sergeant Steiner*. Hollywood: Script City, n.d.

Evans, Max. *Sam Peckinpah: Master of Violence*. Vermillion, S.D.: Dakota Press, 1972.

Fine, Marshall. *Bloody Sam: The Life and Films of Sam Peckinpah*. New York: Donald I. Fine, 1991.

Fleischman, A. S. *The Deadly Companions*. New York: Fawcett, 1961.

French, Philip. *Westerns: Aspects of a Movie Genre*. New York: Viking, 1974.

Goodman, David Z[elag], and Sam Peckinpah. *The Siege of Trencher's Farm*. Hollywood: Script City, n.d.

Green, Walon, and Sam Peckinpah. *The Wild Bunch*. Hollywood: Script City, n.d.

Haskell, Molly. *From Reverence to Rape: The Treatment of Women in the Movies*. Baltimore: Penguin, 1974.

Heinrich, Willi. *The Willing Flesh*. Translated by Richard and Clara Winston. London: Corgi, 1974.

Heston, Charlton. *The Actor's Life: Journals 1956–1976*. Edited by Hollis Alpert. New York: E. P. Dutton, 1978.

Hill, Walter. *The Getaway*. Hollywood: Script City, n.d.

Hoberman, J. "Once upon a Time in America." *Village Voice*, 16 May 1989, p. 63.

Kael, Pauline. *Deeper into Movies*. New York: Bantam, 1974.

Kauffmann, Stanley. *Field of View: Film Criticism and Comment*. New York: PAJ Publications, 1986.

———. *Figures of Light: Film Criticism and Comment*. New York: Harper and Row, 1971.

———. *Living Images: Film Criticism and Comment*. New York: Harper and Row, 1975.

Kitses, Jim. *Horizons West*. Bloomington: Indiana University Press, 1970.

Ludlum, Robert. *The Osterman Weekend*. New York: Bantam, 1985.

Martin, Steve. *Picasso at the Lapin Agile*. *American Theatre* 11 (1994): 33–48.

McKinney, Doug. *Sam Peckinpah*. Boston: Twayne, 1979.

Parrill, William. *Heroes' Twilight: The Films of Sam Peckinpah*. Hammond, La: Bay-Wulf, 1980.

"Playboy Interview [by William Murray]: Sam Peckinpah." *Playboy*, August 1972, pp. 65–74, 192.

Rostand, Robert [pseudonym for Robert S. Hopkins]. *The Killer Elite*. New York: Delacorte Press, 1973.

"Sam Peckinpah Lets It All Hang Out" [interview with Joe Medjuck and another or others]. *Take One*, January–February 1969, pp. 18–20.

Sarris, Andrew, ed. *Interviews with Film Directors*. New York: Avon, 1970.

Sartre, Jean-Paul. *Being and Nothingness*. Translated by Hazel E. Barnes. New York: Philosophical Library, 1956.

————. *No Exit and Three Other Plays.* Translated by Stuart Gilbert. New York: Vintage, 1955.

————. *The Words.* Translated by Bernard Frechtman. Greenwich, Conn.: Fawcett Crest, 1966.

Seydor, Paul. *Peckinpah: The Western Films.* Urbana: University of Illinois Press, 1980.

————. *Peckinpah: The Western Films: A Reconsideration.* Urbana: University of Illinois Press, 1997.

Sharp, Alan. *The Osterman Weekend: A Screenplay.* Hollywood: Script City, n.d.

Shaw, Bernard. *The Bodley Head Bernard Shaw: Collected Plays with Their Prefaces.* Vol. 4. London: Bodley Head, 1972.

————. *Everybody's Political What's What?* London: Constable, 1944.

"Shoot! Sam Peckinpah Talks to John Cutts." *Films and Filming* 16 (October 1969): 4–8.

Simmons, Garner. *Peckinpah: A Portrait in Montage.* Austin: University of Texas Press, 1982.

Simon, John. *Movies into Film: Film Criticism, 1967–1970.* New York: Delta, 1972.

————. *Reverse Angle: A Decade of American Films.* New York: Clarkson N. Potter, 1982.

Slotkin, Richard. *Gunfighter Nation: The Myth of the Frontier in Twentieth-Century America.* New York: Atheneum, 1992.

Thomas, Bob, ed. *Directors in Action: Selections from* Action: The Official Magazine of the Directors Guild of America. Indianapolis: Bobbs-Merrill, 1973.

Thompson, Jim. *The Getaway.* New York: Bantam, 1973.

Weddle, David. *"If They Move . . . Kill 'Em!"* New York: Grove, 1994.

Whitehall, Richard. "Talking with Peckinpah." *Sight and Sound* 38 (Autumn 1969): 172–75.

Williams, Gordon M. *The Siege of Trencher's Farm.* London: Mayflower, 1971.

Wurlitzer, Rudolph. *Pat Garrett and Billy the Kid.* New York: New American Library, 1973.

Index

Bernard F. Dukore is University Distinguished Professor of Theatre Arts and Humanities Emeritus, Virginia Polytechnic Institute and State University. He is the author or editor of more than thirty books and numerous articles and reviews about drama and film.

Typeset in 9.5/13 Stone Serif
with Corvinus Skyline display
Designed by Dennis Roberts
Composed by Jim Proefrock
at the University of Illinois Press
Manufactured by Cushing-Malloy, Inc.

University of Illinois Press
1325 South Oak Street
Champaign, IL 61820-6903
www.press.uillinois.edu